# Major Blunders of the
# Second World War

# Major Blunders of the Second World War

## New Insights into Mistakes and their Consequences

Andrew Sangster

Pen & Sword
**MILITARY**

First published in Great Britain in 2024 by
Pen & Sword Military
An imprint of Pen & Sword Books Limited
Yorkshire – Philadelphia

Copyright © Andrew Sangster 2024

ISBN 978 1 03611 277 6

The right of Andrew Sangster to be identified as Author of this Work has been asserted by him in accordance with the Copyright, Designs and Patents Act 1988.

A CIP catalogue record for this book is
available from the British Library

All rights reserved. No part of this book may be reproduced or transmitted in any form or by any means, electronic or mechanical including photocopying, recording or by any information storage and retrieval system, without permission from the Publisher in writing.

Typeset by Mac Style
Printed in the UK by CPI Group (UK) Ltd, Croydon, CR0 4YY

Pen & Sword Books Limited incorporates the imprints of After the Battle, Atlas, Archaeology, Aviation, Discovery, Family History, Fiction, History, Maritime, Military, Military Classics, Politics, Select, Transport, True Crime, Air World, Frontline Publishing, Leo Cooper, Remember When, Seaforth Publishing, The Praetorian Press, Wharncliffe Local History, Wharncliffe Transport, Wharncliffe True Crime and White Owl.

For a complete list of Pen & Sword titles please contact

PEN & SWORD BOOKS LIMITED
47 Church Street, Barnsley, South Yorkshire, S70 2AS, England
E-mail: enquiries@pen-and-sword.co.uk
Website: www.pen-and-sword.co.uk
or
PEN AND SWORD BOOKS
1950 Lawrence Road, Havertown, PA 19083, USA
E-mail: uspen-and-sword@casematepublishers.com
Website: www.penandswordbooks.com

# Contents

| | | |
|---|---|---:|
| *Acknowledgements* | | vii |
| *Preface* | | viii |
| *Introduction* | | x |
| | | |
| **Chapter 1** | Blunders or Misjudgements | 1 |
| | Roosevelt in Personal Danger | 2 |
| | Rommel's Innocent Spy | 3 |
| | Mechelen Accident | 4 |
| | A General's Misjudgement | 7 |
| | Calculated destruction of a famous Monastery | 12 |
| | Sinking the French Fleet | 19 |
| | Bio-Chemical Warfare | 27 |
| | | |
| **Chapter 2** | The Dieppe Disaster | 38 |
| | Why it was Deemed Necessary | 38 |
| | A Plan to ease Political Pressures | 42 |
| | Town of Dieppe | 44 |
| | Operation *Rutter* | 45 |
| | Canadians | 50 |
| | Committee Work | 52 |
| | *Rutter* becomes *Jubilee* | 54 |
| | *Jubilee* Battle | 57 |
| | First Postmortem | 60 |
| | Further Ramifications | 61 |
| | The Focus on Mountbatten | 63 |
| | Political Driving Forces | 72 |

vi   Major Blunders of the Second World War

| | | |
|---|---|---|
| **Chapter 3** | Edward VIII, A Judas? | 79 |
| | Introduction | 80 |
| | An Overview of Modern Monarchy | 81 |
| | Early Life of Edward VIII | 87 |
| | Character, as revealed in private love letters | 89 |
| | The Interbellum Years | 92 |
| | Wallis Simpson | 95 |
| | The Divisions at Abdication | 99 |
| | Nazi Sympathiser or Traitor? | 106 |
| | The Second World War | 109 |
| | Bahamas | 117 |
| | Postwar | 121 |
| | Final Observations | 126 |
| **Chapter 4** | U-Boat War, was Dönitz Guilty? | 130 |
| | A U-Boat Commander's Autobiography | 131 |
| | Submarine Warfare in the First World War | 134 |
| | Interbellum Years | 135 |
| | Submarine Warfare in the Second World War | 136 |
| | The Crewmen | 143 |
| | U-boat Conduct of Warfare | 145 |
| | Karl Dönitz to 1918 | 155 |
| | Interbellum Years | 157 |
| | The Second World War | 162 |
| | Post-Hitler | 171 |
| | Introduction to Trial | 173 |
| | Trial Papers | 176 |
| | Final Judgement | 181 |
| | Observations on the Trial | 182 |
| | Spandau then Freedom | 184 |
| | Dönitz, A Misjudgement or Not | 186 |
| *Final Observations on Case Studies* | | 190 |
| *Notes* | | 198 |
| *Bibliography* | | 205 |
| *Index* | | 208 |

# Acknowledgements

Over the years I have been very grateful to those who work and administer the various archives, and for the work of fellow historians with their various insights and perceptions.

However, I am exceptionally grateful to my wife, Carol Ann, for her incredible patience as I disappear into archives and rarely emerge from my study. I am also grateful for the support and encouragement of my friend and colleague the Revd Dr Canon Peter Doll, Vice-Dean of Norwich Cathedral.

The Revd Dr Andrew Sangster

# Preface

In the history of any human organisation, whether business, industry, the professions, the church, the military, or government, there are countless moments of blunders, mistakes, incompetence, and misjudgements. These descriptive words may overlap, but they hold their own distinctive nuances. A mistake is an error of judgement, a blunder is a mistake caused by carelessness or ignorance, implying a degree of incompetence. A misjudgement tends to imply a miscalculation even after lengthy consideration. As soon as they occur, they are leapt at by journalists and reporters. This is of special interest to the public when it is a matter of 'how are the mighty fallen', when important people and leaders are implicated. However, incompetence, blunders, errors of judgement have been, since recorded history, recognised as a human propensity for frailty with a variety of reasons. These can be based on such issues as greed, power, egotism, but the list is endless because of our human nature. The author of this book may be making a misjudgement in writing on this subject, because some elements of misjudgement in human history remain either highly contentious or need to be placed in the locked amnesia cupboard. In the history of war blunders and misjudgement can have major ramifications both at the individual and corporate level. Even a mistake made by a relatively insignificant individual can have serious repercussions. A schoolboy may have thought he was creating an amusing joke by throwing a firework into the classroom, but a burnt down school with casualties becomes a serious issue.

A sailor not checking whether a torpedo is armed is even worse, and a general who decides that he is going to risk the lives of hundreds of men to save a family member is just as bad. These last two examples happened, the first was a blunder which could have had deadly ramifications, and the second a misjudgement resulting in unnecessary deaths. This book has selected ten case studies from the Second World War, some very brief because the event was singular and straightforward, more time is spent on three more controversial issues. There will be historians who disagree that an event was a misjudgement, and this creates a distinctly grey area, such as the sinking of the French fleet at Mers-el-Kébir. Some issues are better known than others, but a historian's task is to present the known facts where possible, and then leave the reader to draw their own conclusion despite inbuilt views by the writer.

# Introduction

Some of the contentious issues focused on in this book have already had studies written on them by historians and journalists, so the question is why do it again. Hundreds of thousands of words have been written on some of these subjects, but this study is basically to provide a brief summary of the main issues, underlining the critical points and often with new observations. It is intended as an appetiser for each individual reader, for those who want to know the information without having to read hundreds of thousands of words, for those who are curious, or who had no idea about the various problems. The task of the historian is to outline the known facts, hear the views of others, both those who witnessed events, and the opinions of others since. Inevitably judgements can only be hinted at in these case studies, but it is up to the reader to reach his or her own assessment.

Throughout the Second World War incompetence, blunders, mistakes, and misjudgement played a role in nearly every activity and aspect of the war, many are well known others less so. It is often the case, but not always, that blunders or mistakes reflect a misjudgement higher up the command ladder. These various issues can be observed in individuals at the lowest levels of command responsibility to those at the very top. The unsavoury but eventually successful leader of the Soviet Union, Joseph Stalin, refused, despite constant sound advice from his own intelligence sources and countless others on the international scene, to believe that Hitler was about to launch an attack on Russia, which, when it happened, virtually left him isolated and worried about his personal future. For their part, the British leaders have often been accused of not preparing for what, especially with the benefit of hindsight, was an inevitably major war with Nazi Germany. They refused to listen to Churchill's warnings, seeing him more as a belligerent problem child, sought appeasement, and failed to prepare their military adequately for the incoming conflict.

In France, with the largest European army there was a lack of any foresight, as with the British still suffering from memories of the Great War and wanting peace at all costs. When war broke out the French army appeared poorly led and the equally unprepared British sent a small expeditionary force. Despite the signs of the day and the diplomatic warnings, the King of Belgium believed that his stand on neutrality would save his country from a man like Hitler. These were, again with the benefit of hindsight, major misjudgements often made worse by political and military incompetence, a very human feature.

This book explores ten cases of blunders and misjudgement which occurred during the war, and the first chapter explores various incidents caused either by blunders or misjudgement or both. Some are hardly mentioned in general history books, but all had potentially serious ramifications. As the first chapter unfolds the incidents range first from a time when an American destroyer fired a live torpedo at the battleship conveying President Roosevelt across the Atlantic. This is followed with other incidents of blunders and misjudgement concluding with the final account of how the Allies left gas shells open to attack causing widespread death. The following longer chapters reflect first the Dieppe Raid disaster, exploring the ineptitude of the planning, who actually authorised the raid, and the disastrous role of Mountbatten. The behaviour of King Edward VIII is explored, a monarch often regarded as a potential traitor, whether this could have held firm in a court room is debatable, but his dubious conduct was highly questionable. The final chapter explores the U-boat war and questions whether Admiral Dönitz was guilty of the charged crimes at Nuremberg, and whether his prison sentence reflected a sense of revenge for his initial success in the battle of the Atlantic and being Hitler's nominated successor, being seen by some as casting a slur on the Nuremberg Trials.

Chapter One

# Blunders or Misjudgements

## Author's Notes

The first incident is a brief mention of the time when an American destroyer fired a fully armed torpedo at an American battleship transporting President Roosevelt across the Atlantic. This was decidedly a blunder because of incompetence and sent a warning about this potentially dangerous and embarrassing human problem.

The second explains how an American officer innocently supplied Rommel with all the British secrets and movements in North Africa. This was again a mixture of blunder and incompetence for using a broken code, a misjudgement for agreeing to such information being shared.

The third deals with a German mistake when one of their pilots flying over enemy territory was obliged to crash land in Belgium, while carrying all their plans for invading France, causing mayhem in the German High Command, a blunder indicating sheer incompetence.

The fourth deals with an Allied military commander, many of whom have been written about with accounts of their achievements, their blunders, misjudgements, and some suffering from egotistical leanings which led to discord in the Allied alliance. This section deals with an almost unbelievable misjudgement when a famous American general sent an armoured task force into enemy territory, in a futile effort to rescue his son-in-law from a PoW camp. It was a serious misjudgement as he lost over 200 men and much equipment only to fail in saving a personal family member.

The fifth incident follows a major misjudgement when Allied commanders in Italy decided to obliterate by bombing the world famous and ancient Benedictine Monastery at Monte Cassino. It cost more Allied lives than the enemy, many innocent civilians were killed, it assisted the German defence, which continued

## 2 Major Blunders of the Second World War

*to hold onto their valuable vantage point for a few months longer than anticipated, and it was regarded as a Philistine act to this day.*

*The sixth incident is examined because whether it was a misjudgement or not, it is still highly debatable and certainly contentious. This explores the time when the British Royal Navy sank part of the French fleet following the armistice, when technically, although having surrendered, they were still seen by many as Allies to Britain. There remains from the time of the incident strongly divided opinions as to whether it was an essential act of aggression for Britain's safety or was a serious misjudgement.*

*The final and a major section in the first chapter explores the time during the battle for Italy when American gas shells released their deadly load after a Luftwaffe attack, with the Germans realising what had happened before the Allies had identified the problem which was not publicised for years. It led to many deaths of the Allied military and Italian civilians and was so embarrassing that this issue, resulting from both incompetence and misjudgement, was highly embarrassing. It also notes Himmler's effort in bacteriological warfare.*

*These classical examples are selected at random to demonstrate that more often than not, blunders are the result of incompetence and misjudgement. These issues reflect the nature of human behaviour highlighted in war and therefore with serious repercussions.*

### Roosevelt in Personal Danger

The new battleship *Iowa* in November 1943 was carrying the American President Roosevelt to Cairo and Tehran for major conferences. The *Iowa* was just off Bermuda when a torpedo was fired in the battleship's direction, and not by a German submarine, but by an accompanying destroyer the USS *William D. Porter*. This vessel was named after a nineteenth century commodore, and it was better known by its nickname of the *Willie Dee*. The vessels had been practising a defensive measure, and it is believed that the destroyers were simulating an attack, but *Willie Dee* by mistake released an armed torpedo, causing the *Iowa* to take diversionary measures. There were orders for radio silence and the destroyer tried to indicate the danger by signal lamp, but then indicated the wrong direction the torpedo was travelling. It was a fraught situation, so the destroyer had to break radio silence.

Roosevelt watched the torpedo explode in the battleship's wake, and Admiral King ordered the *William D. Porter* back to port with the whole crew under arrest, which was a first time in American naval history. This destroyer appeared to have a record of mishaps, the previous day losing a depth-charge overboard which rocked the *Iowa*, thereby leading to the misapprehension they were under U-boat attack.

The officers were given land duties, and the torpedo man who had not removed the fuse was given hard labour, but Roosevelt intervened on the grounds it was an accident. This was a mishap probably caused by inexperience or even poor training, but it was an incident of sheer incompetence probably caused by inadequately trained officers and crew which could have led to catastrophic results.

## Rommel's Innocent Spy

Rommel had the reputation of seeming to know all the British plans; one of the problems was not the Desert Fox's magical gifts, but a US Military attaché in Cairo, a Colonel Bonner Frank Fellers who was sending constant reports back to General George Marshall in Washington. These were comprehensive reports including locations, casualties, intentions, and plans; what he did not realise was that the US diplomatic code he was using had long been broken and accessed by the Germans. Until Fellers was removed in July 1942 his information was unbelievably valuable to Rommel.

This was an accident and not the work of a traitor, but just as much of a serious catastrophe. Colonel Fellers was the military attaché in the American Embassy in Egypt, and his task was to report to his base everything the British were planning, which the British were happy to communicate, granting him full access. He had been using what was called the *Black Code* which had been stolen by the Italians and decrypted by the Germans. His information gave detailed reports about troop movements and intentions. This included convoy movements,

## 4    Major Blunders of the Second World War

details about Malta, and every possible form of information, which led to immediate German response who were prepared for the movements; this cost many lives of British, Commonwealth troops and Free French forces. The Ultra sources indicated there was a leak and Fellers came under suspicion, but it was not until 1942 this was confirmed when an Australian troop overran a German Intelligence unit, and Fellers was identified. He was found not guilty and returned to the USA where he was decorated with the Distinguished Service Medal and promoted. The world of subversion, spies, and secret intelligence was as prone to incompetence and misjudgements as the front-line military forces. As a matter of curiosity, the *Abwehr* (German Intelligence) had operated a spy ring in Egypt, and they used Daphne du Maurier's novel *Rebecca* as their cypher key. This was turned to British advantage and fed wrong information back; the irony being that Daphne du Maurier was married to General Browning, but Fellers by sheer accident had provided the best information. Some would regard this as incompetence for taking the reliability of a code system for granted, which had been an error reflected by the Germans in assuming their Enigma machine was impenetrable. Others that it should have been worked out that Rommel and his team knew too much and must have had an Allied source tapped. Some would argue whether it was necessary to send such details of this nature to America which verged close on incompetence. Given the fraught exigencies of the day this incident falls between misjudgement and incompetence, but it cost untold lives.

## Mechelen Accident

It was not just the British who were embarrassed by incompetence and misjudgement; the myth of German efficiency and never allowing personal matters to interfere with work, was shattered by an early incident in what was to be later known as the Mechelen incident. On 10 January 1940, a Messerschmitt BF108 made an emergency landing inside the Belgium border near Vucht in the area of Maasmechelen, located on the Meuse River in the province of Limburg. The pilot, a Major Erich Hoenmanns

Blunders or Misjudgements 5

needed extra flying hours, and wanted to do something as mundane as taking laundry to his wife in Cologne, so he offered a lift to his friend Major Helmuth Reinberger. Flying through fogbanks he lost his bearings and inexplicably switched off his fuel supply and had to crash land; the plane was damaged beyond repair, but the officers survived. It was then that the pilot realised that Reinberger was in a state of panic because he was carrying plans of *Fall Gelb* (Case Yellow) the German invasion of the Low Countries; he had been travelling to Cologne for a staff meeting. He made several attempts to burn the plans, even borrowing a match from a farm labourer. They were picked up with the remains of the plans by two guards and taken to a Belgium border guard house near Machelen-ann-de-Mass, where there was another attempt to burn the plans in the stove. When this failed it not only drew the attention of the guards to the importance of the documents, but Reinberger tried to snatch a guard's pistol to commit suicide. As a matter of interest both became, later in the war, part of a prisoner exchange and were partially pardoned.

The plans, or their remains were placed under intense scrutiny, and it soon became clear that they were looking at the specifics of the German invasion plan. Hitler was furious, and he went straight to the top and fired General Felmy in charge of Luftflotte Fleet II as well as his chief of staff, Colonel Kammhuber. Kesselring was brought in from Poland to take over, and in his memoirs describes how Göring was 'down in the dumps' because Hitler had started his outbursts by blaming him as head of the Luftwaffe.

General Jodl believed the loss of the plans was a total disaster, but the Belgians managed to convince the Germans they had been destroyed. The Belgians interrogated Reinberger to discover what was in the papers, implying they did not understand them; they bugged the room when he met the German Attaché to hear him explain that the papers had been destroyed by the fire. General Jodl at OKW on hearing this believed all was secure. The Belgians, a little uncertain and suspicious, had been warned by Mussolini's son-in-law Ciano, that the Germans had planned an attack around mid-January. The King of Belgium, Leopold III informed

6 Major Blunders of the Second World War

his Minister of Defence, the French Commander Gamelin, and Lord Gort of the British Forces were all warned.

The Chief of French Military Intelligence, Colonel Rivet was sceptical, but Gamelin thought it might provide the impetus to persuade the Belgians to let the French and British into their territory; something Leopold was stubbornly refusing. Gamelin was thinking both offensively and defensively, and he gave orders for the 1st Army Group and Third Army to move towards the Belgium frontiers. Many believed this incident of a crashed plane was not an accident, including General Brooke, who in his diaries wrote that he thought it was a ruse by the Germans to encourage the Allies to panic, and enter Belgium thereby providing the Germans with an excuse to invade that country. Brooke always had a high respect for the German military, and he found it impossible to believe they could have an accident over laundry problems.

However, more information arrived which was claimed to have come from the German Colonel Hans Oster implying an attack was imminent, and this was relayed to all Belgian army commanders. A Chief of General Staff, van den Bergen used the public radio to call in all Belgian troops on leave, and prepared to have barriers removed in case the French and British troops needed to move in. The Belgian King was furious that this was done without his orders, and the Germans realised the Belgians appeared to know their intentions. Van den Bergen, who may have done this with Gamelin's knowledge to bring Belgium in on the Allied side was in disgrace, and later resigned. There followed a confused and much debated period of whether Leopold was or was not allowing access to the French and British depending on certain guarantees. Sir Roger Keyes, the liaison man had a version that favoured Leopold which he fervently held as correct against all opposition. The Belgians remained hesitant and nervous, and the Allies remained reluctant to penetrate Belgium's neutrality without permission.

The Germans changed their date, probably not so much because their plans had been compromised, but by the weather which had turned to snow and freezing. The motivation as to why they changed their plans remains elusive, but the commotion caused by the plane accident indicated to the Germans the way the Allies would react. Gamelin failed to change his plans or strategy given the likelihood that the Germans would now alter their plans, a mistake for which he has been frequently criticised.

One accidental mistake by a German pilot upset the applecart, created panic both sides of the divide, and was misread by nearly everyone involved. The human propensity to make mistakes and have accidents in war can have wider ramifications than landing up in the casualty unit. However, a trained Luftwaffe pilot and any officer would know that carrying military plans by air over enemy or even neutral territory ran too many risks, so although it has blunder elements within this account, there is no question that it was sheer incompetence and his route a serious misjudgement.

## A General's Misjudgement

The history of military commanders frequently provides a kaleidoscope of human behaviour most of which is well known. During the Second World War many major commanders became heroes in the public eye and world famous, but as time passed many of these figures have lost the initial gloss as various acts of incompetence and misjudgement have come to light. It is of course a human failing, but it carries a sense of greater responsibility for a military commander because the lives of many are dependent on his decisions. After the victory of El Alamein Montgomery was regarded as a great leader and built up as such because Britain had needed a victory. He was not always the military genius as depicted, and many historical critics have pointed out his flaws and misjudgements. His egotistical personality caused havoc in the occupation of Sicily; he was criticised for taking his time in Italy for his somewhat ponderous movement towards Salerno. Later in D-Day Normandy his problems over Caen caused delays, his *Market Garden* Operation lost lives at Arnhem, and he strained Anglo-American relationships following his gross boasting after the Battle of the Bulge. Some of his plans were misjudgements, but at the time the Allies needed heroes.

It was the same with the equally egotistical American General Mark Clark who was almost dangerously Anglo-phobic, and surrounded himself

8    Major Blunders of the Second World War

with a huge assemblage of chosen journalists and photographers who were instructed to photograph him in poses and places he carefully selected. His near failure at Salerno, his flawed planning for the Anzio landings, his occupying Rome for propaganda purposes and not trapping a German Army have met with considerable criticism. Earlier, Clark ordered the crossing of the Rapido River against the advice of his senior officers and consequently lost many men. Later, his own soldiers demanded a postwar Congressional Hearing, where he was found not guilty, on the probable instinct the world needed heroes.

### General George Patton

A whole book could be devoted to the incompetence and misjudgements of military commanders: being human they are prone to error, incompetence, and misjudgement, but one little known incident in particular is to be explored to expose the dangers of poor judgements made by senior military commanders. This relates to General George Patton one of the best-known figures of the war amongst generals, who, to rescue his son-in-law from a German PoW camp, lost soldiers, and valuable resources in an inexcusable and futile operation.* According to Field Marshal Gerd von Rundstedt, when questioned about enemy commanders said, 'Patton was your best'.[1] Journalists simply loved him because there was always a story for better or worse. For a brief time, the world believed Patton had relieved Paris because of the journalistic zeal to demonstrate his ability in war.[2] Legends and myths grew around him while he was still alive and active. It is true that 'Old Blood and Guts', which was a partially self-invented nickname dating back to the days he fought rebels on the Mexican border, had a reputation that even Stalin, as he watched the Third Army's progress across France, admired. It is equally true that he forced the pace, and like the earlier German blitzkrieg advances used armour to its best effect. This was especially true when he felt in opposition not so much with the Germans, but with Montgomery for whom he had a deep contempt, and not without some cause. It was once noted that Patton was

---

\* Only Rommel and Patton have had films made about them, and they remain popular in the public image.

'obsessed with beating the British on the battlefield, both to satisfy his personal vanity and to demonstrate that the American soldier was second to none'.[3] The behaviour was childish: Montgomery referred to Patton as a foul-mouthed lover of war, while Patton described Montgomery as that 'cocky little Limey fart'. Much later when he crossed the Rhine on 22 March 1945, he telegrammed Omar Bradley 'For God's sake tell the world we're across...I want the world to know the 3rd Army made it before Monty'.[4] Patton was loved and hated, admired and despised, regarded as Guderian's equal by some; others saw him as a self-centred buffoon whose death in an immediate post-war car accident saved him from causing a political embarrassment with the Soviets. One of the best loved cartoonists of the war, Bill Maulden, was hauled in front of Patton to be bawled out for too many anti-officer cartoons.

The historian and World War veteran Dwight Macdonald called Patton 'a swaggering bigmouth, a Fascist-minded aristocrat...brutal and hysterical, coarse and affected, violent and empty...compared to the dreary run of us, General Patton was quite mad'.[5] In 1943 Field Marshal Alan Brooke wrote of Patton that 'I had already heard of him, but I must confess that his swash-buckling personality exceeded my expectation. I did not form any high opinion of him, nor had I any reason to alter this view at a later date. A dashing, courageous, wild, and unbalanced leader, good for operations requiring thrust and push, but at a loss in any operations requiring skill and judgement'.[6] Patton was probably one of the most controversial of the Allied generals, known for his ivory handled handgun, his outspoken views, and sense of bravado, often at the expense of other's lives.

When in Sicily some out-of-control American soldiers massacred Italian prisoners of war in cold blood they were not prosecuted, and as Hastings wrote, 'Patton, whose military ethic mirrored that of many Nazi commanders', claimed these killings had been thoroughly justified.[7] Patton is probably best known for the notorious incident of slapping shell-shocked soldiers during a hospital visit, and despite a public apology, appeared at one time to have been seemingly side-lined, talking to the Mothers' Unions and Women's Institutes in England. He was soon

## 10   Major Blunders of the Second World War

returned to action in France where his ruthless cut and thrust approach increased his reputation as a military commander who could 'get things done'. His assistance in resolving the Battle of the Bulge further enhanced his reputation, carrying out a military movement which astounded many, relieving Bastogne and disrupting the German advance. It has even been suggested that he had prior knowledge of the German intentions which enabled him to react so swiftly, knowledge he kept to himself. He damaged this reputation by making an inane decision which epitomised the dangers of misjudgement.

### Misjudgement

Just inside Germany was the Prisoner of War camp near Hammelburg (*Oflag XIII-B*) in which, Patton had been informed, his son-in-law Colonel John Waters, (married to his daughter Beatrice) who had been captured in Tunisia, was being held prisoner.* Patton behaved recklessly, perhaps immorally, sending a task force into enemy held and dangerous territory for a family member. It was a total fiasco, and all but a few of the three hundred men sent were killed, wounded or captured.** Patton ordered a Captain Abraham Baum with the task of penetrating nearly fifty miles of enemy home-territory with some sixteen tanks, nearly thirty half-tracks and approximately 300 men. It was known as *Task Force Baum*. They were hampered by a lack of maps and no exact location for the prison camp. The column was spotted and traced by a Luftwaffe spotter plane, and they had to contend with some resistance. On the day (27 March 1945) they arrived at the camp there was little resistance. The camp commandant, a General Gunther von Goeckel asked Patton's relative John Waters to act as 'a go-between.*** It was deemed essential for Waters to make some form of contact with the Americans because they were pouring lethal fire into the Serbian prisoners because their uniforms looked similar to German ones. This prison camp had been originally

---

\*   In February 1943
\*\*   Only 15 survived according to Kershaw A, *The Liberator* (London: Hutchinson, 2012) p.236
\*\*\*   General Gunther von Goeckel was not seen as a war criminal, he was released on 28 February 1947

for Serb PoWs, so it was no surprise there were many there. A German soldier not knowing the situation shot Waters in the backside which meant he needed immediate medical attention. There were far more prisoners than first realised, most of them were too ill, exhausted, or underfed, and rather than walk back to American lines they opted to stay. The return journey was dangerous, there was no moon, no lighting could be used, and the tanks betrayed their whereabouts. They were ambushed at Höllrich, and most of the escaping men realising the situation they faced, headed back towards the *Oflag* which they had just left. In the ensuing battle it was everyman for himself; most were taken prisoner. Captain Baum was shot and landed up alongside Waters being cared for in the Serbian hospital. They were liberated less than two weeks later, but most of the other prisoners had been marched deeper into Germany. Baum received from Patton the Distinguished Service Cross. Many thought that it should have been the Medal of Honour, but this would have meant an investigation which would have been embarrassing to Patton.

Patton later claimed the taskforce was to distract the Germans from a main force, but it is known that he had written to his wife on 23 March stating that 'we are headed right for John's place and may get there before he is moved'.[8] Then on 30 March he told his son George 'the other day I sent an armoured column out to recapture a prison camp...I am afraid that this was a bad guess, and that the column has been destroyed so I lost 225 men'.[9] In fact he lost a great many more, his relative was wounded but because of that was not marched away. Whichever way the incident is viewed it should have ruined him much more than the slapping incidents, but it was 'quickly covered up and its survivors sworn to silence'.[10]

Unbelievably, according to Bradley, Eisenhower severely reprimanded Patton orally, but took no official action. In communicating with George Marshall about the incident, Eisenhower wrote, 'Patton is a problem child, but he is a great fighting leader in pursuit and exploitation'.[11] A few weeks later in April 1945 he was promoted to a four-star general and hailed as the outstanding American general of the war.

The general thrust into Germany in this area was to take Aschaffenburg on the Main River and then through Bamberg to Nuremberg and

## 12  Major Blunders of the Second World War

down to Munich. Patton's reckless and costly adventure meant that his special mission had to by-pass areas such as Aschaffenburg which was being heavily fortified by SS troops. The Germans were led by a man called Lamberth whose strategy was to hold off the Americans as long as possible. In the biography of a Colonel Felix Sparks, Alex Kershaw described how Sparks led his men towards Aschaffenburg anticipating that Patton had taken the place, only to discover that they had by-passed it on the ridiculous mission to rescue John Waters.[12] It was fortunate that Sparks checked first since it became an area of such bitter fighting that 'for the first time in Europe in the Second World War, it was reportedly decided to use napalm on a civilian area'.[13]

Patton had ignored all the hazards, and risked his men for one relative, leaving a dangerous battle area for Sparks and his troops to fight through. It would not be the first time that a military commander has risked and ruined the lives of his men for the sake of a relative; wars have more often than not been waged over family issues, but the world wars were not the place or time for such medieval romancing and gestures.

There is no doubt the German view of Patton that he was the Allied top general was true for many because of his 'thrust forward' attitude, it is equally true that he had moments of success, most especially in the battle of the Bulge. Much myth has emerged around the life of General Patton, much has needed to be forgotten which allows conspiracy theories to flourish. In reality he was the flawed hero, a 'problem child' as Eisenhower described him. However, in risking his men to save a family member, it not only failed but was a total misjudgement.

**Calculated destruction of a famous Monastery**

The bombing of the ancient monastery and town of Monte Cassino in the battle for the Gustav line in February 1944 was seen at the time as essential to break the deadlock for the Allied forces to reach into northern Italy. The fighting for the Gustav line was a series of battles but the dominating height of the monastery had proved impossible to wrestle from the hands of the defending German troops. They had used all their skill in defending this site, and 'in November the Germans had put 100 steel shelters into the Cassino position, and they added more later, as well as 76 armoured casements and a number of armoured machine-gun nests', and it was costing too many lives.[14] Field Marshal Kesselring admitted the use of the 'natural features with concrete armoured positions and enfilading fire' made defence easier than attack.[15] They had prepared their defence points and 'their skilled commanders were determined to hold out whatever…they were assisted by Allied ineptitude in the first three battles'.[16] Italy was easier to defend and attack because of the nature of its terrain, but Monte Cassino had become a serious deadlock, and after much discussion it was decided to annihilate the monastery and its immediate environs.

On 3 February, Alexander had ordered the New Zealand 2nd Division and the 4th Indian Division under General Freyberg to join General Clark's 5th Army, but Freyberg believed that Cassino and the area it dominated could not be taken unless the Abbey were obliterated. Freyberg was utterly convinced the Abbey was an observation point and demanded its destruction, and it has been suggested that this extreme policy may have been influenced when he had heard that his only son was missing at Anzio.[17] There is no question that it was not just Freyberg's decision but was widely discussed within the Allied camp, and the question of whether it was a misjudgement still dominates the history books and memoirs to this day, not least because it played into Field Marshal Kesselring's hands as if he had been handed a victory.

Within the Allied command structure there were naturally fluctuating opinions, claims and counterclaims which continued after the war. Many argued Monte Cassino could have been outflanked, including Major-General Tuker and the French Commander General Juin.* Tuker claimed Freyburg 'should never have been put in charge of a corps, he had not the tactical understanding' nevertheless Freyburg had Alexander's support.[18] 'Tuker could not understand why Cassino town, monastery and point

---

\* Hoyt, *Back*,p.159 claims it was Tuker who asked Freyberg to bomb the abbey and recently two New Zealand historians have claimed the same, Harper, *Battles*, p16.

## 14 Major Blunders of the Second World War

593 be made point of attack' unless the bombing could guarantee total destruction of resistance, otherwise he argued it was better to outflank along the northern route and Gari river, stating 'I went on arguing this from hospital by letter through my divisional headquarters'.[19] Military students since have often supported this possible strategy. Later Alexander wrote that a misinterpretation of a German radio message prompted the Allies to think the Germans were inside the Abbey. Field Marshal Lord Alexander wrote in his memoirs that an American officer had 'picked up on the wireless…conclusive proof that the Germans were inside the monastery. The interpreted conversation ran: "*Wo ist der Abt? Ist er noch im Kloster?*" *Abt* is the Germany military abbreviation for 'Abteilung' meaning a section. Unfortunately, *Abt* also means Abbot, and since *Abt* is masculine and *abteilung* femine, (sic) the conversation referred to the Abbott…a little knowledge of a foreign tongue can be a dangerous thing'.[20]

It is extremely unlikely that the Germans used the Abbey despite what the occasional spotter-plane and misunderstood radio-messages claimed. Kesselring had promised to safeguard the Abbey and he refused the use of the Abbey to his men, having 'given his assurance to the Vatican on 11 December 1943'.[21] Westphal confirmed that Kesselring had the Abbey cordoned off by military police for its protection.[22] The Abbot said the Germans had not broken the agreement; the Abbot's secretary, Don Martino Matronola's diary recorded that the Germans never entered the premises.[23] General von Senger, a cultured, educated and civilised German general who was a Lay-Benedictine attended mass, and later said he was the only German present; even Churchill later admitted that the evidence indicated there were no Germans.[24] However, many in the Allied camp could not accept the possibility that the German promise to stay out of the monastery could be believed.

The military theorist J.C.F. Fuller described the bombing as 'not so much a piece of vandalism as an act of sheer tactical stupidity'.[25] The Germans were dug in below the buildings on that formidable hill, and the antiquity of the religious site was a secondary consideration to Freyberg and Alexander who decided human life was more important; yet they were aware 'that as many as 3,000 Italian civilians had sought shelter within the monastery's walls'.[26] The Germans had declared a 300 yard wide non-combat zone around the abbey, which in terms of the sharp decline is still within the shadows of the walls. To preserve the Abbey meant avoiding the mountain, but it was militarily out of the question for the Germans, so whether the monastery was occupied or not was a fatuous debate, because Monte Cassino hill dominated the area, and if they had declared it an 'open site' that would not have bound the Allies to the agreement.*

On the morning of 15 February the 96th Bombardment Group in Foggia read their brief which stated that the Abbey *'is a huge ancient monastery which the Germans have chosen as a key defence and have loaded with heavy guns. The monastery has accounted for the lives of upwards of 2,000 American boys who felt the same as we do about church property and who paid for it because the Germans do not understand anything human when total war is concerned. The monastery MUST be destroyed and everyone in it as there is no one in but Germans'.*[27] The latter statement was a total deceit as it was known the religious body of men had stayed and were giving shelter to Italian citizens driven from their homes. It was probably issued this way to protect pilots and their crew feeling reluctant to bomb a world-famous religious site with clergy and innocent lay people inside. Later that day over 400 tons of bombs were dropped on the Abbey killing sheltering Italians and monks, and totally destroying the buildings: according to Senger no German was killed.**

The bombing will always remain contentious, and the Germans made propaganda from the 'Philistine' act. A Berlin diarist wrote that 'photographs of the battle of Monte Cassino are piling up. The destruction of that beautiful monastery is horrifying. What will happen to Florence, Venice, Rome?'[28] In Dublin de Valera took a brief moral advantage to send an appeal to the belligerent governments and to Roosevelt personally on behalf of Rome.[29] Kesselring said the bombing 'was not only quite unnecessary but prejudicial to the subsequent conduct of the battle'.[30]

---

\* Today the Abbey sells an account and castigates the Allies for the destruction.

\** In the morning 257 tons of 500 lb bombs, 59 tons of 100 lb incendiaries; in the afternoon 283 tons each weighing 1000 lbs.

## 16  Major Blunders of the Second World War

In this Kesselring was accurate; the German parachutists, led by Major Rudolf Bohmler, used the rubble as a defence, holes and gaps in the debris proved as useful as concrete bunkers and easier to hide from prying enemy binoculars. Senger wrote, 'now we would occupy the abbey without scruple, especially as ruins are better for defence than intact buildings', and after the bombing the Germans could in good faith occupy the dominating top of the hill. [31] Bohmler later wrote that if the Allies had attacked immediately with a flanking movement, they would have won the hill, but the paratroopers had time to turn the rubble into a fortress.[32] It created shelter, defence, and advantage points; it is easier to fight from rubble than from a building. One historian noted that it had been said that from the Allied perspective 'there did not appear to be a glimmer of intelligent leadership anywhere from division up'.[33] This episode raised the question that amongst the top commanders no one appeared to have foreseen the tactical disadvantages of post-bombing, namely it is easier for defence to fight from rubble and ruins than a well-known building still intact.

Questionable leadership by the Allied command has been the subject of much investigation, especially with Mark Clark, one historian noting 'there is no doubt that the tactics adopted by Clark's 5th Army at Monte Cassino were poor'.[34] The historian Ellis in his book on Monte Cassino concludes with the powerful indictment that both the 5th and 8th armies were 'poorly led during the Cassino battles'.[35] The bombing which created defensive strong points and the late, untimed, infantry attack were indicators of this poor planning, and made the German defence easier, and helped create the image of Kesselring as the great commander of defence.

The debate will undoubtedly continue while historians and others investigate the past. The Germans appeared to have respected the Abbey and its treasures, but they could not ignore the dominating mountain on which the Abbey stood, and the non-combat zone was pointless. The Allies were right to place lives before ancient monuments, but the bombing provided excellent defensive rubble for the paratroopers. Monte Cassino had some positive repercussions, in that property of an historic nature such as the Ponte Vecchio in Florence and Venice were spared by Kesselring, and on 17 February, forty-four days after the bombing, Alexander sent a belated letter to commanders about preserving 'property of historical and educational importance in Italy'.[36] In the postwar period the debate intensified with Clark claiming he was always against the venture, but Freyberg, then New Zealand's Governor-General in a letter to Kippenberger wrote that Clark had said 'nothing would do but to bring in the heavy fortresses'.[37] Personality conflict in the Allied coalition during and after the war was part of the failing which resulted in such serious misjudgements.

On Wednesday 15 March there was another bombing raid on Monte Cassino. Over 1,400 bombs were dropped but, because of the safety of the rubble from the initial raid, the parachutists were safely dug in, and although they could only move at night, still put-up formidable resistance. Churchill complained about the failure to take Monte Cassino to Alexander, who in his reply wrote that lack of success was that 'the tenacity of these German paratroopers is quite remarkable...I doubt if there are any other troops in the world who could have stood up to it and then gone on fighting with the ferocity they have'.[38] Despite warnings from the airman Eaker the rubble created by the bombing stopped the proposed use of tanks, and again the infantry were sent in late and in small numbers, and they 'dribbled in' according to Kippenberger.[39]

The use of air superiority was questionable at this stage. Kesselring and his Luftwaffe commanders had few aircraft at their disposal. In January 1944 they had 370 planes whereas 'the Allies had close to 4,000'.[40] It would appear the Allies failed at this juncture to use their supremacy appropriately; it was 'sadly inadequate'.[41] The actual bombing raid on Cassino town damaged towns away from Cassino and killed Allied troops by hitting '8th Army HQ, General Juin's HQ, Allied gun-positions, the 4th Indian Division's B Echelon and a Moroccan military hospital'.[42]

The poor planning by Clark, 'perhaps the most egocentric Allied general of the War', and Alexander, who 'acquired a false reputation as a great commander in the field', along with Freyberg's mistakes meant that Kesselring's defence strategy worked better than it should have done given the over-powering numbers.[43] 'On the whole both 5th and 8th

## 18   Major Blunders of the Second World War

Armies were poorly led during the Cassino battles, where operations were consistently marred by lack of strategic vision and slipshod staff work'.[44]

The bombing of Monte Cassino killed innocent clergy and Italian civilians, and also misdirected bombs created many Allied casualties, the 'blue on blue' deaths and injuries may never be known. The Germans lost very few men, the bombing helped them have natural defensive positions, whilst the rubble increased problems for vehicles, especially Allied tanks. The hill was not taken until the middle of May after a major effort by New Zealand infantry followed by violent hand to hand fighting by Polish troops.

Militarily the bombing had proved to be a disaster and it still took months to chase the Germans from their vantage point. The bombing killed few if any Germans yet created havoc elsewhere. The number of lives lost in fighting over this massive hill over the months was horrendous, and the figures in various history books and other archival texts vary. It also brought down on the Allied commanders criticism at the time, and growing since, for the reason of destroying a world-famous ancient monastery. Many at the time and since have regarded the bombing as a sheer act of senseless vandalism. Any visitor to the monastery today is met by reminders of the Allied bombing in terms of the history and pamphlets, but not least in looking at a staircase where relics dug from the bomb rubble now adorn the wall. It was diplomatically embarrassing for the Allies, and it is viewed by many as unnecessary and a morally wrong use of aerial destruction. The German Field Marshal Kesselring once claimed that fighting in Italy was like fighting in a museum, and while Alexander was right that lives came before ancient buildings, it was nevertheless, a gross misjudgement by Allied military command on the spot. It was no mere accident or blunder, there was a degree of incompetence in ordering the aerial bombing given the lack of preciseness in bomb-aiming and target areas, and the lack of foresight in bettering the German defence positions. Given the facts that it was such a major misjudgement many of those involved in the postwar era have tried to distance themselves from any involvement in the decision making.

## Sinking the French Fleet

On 3 July 1940 there was a German air raid on Cardiff, Haile Selassie of Ethiopia left Britain for Khartoum in the hope of regaining the country from Italians with British help, and the French fleet was attacked by the Royal Navy at Mers-el-Kébir to ensure it did not fall into German hands. France had been defeated and the British had retreated via Dunkirk back to home shores. Britain stood alone with its army now on the defensive and badly mauled, the only offensive against the Nazi onslaught was RAF bombing, and the Royal Navy fighting to protect British shores and supplies from U-boat attacks. There was a nagging fear that the dangers would increase exponentially if the French Navy fell into German hands. Technically the French were Britain's Allies and the decision to sink the French fleet raised many questions. This section is included because the question of incompetence and misjudgement is not always clear even over 80 years after the event. There are some who would argue there was no choice but for the British to attack their beaten Allies, others that it was precipitate, too impulsive, and more time should have been given to find alternatives and the French to collect their thoughts. Many at the time and since thought it was an immoral act, and there are those who argue that it was an appalling error of judgement, and even with the benefit of hindsight there are no clear answers. It is over to the reader to arrive at their own conclusion when the account and the reasons are explored.

### *Mers-el-Kébir*

As soon as the French had signed the Armistice there was considerable concern in British circles as to what would happen to the powerful French fleet. The Italian fleet was now on the side of the enemy, and it would be a potential disaster if the more powerful French vessels fell into the hands of the Germans. At this stage the Royal Navy was considered the most powerful European fleet, but with Italy aligned with Germany and fear of the French fleet coming under Nazi control, the traditional balance of naval power would change dramatically. This possibility was regarded 'as an intolerable risk by the British government'.[45] Control of

## 20    Major Blunders of the Second World War

the seas was a dominant feature of the Second World War as with most international conflicts. The German navy was rapidly developing both its submarines and major surface vessels such as the *Tirpitz*, *Bismarck* and so forth. The French fleet was also powerful and if it fell into German hands, the implications spelt potential disaster. It could mean the seizure of the Mediterranean. The Atlantic trade routes were now even more critical and had come under U-boat threat, and even a German cross-channel invasion (*Sea Lion*) would be made more feasible.

The British were especially concerned because they had noted that Article 8 of the Armistice indicated that French ships should return to their home ports; it took little imagination to understand how easy it would be for the Germans to take control; Hitler's promises could never be trusted. There were discussions at the highest level, and Toulon port was guarded by shore artillery, so the focus became the North African base, under plans known as Operation *Catapult*.

In Mers-el-Kébir there was an attempted discussion with the French naval commanders. Admiral Somerville set up a four-headed ultimatum for discussion. This was led by a preamble that it was important the French should not allow their vessels to be used by the common enemy, and that after the war they would be returned, or compensation given. The ultimatum's first demand was for the French fleet to join the British and continue fighting the Germans. The second was to sail with reduced crews to British ports and those men who wished would be repatriated. The alternative was to sail with a reduced crew to faraway French ports such as Martinique where they could be demilitarised or cared for by the USA. The fourth ultimatum was an order to scuttle the ships within six hours otherwise force would be used to prevent the vessels falling into German hands. The demands were clearly explicit, but the Admiral gave them to the French-speaking Captain Cedric Holland (Commander of HMS *Ark Royal*) but the French Admiral Gensoul was affronted that negotiations were taking place through what he considered a junior officer. This sense of rank and social class was not helpful. As a consequence, Gensoul sent his lieutenant, a Bernard Dufay which led to long delays and much confusion. This whole episode remains somewhat confused as to what actually happened, but as it transpired it appeared Admiral Darlan never received the full text, particularly the option of sailing to American waters. Darlan had little time for the British and it remains questionable as to what his response would have been even if he had been aware of the full details.

'Captain Holland kept trying but Gensoul refused to change his original reply', and the human pride of resenting having to talk to what was deemed a junior officer led to disaster.[46] The result was catastrophic in so far that only one French battleship escaped, the *Strasbourg*, the rest of the fleet was sunk or seriously damaged, and some 1,300 French sailors died. Britain and France were virtually at war without a formal declaration, and this remained the situation through most of the time of the Vichy regime. Everyone must have found the whole affair confusing and distasteful; even Stoker 1st Class Vernon Coles recorded that 'at 1755 we opened fire. It was a sad irony. We were not attacking the Germans or Italians, but the Royal Navy's oldest enemy and our twentieth-century ally'.[47] The British felt they had no choice but to neutralise or sink the French fleet which they did at Mers-el-Kébir on 3 July as soon as no clear answer was received from the French.

The French must have known how the British felt about their fleet being in danger of Nazi control or oversight, because in anticipation of this problem 'the sailing of French warships to British ports had been Britain's absolute condition for relieving France from its promise not to make a separate peace'.[48] The British had also noted that the French government while in Bordeaux had refused permission for the French ships to sail towards British ports. The possibility of the French fleet falling into German hands was too immense, and even having to keep an eye on them would be a waste of precious time and resources. The British experienced this when the battleship *Richelieu* left Dakar for France and the Royal Navy had to chase it back. The question as to the rights and wrongs of the British decision are still debated to this day. One historian wrote that 'however distasteful this attack on an erstwhile ally, those who preferred keeping their new agreement with Germany to observing their prior treaty commitment to Britain could hardly expect

## 22 Major Blunders of the Second World War

greater consideration from the latter'.[49] There was serious Anglophobia in Vichy France, and the feeling was mutual, especially since the newly installed Vichy regime had just released some precious 400 Luftwaffe pilots which the French had promised to hand over to the English for safe-keeping.[50] Admiral Darlan was well-known for his long history as an Anglophobe, and later when he assumed more authority in Vichy he was more prepared than Laval or Pétain to link military arms with Germany. One of Darlan's ancestors was reputed to have fought the British at the Battle of Trafalgar.

### Reactions

Even so, there is no doubt that the Royal Navy probably found the whole task appalling, and 'yet this one-sided battle had an extraordinary effect around the world in its demonstration that Britain was prepared to fight on as ruthlessly as it needed. Roosevelt in particular was convinced that the British would not now surrender'.[51] The American Secretary for State entered in his diary that 'it is very interesting to see how the tide of opinion has swung in favour of the eventual victory of Great Britain. The air of pessimism which prevailed two months ago has gone'.[52] At this stage America retained its isolationist policy and Churchill fully understood the need for American support, money, resources, and military. He was determined that the American administration would note Britain's ability to fight ruthlessly against the odds and encourage Roosevelt to support and enter the conflict.

Churchill, unlike his predecessor was by nature offensive rather than defensive, and he was determined to find a way of expressing his warlike nature in actual action; he was good at doing so verbally. As previously observed some historians have even claimed that the sinking of the French fleet at Mers-el-Kébir was merely an expression of that frustration of needing to show aggression. Forczyk claimed 'that Operation *Catapult* was an idiotic display of military force and represented the nadir of British strategy in the World War II'.[53] Although somewhat powerfully expressed, it was nevertheless true that Britain did not have the resources to fight a war against Germany. This is probably why Churchill was obliged to turn to peripheral activities because Britain lacked the resources to fight a major war on the European mainland.

Even Ciano noted in his diary that 'it proves that the fighting spirit of His Britannic Majesty's fleet is quite alive, and still has the aggressive ruthlessness of the captains and pirates of the seventeenth century'.[54] His reference to pirates of the past, because of his style of humour, did not necessarily imply he thought the act necessarily unjustified, but merely as a feature of determined reaction.

Operation *Catapult* certainly underlined to the Nazi regime that Britain was intensely serious in its intentions to fight on. In Vichy France where there was already a rampant Anglophobia, this now turned to a visceral hatred and a breaking down of diplomatic relationships. Both then and now Churchill had his critics. It has been argued that Churchill should have given more consideration on the effect on Franco-British relations; that it was an unprovoked attack, and that it 'hindered de Gaulle's efforts to recruit Frenchmen and was an unnecessarily rash action'.[55] It has also been noted that 'Admiral Somerville was ashamed by his role...and called it the biggest political blunder of modern times'.[56] Even British contemporaries of the time were confused as to whether it was a gross misjudgement or not.

### Vichy France

On 5 July the Vichy government severed diplomatic relations with Britain because of Mers-el-Kébir, and Admiral Darlan ordered the French fleet to attack the British navy, but he was overruled by the foreign minister Paul Baudouin and Pétain. The French were outraged as the British had sunk a battleship, damaged others, including cruisers and destroyers, killing or wounding well over 1,200 French sailors, and though Darlan was thwarted from naval retaliation, the Vichy regime ordered a bombing raid against Gibraltar.

One thing is certain, that not long after the Mers-el-Kébir attack by the British Navy, the French Foreign Minister Paul Baudouin, on behalf of Pétain and through the mediation of the original armistice contacts in Spain, sent a request to meet Ribbentrop to discuss the possibility

## 24   Major Blunders of the Second World War

of becoming what has been described as an *associated power*, this was confirmed at Pétain's trial.[57] The immediate motivation behind this approach was clarified when in August of that year General Huntziger informed his contact von Stülpnagel that he needed to speak to Keitel. It has been generally understood that following the clash with the Royal Navy, Vichy was now seeking some kind of Mediterranean partner and even a possible cohort in Europe. It is difficult to speculate how far Mers-el-Kébir had affected the Vichy mind-set, but it was probably a significant factor in turning their minds towards a form of political collaboration with the occupier. Vichy France, through Charles Huntziger's office at Wiesbaden (where armistice details were continuously under discussion), talked to the Germans about Fortress Europe and suggested the French look after the problem of overseas possessions, looking to the British territories as some form of compensation.* After Mers-el-Kébir diplomatic relations with England were broken and never restored, but most of the military men did not want a war with Britain which some were suggesting.

This British Naval attack certainly prompted the turning away from the old alliance, and it encouraged Laval's belief that France had more in common with Germany than Britain. Britain's action at Mers-el-Kébir may have been deemed right by the British perception of naval superiority and the need for decisive action to be seen, but it has left a mark on Franco-British relationships even to this day. It was a period of deep enmity between the old Allies of France and Britain. Most of this hostility arose from Mers-el-Kébir, the Dakar expedition, and the virulent presence of de Gaulle now regarded as a British agent. As the memory of Dakar and Mers-el-Kébir faded there was a slight relaxing of the approach towards Britain, but it was more a degree of caution. The British Ambassador in Spain, Hoare, had made it clear that that any activity against de Gaulle in Africa could lead to war with Britain, which most recognised as a serious threat. France, still technically at war with Germany could not afford to fight her former ally. Nor could France afford

---

* Charles Huntziger had commanded the French 2nd and then 4th Army Groups in the war; he was a staunch support of Vichy holding many posts, but he was killed in a plane accident on 11 Nov 1941 near Le Vigan Gard.

to alienate the country whose Royal Navy was still considered powerful. There were already serious problems with the food blockade, and Vichy continually sought American assistance to persuade the British to allow food supplies into the country. Laval and Pétain became conscious of the need to avoid an outright British war.

## *Elsewhere*

On 3 July, Operation *Catapult* had started with the seizure of French ships in British ports. According to the French historian Henri Michel it was a 'treacherous' act.[58] There were French ships scattered in British ports in Egypt and Britain and those in Plymouth and Portsmouth were boarded without notice. The French submarine the *Surcouf* (the largest in the world at that time) offered resistance leading to the deaths of three Royal Navy personnel and a French sailor. Two older French battleships, the *Paris* and *Courbet*, two destroyers, eight torpedo boats and five submarines were taken over. Many were later used by the Free French, but it created a sense of understandable anger amongst the French, especially de Gaulle, and many French sailors demanded and were given repatriation to France. It may have been that discussion may have won the day, but there was a sense of urgency in the British self-interests based on the need to survive at all costs; it was not regarded as a time for civilised niceties.

In Alexandria talks were held between Admiral Cunningham and Admiral Godfroy which led to the fortunate agreement that the French ships could be neutralised without resort to violence; here personal discussion worked. The British were under extreme pressure. With the loss of France and the potential threat to the Empire from a Mediterranean attack they took measures to ensure control of the region, seizing a French naval squadron in Alexandria on 3 July 1940.

## *Final thoughts*

For the Americans and the rest of the world it was 'realpolitik' and clearly indicated Britain's intention to fight. For France it was a palpable stab in the back and a profound betrayal. To this day many French people still view it as a despicable over-reaction, an act of self-seeking treachery.

Although war was never formally declared, from the time of that incident it was a *de facto* war between the two one-time allies.

Critically, in viewing this incident later in the war, the remaining French fleet then scuttled itself at Toulon, where it was supposed to be safe from German interference, but the deed was done after the occupation of Vichy France because of the realistic fear of the vessels being taken over by the Germans. This action provoked the feeling 'that we told you we would, you should have trusted us'. Various viewpoints of the French fleet destruction at Toulon have been expressed, some sympathetic others less so, one historian describing it as a 'melancholy conclusion to an armada about which there had been so many hopes, fears, and premonitions'.[59] Because of this Vichy reaction it could be argued that the French could have been trusted; on the other hand, in July 1940 the French were in a very fragile state and confused.

This incident will never be satisfactorily resolved, but the fact that the armistice demanded the French warships return to their home ports, the total untrustworthiness of Hitler, and that Britain could not allow its Royal Navy to be outstripped for many commentators the argument bends in favour of Churchill's decision. The necessity of the power of the Royal Navy was abundantly clear to friend and foe, and in view of *Sea Lion* it could be regarded as essential to survival.

Others argue killing French sailors, before their national defeat a few months before, was simply wrong. It caused deep resentment amongst the French, persisting to this day. Only a few years ago this writer sat listening in a French bar to young, middle-aged, and elderly customers in rage over Brexit, somehow connecting it to the sinking of the French fleet and was grateful they assumed the listening stranger was not British. It caused de Gaulle problems in recruitment and made him even more resentful of his British hosts. It may well have played a part in turning some Vichy leaders into a more pro-German view, and certainly brought Vichy France and Britain into a deeply mutually suspicious relationship which at times verged on outright war.

This contentious issue remains in a very grey area. The arguments for Operation *Catapult* are strong, there were some doubters at the time, not least by the Royal Navy called upon to do the killing. The bitterness in France remained, not least when the French fleet in Toulon scuttled itself, and since many have regarded it as catastrophic misjudgement in terms of international relationships.

## Bio-Chemical Warfare

*Dulce et Decorum Est*, by Wilfred Owen, 1917

*GAS! GAS! Quick, boys! An ecstasy of fumbling,*
*Fitting the clumsy helmets just in time;*
*But someone still was yelling out and stumbling.*
*And flound'ring like a man in fire or lime...*
*Dim, through the misty panes and thick green light,*
*As under a green sea, I saw him drowning.*
*In all my dreams, before my helpless sight,*
*He plunges at me, guttering, choking, drowning.*

### Introduction

If a fire breaks out in a huge public building and nobody knows the whereabouts of the fire-extinguishers, then disaster will follow. Extending this analogy, an administrative blunder mixed with a degree of over-confidence led to the deaths of countless military and innocent Italian citizens in an incident which was kept secret for many years. It involved the feared and internationally outlawed use of gas weapons. The individual soldier in the front line of the Great War faced machine guns, artillery attacks, mortar bombs, hand grenades, aircraft, but the most feared were the gas attacks.

Gas weapons were not a feature of the Second World War, but it lurked ominously in the background, not least because the Italians had deployed gas in a colonial conflict during the interbellum years. It was because of the ever-present threat that gas weapons were kept in many Allied mobile arsenals to be used as retaliation if the enemy resorted to them, and thereby deter them.

## 28   Major Blunders of the Second World War

It was this which led to a major disaster in Italy, and it could have triggered a greater disaster by prompting an interchange between the enemy armies by using the gas as seen in the Great War. This disaster happened because the Western Allies believed that the Luftwaffe was crushed in Italy, and they felt confident that they could unload vital supplies at night in the port of Bari with all the lights on, and seemingly unaware of the whereabouts of gas shells and bombs within their itinerary. The result was total disaster, politically risky, militarily dangerous, and kept quiet for these reasons. The bombing raid was one thing, the consequential release of gas another.

### Gas as a Weapon

Wars are provoked under many excuses, from pure aggression to defence, preventative wars, wars of intervention for claimed moral reasons, the list is endless. Only one factor remains permanent: the main feature of war is the emerging power of total destruction, brutality and the growing sense of sophistication and human ingenuity in devising new methods of mass destruction of life and land. Gone are the days when tribal warriors would sally forth seeking more land, power, resources, and self-importance. In recent history there was a time when battles had visitors watching from a safe distance with their picnic baskets and feeling reasonably safe. The American Civil War has often been quoted as the first modern industrialised war, but the wars of the twentieth century took barbarity to repulsive depths. Mass killings on the battlefield, carpet bombing, ethnic cleansing in the Holocaust are only a few examples. The Second World War was concluded by nuclear bombs, which with today's rapid delivery systems still casts a shadow of fear across the globe. Many people still find the fear of chemical and biological warfare even more frightening than disappearing in a nuclear vapour. During Mussolini's time in power, he ordered the Pontine Marshes (in the Lazio region of central Italy) to be cleared of malarial carrying mosquitoes, and thereby established a region capable of agricultural potential and made human life more tenable. Himmler ordered these marshes to be flooded, and the malarial mosquitoes re-introduced thereby creating one of the first forms of biological war. It was in a sense evolving the system of the unseen weapon such as the long-deployed use of poisoning the food or drink of an individual who was deemed necessary by others to be killed. In the modern era this process has moved from the attack on the individual to whole armies and even communities.

During the 1914–18 war gas was used for the first time with devastating results. The intention was to injure, demoralise and kill the opposition. The French were the first to use tear-gas grenades, and the Germans later deployed fragmentation shells with chemical irritants which sometimes went unnoticed by their enemy. In 1915 the Germans used artillery shells with xylyl bromide tear gas on the Russian front, and later introduced the first killing agent chlorine. The British called it cowardly, and they rapidly developed chlorine, but in its first use failed to take note of wind direction as it blew back over their own ranks. Phosgene was soon developed and the most common was the well-known mustard gas which led to devastating results. The rapid-firing machine guns and artillery bombardment were feared by everyone, but not as much as the use of gas against which only a gasmask could provide some limited defence. After the war, on 17 June 1925 the Geneva protocol was signed by 132 nations outlawing the use of this weapon, but the threat remained.

In the Great War it was estimated there were some 90,000 fatalities from a total of 1.3 million casualties. The gas mask was the only means of protection, but the use of gas has often been regarded as the initiation of weapons of mass destruction. When it was used in the Great War it was technically illegal in so far that it violated the 1899 Hague Declaration concerning Asphyxiating Gases, and the 1907 Hague Convention on Land Warfare which prohibited the use of poison in warfare. Overall, most people were against the policy of using gas, but the problem with war is that it rapidly becomes out of control. Most people are more concerned with survival and winning than by international legal and ethical agreements. Nevertheless, there has been a sense of taboo about the use of gas, which was emphasised in the 1925 Geneva Protocol banning chemicals and bacteriological weapons. The 1925 Protocol underlined the

## 30 Major Blunders of the Second World War

international nature of the law, and it was given additional commitment in the Conventions of 1972 and 1993.

The danger of gas, perceived during the First World War, was that it could be as indiscriminate as high-level bombing with what is often dubbed 'blue on blue' damage, but a sudden change of wind, as experienced by the British, could blow it back and wreak havoc amongst the perpetrators. It caused death like any shell, but it often created blindness and long-term psychological ramifications. A recent study analysed the effects and found that gas consumption created a range of somatic symptoms [any form of mental disorder that manifests as physical symptoms], respiratory and neuropsychiatric symptoms.[60] It does not need medical expertise to stress the dangers and sheer hostile nature of gas, which the vast majority of people still regard as immoral even in a war where survival is the major issue, but moral standards or views are frequently ignored by military commanders, politicians, and the soldier on the front line. As such, the use of bio-chemical warfare continues as an issue in today's world. It was used after the Great War, and was considered during the 1939–1945 conflict, and has been deployed in recent decades. When Britain was in danger of invasion by the Germans following the fall of France, the situation was desperate, and international protocols, already broken by the Italians, were shelved, and in a Cabinet meeting it was decided that gas must be ready in case the Germans used it against the Russians.[61] Earlier General Alan Brooke, who was responsible for home defence, had decided to use gas in the crisis of a German seaborne attack to repel the invaders, and he had visited Porton Down to discuss the possibilities.[62] He was prepared to go this far although he and others knew that the offshore wind could sweep the gas ashore with a sudden change of wind, destroying British forces and civilians. This policy underlined that the more serious the threat the more likely gas would be used. High principles and any sense of keeping to the rules would be abandoned in the light of an overwhelming threat. This attitude shared by other nations illustrates that in total war there is no such thing as a clean war. The keeping of bio-chemical weapons by many nations has been excused by the reason that it is necessary just in case the other side uses them first.

During the Second World War it has been estimated that America held some 135,000 tons of chemical agents, Germany 70,000, Britain, 40,000 and Japan about 8,000. These stockpiles varied in content. Many were the old suffocating chlorine and phosgene agents, the blistering mustard gas, but the German nerve gases reportedly were much deadlier. Hitler had experienced gas attacks in the Great War, and as far as is known there was no serious threat of them being deployed by the Germans. (It is believed that during the Great War, Hitler had been temporarily blinded by British gas.) There were certainly discussions by Churchill and some American generals about using them against Germany and Japan, but as with Hitler, most probably there was the constant concern that the other side would retaliate in kind; not using gas was not based on any moral argument, but out of fear.

Italy had used gas in the attack on Ethiopia in the full and certain knowledge that the tribesmen they were attacking could never retaliate in kind. Italy had signed the protocol and ratified it in October 1935. By December of the same year the Italians dropped mustard gas or phosgene bombs in 103 attacks and 'Mussolini had personally approved it in a telegram to the Italian commander, Marshal Rodolfo Graziani, on 27 October'.[63] It was hardly surprising the tribesmen had surrendered not long after these attacks. Later in the Anglo-Italian war in North Africa the German Field Marshal Albert Kesselring had to advise Mussolini not to use gas against British troops, whether out of moral reasons or fear of retaliation may never be known.

### Danger of Storing Gas Weapons

Probably because of the fear of chemical weapons their existence in the stockpiles of various countries was kept as a highly guarded secret both during and after the war. There was a general understanding by all sides that gas would not be deployed, and despite the desperate situations which arose for all sides they were not deployed. Mussolini had been tempted having used them successfully, but the Germans were the masters in the Italian field of operations and advised against their use. It was clear that both sides of the divide knew such stockpiles must be in place, and the

## 32    Major Blunders of the Second World War

sheer fear of retaliation meant one belligerent would think twice before activating such a weapon. However, by the same sense of nervous fear they were sometimes kept close to the frontline just in case their use was required in retaliation. Stockpiling such weapons was in many ways more dangerous than any normal ammunition dump, and the greatest care and secrecy was essential. Escaping released gas was far more difficult to cope with than exploding bombs. There was one incident during the Italian campaign when an Allied stockpile was exposed, attacked in an air raid, the gas was released causing considerable damage to military and civilians alike. At the time and for a long period after the war, such was the gravity of this incident it was kept under cover. It occurred in the Italian port of Bari, how and why it happened, and the consequences will be explored in the following subsection of this chapter.

### *The Bari Incident*

Field Marshal Kesselring was fighting a retreating defence in Italy with some skill, and some historians such as Carlo D'Este have made the claim that 'Kesselring was one of the outstanding commanders of the war'. Logistically the Allies were far better resourced than the German occupying forces, but the Italian terrain was easier to defend than attack. However, the Allies had total air-superiority, their naval forces were powerful, and American resources appeared unlimited. Naples had been the main port for supplies, but Bari on the east coast of Italy was the main supply for both the air force and the army battering away at the Gustav line.

In late November 1943, Kesselring had held a conference at his HQ in Frascati with von Richthofen, Dietrich Pelz, Baumbach and all the Luftwaffe senior officers. The discussion was how to slow down the inexorable Allied advance by attacking their supply routes. At first it was decided that the Foggia Allied airfields were the most obvious option. On the other hand, von Richthofen persuasively argued for Bari because of the immense flow of supplies passing through the port, and Kesselring soon agreed. On the other side of the divide, Sir Arthur Coningham had claimed the Luftwaffe was finished, stating that 'I would regard it as a

Blunders or Misjudgements  33

personal affront and insult if the Luftwaffe would attempt any significant action in this area'.[64] Richthofen pointed out that his spies had informed him that such was the over-confidence of the Allies that Bari port was unloading incoming convoys at night with all the lights on. When the raid took place on 2 December the complacency of the Allies was evident, and the port and town were so bright and lit up, it was easy to see from above where to attack. Navigational aids were hardly necessary as the essential parts of the port were shining like a funfair.

The Luftwaffe carried out the raid on the port so efficiently the attack became known as the 'Little Pearl Harbour' or 'Second Pearl Harbour'. The Luftwaffe managed to sink seventeen ships, and damaged many others, along with many of the dockyards.* Amongst these vessels was a Liberty ship called the SS *John Harvey*, captained by Elwin Knowles; this ship was carrying mustard gas bombs.** The port of Bari had been in a hectic state of unloading, but Captain Elwin Knowles could not ask for priority because of the secrecy of what he was carrying. Such was the silence surrounding gas-weapons, the vast majority from dock-labourers to senior officers had no idea of their existence. The enemy only had to have a hint that gas weapons were in the area to provide an excuse for retaliation with the same type of warfare. Captain Knowles was to die with his entire crew. Curiously, some of the crew had speculated about the vessel's contents because of the presence of an officer called Beckstrom who, with his men, were trained in the handling of such weapons. At least they were aware of the dangerous cargo: in Operation *Husky*, the invasion of Sicily, ordnance officers mistakenly sent poisonous mustard gas shells to the Mediterranean, and 'no one knew precisely where in the holds of one or more ships bound for Sicily' they were stored.[65] Again at the battle for the Rapido American troops had 'to check shells for some gas ones had been issued by mistake'.[66]

The SS *John Harvey* vessel's manifesto remained a secret for many years, because she was carrying 2,000 M47A1 mustard bombs from Oran in

---

\* 5 American, 5 British, 3 Norwegian, 2 Italian, 2 Polish and 7 more seriously damaged.
\*\* Built in North Carolina and launched on 9 January 1943.

## 34   Major Blunders of the Second World War

Algeria; it is claimed that they were sent into a theatre of operation in case the Germans resorted to chemical warfare.* It had been authorised by President Roosevelt, even though the use of chemical weapons had been outlawed by the 1925 Geneva Protocol mentioned above, though ironically there was no ban on their manufacture and transportation until 1972. This had supplied a convenient loophole for keeping gas weapons near to the activity of the frontline, but in a state of war the necessary efficiency was lacking, since they were only needed if the enemy used their gas weapons first.

There were claims that 'Ominous reports had begun to reach Washington and London that indicated Adolf Hitler…was planning to resort to the use of poison gas'.[67] It was only rumour, and no reliable evidence exists that this was a German policy. It had also been rumoured that the Germans were storing up a quarter of a million tons of toxic munitions, including a new colourless and almost odourless gas called Tabun, possibly of Italian manufacture. Roosevelt had clearly stated that 'we shall under no circumstances resort to the use of such weapons unless they are first used by our enemies'.[68] Eisenhower was aware of the presence but not the whereabouts of the gas bombs and shells, knowing that they would only be used as an act of retaliation. In a total war it is always too easy to suspect the enemy of any new tactic to gain the advantage, but there had never been any reason to believe the Germans would use gas except for retaliation and their own safety. The Axis had not used any toxic agents in any military theatre of war; the Americans had trained their combatants in their use but 'few of the trainees took the schooling very seriously'.[69] It was generally believed by many experts that Hitler would not authorise its use because he had a personal antipathy to gas warfare, having lived through the First World War as a corporal. Others supplied information that they were convinced that the Wehrmacht military training did not include toxic warfare, and it was believed that the German High Command would not want to outrage world opinion. The Germans, like the Allies, held toxic weapons in store, and

---

\* Each bomb held up to 100 lbs of mustard gas , which is a toxin known as dichloroethylene sulphide.

it was particularly feared they had *spitzen K-stoff*, which an officer noted 'presumably [meant] some especially important or virulent form of gas'.[70] As late as mid-April 1945 Ultra revealed that Hitler was retaining the right to order their destruction or removal to a safer place like the coast.[71]

When the SS *John Harvey* during the Bari German air attack literally exploded, the mustard-gas infiltrated both the water, the air, and especially the oil, which attached itself to many fighting for their lives in the harbour waters. In the Great War gas had been breathed in as vapour, but in the waters of Bari much of the toxic material was mixed with oil and water, and the effects had never been seen before by the few medical experts available. Many had noticed the unusual smell of garlic, but there was complete confusion over how to treat the accumulating victims. Many were left in their originally contaminated clothes, so they continued to breathe in dangerous fumes. Only those who were capable of stripping and washing themselves increased their chances of survival. A Captain Denfield, a medical doctor, was suspicious about what he was seeing, but he came upon a wall of silence until a stevedore sergeant told him that chemicals were sometimes contained in ship holds. A Lieutenant Colonel Stewart Alexander flew in and confirmed that it was gas: Alexander was an expert from Edgewood Arsenal in Maryland, the equivalent in Britain of Porton Down where such weapons were studied. In this confusion of ignorance, the medical teams took considerable time to realise that the main problems were men going blind and in terrible agony. Some historians claim that over a thousand soldiers and sailors died as well as many Italians from the mustard-gas.[72] Other sources are a more conservative, but even at the lowest end of speculated deaths it has been claimed there were 628 military victims, 83 fatal and many more civilian deaths from the gas-vapour that infiltrated the town. HMS *Bicester* rescued some 30 survivors, but this vessel had to be towed to Taranto because of damage caused in the attack; in Taranto they found that many of the rescue crew were soon suffering from chemical burns and blindness.

In the early stages it was suggested that the Germans had dropped mustard gas bombs, using propaganda style news to indicate they had been the first to use them in the Great War (22 April 1915). It was not until

## 36    Major Blunders of the Second World War

a damaged M47A1 shell was found that it was realised the root of the problem was an Allied logistical blunder. Some of the Allied commanders had worried that a 'retaliatory raid might be made by mistake before the rumour was discounted', which would have increased the already mounting horrors of a total war.[73] There is no doubt that for several hours the military situation was precariously balanced with few knowing what had happened, and those who knew being uncertain how to react. The British port authorities at first declined to acknowledge its existence and Churchill also refused, claiming that the symptoms were not the same, and finally demanding that the causes of the protracted deaths be put down as NYD (Not Yet Diagnosed) dermatitis, or burns caused by the enemy. Unquestionably Churchill was concerned about public opinion, and not letting the enemy know of the existence of such toxic weapons, but the German spy work was efficient and soon *Axis Sally*, sometimes known as the *Berlin Bitch* was broadcasting that 'I see you boys are getting gassed by your own poison gas'.[74] There was the constant fear that if the enemy were aware that this weapon was contained close by or in the battle scene there could be a prompt retaliation with the same type of weapon.

Sadly, the statistics were appalling: 'Of the 70,752 men hospitalised for gas in the First World War only two per cent died, as against thirteen per cent in Bari'.[75] This was probably because the medical officers had no idea what they were dealing with, and it was the first time such gas had infiltrated the human bodies by oil and water. Ironically, as a result of the pathological tests carried out post-war on the many who died, medical research found in these toxins a clue towards curing some elements of Hodgkin's disease and various forms of leukaemia.

The port was out of action for many months, and the disaster was not given any publicity because of the censors. The event was well-known by those who were there, but it was kept out of the public eye in America and was only de-restricted in 1959. This restriction on events was because it had been such a terrible almost self-inflicted disaster causing a major embarrassment at both political and military levels. The secrecy cost Italian lives because the civilian hospitals were kept in the dark. The *Washington Post* mentioned the attack, but it did not refer to the gas or the amount of damage, probably worried about stirring public opinion as to how the government was running the war. Churchill had all the records purged and the whole incident remained obscure until the late 1960s. As recently as 1986 *The Times* reported that some 600 contaminated British seamen would receive back-dated war pensions.

The Luftwaffe air raid put the port of Bari out of commission for a long period of time; it was the second greatest shipping disaster for the Allies during the Second World War, and Kesselring's raid had some serious effects on the Allied campaign. Not least amongst the problems was lack of supplies to the 15th Air Force at Foggia which had been dependent upon Bari's imports. It also 'prevented Mediterranean Allied Air Forces from attacking German airfields prior to the amphibious landing at Anzio'.[76] From Kesselring's point of view it was an outstanding success, but it succeeded because the Allied air command was overconfident and mistakenly thought the Luftwaffe was finished. Allowing the lights to stay on when just a few miles from the enemy lines is almost beyond belief, especially with so many valuable merchant vessels moored side by side. Some historians believe the ramifications of the Bari raid stretched as far as Normandy.[77] This may be putting too much weight on the German success, but it caused serious problems for the Allied campaign and cost far too many lives and long-standing casualties. Having gas weapons not only close by and ready for action, but not knowing where or how many created a serious blunder. It could have been simply poor administration, inexperience, frenetic activity, or the heat of war, but it amounted not only to sheer incompetence but a major misjudgement, and the consequences were far reaching, and for those involved an unnecessary tragedy.

Chapter Two

# The Dieppe Disaster

## Author's Notes

In August 1942 a cross-channel attack was made by the British on the port of Dieppe, involving over 6,000 men which lasted only six hours and resulted in a 60 per cent casualty rate. The soldiers fought bravely against overwhelming circumstances but were badly let down by those who had prepared, planned, and initiated the attack. This study is an attempt to unravel why the raid happened in the first place, it will provide a brief synopsis of events, but not deal with the battle in detail. The raid itself is simply summarised, as there have been many excellent studies on the battle itself. One of the better earlier studies was written by Ronald Atkin, and more recently an outstanding study by Patrick Bishop.[1] The central focus of this brief study is to question the responsibility of those who wanted the raid, why they decided it was necessary, and who was mainly responsible. This exploration outlines the contentious reasons behind the Dieppe raid, its planning, and the debates which followed.

The main thrust of the accountability for this disaster and major misjudgement wavers between factors such as political pressure, or the personal aggrandisement of a military commander, namely the well-known Mountbatten, trying to enhance his reputation. There have been many accounts and explanations by historians and the participants, and it remains something of a clouded mystery. This study has no definitive answers, but will try and balance the evidence as far as possible for the reader to evaluate their own opinion.

## Why it was Deemed Necessary

Churchill realised that Stalin's demands for a second front were important because the Soviets were hard pressed and bearing the brunt of the Nazi war. The Allies, especially the Americans were concerned that it might cross Stalin's mind to make a separate peace with Hitler, which would possibly mean another concerted attack on Britain. Mussolini and his Foreign Minister had questioned Hitler as to whether he should seek some form of agreement with Stalin, but this was not Hitler's way of thinking. Apparently, Stalin had hinted at this possibility in an effort to whip his allies into a more pro-active warlike attitude because of the pressure the Soviet forces were under. The Americans were equally enthusiastic on starting a second front not in Africa or Italy, but directly across the channel, heading for Berlin by way of France. It took the notable Chief of the Imperial General Staff, Alan Brooke, to convince them that an early attempt to cross the channel would be disastrous, which was not well received. The American General Omar Bradley in his later memoirs acknowledged Brooke had been right, writing that 'in Africa we learnt to crawl, to walk and then run. Had that learning process been launched in France it would surely have, as Alan Brooke argued, resulted in an unthinkable disaster'.[2] This debate over the war in North Africa resulted not just in tension between Stalin and his Western Allies, but within the Western camp as well. Churchill was aware that the British public and parliament demanded some success. In early 1942 Britain had its back to the wall, nothing was going well, and the North African campaign appeared somewhat unfruitful. The occasional raid across the channel or into Norway seemed to be the only way the hitherto defensive British could appear to be offensive and aggressive. Churchill once referred to such attacks as a 'punch on the snout' and hoped thereby to impress not only the Soviets and the Americans, but also the general public who were becoming cynical about the series of disasters which seemed to occur one after another. The only other offensive against the Nazi enemy were the RAF bomber raids. Churchill's hopes for a success and survival had risen when America joined the fray, but as much as he needed some form of victory, both he and Brooke realised they needed more time to launch a full-scale invasion across the often-turbulent English Channel, with the American troops at this stage being inexperienced against a highly professional German army. Roosevelt had eventually agreed to attacking

French North Africa first, but the need to cross the English Channel was constantly fermenting, and Churchill was under considerable pressure on this matter, not least with the Americans, who having the necessary power and money, kept pressing for a date to drive straight to Berlin from the French coast. Roosevelt's top military adviser George Marshall remained cynical about the African invasion and kept the channel crossing on the agenda, with Roosevelt questioning British colonial motives in North Africa. As a consequence of this political pressure 'to do something', and thereby supporting Stalin, encouraging the Americans, and appeasing public opinion, Churchill started looking to the suggestion of some form of snatching a holding area (lodgement area) in occupied France, and consequently a plan emerged, originally coded Operation *Sledgehammer*. Various coastal areas were examined to find a place on the French coast which could be attacked and occupied, and possibly held ready for a major invasion as projected later in Normandy D-Day. The main concern remained keeping Stalin fighting, as there was the rumour that he might start looking for some form of settlement with the Nazi regime. If true, it was undoubtedly his heavy-handed effort to encourage some diverting attention for the German forces in the West, using their troops on the Eastern Front to assist an attack in the west. It was also hoped that such an operation would please the Americans who were all too enthusiastic about a direct attack into the heartland of Germany. The whole episode of invading a portion of German occupied France at such an early date was driven by political needs as perceived by the British, because of the pressure applied by their stronger allies.

The Dieppe Raid must be explored within this fraught political backdrop. Churchill had faced a series of defeats in Norway, the Low Countries, France, Greece, Crete, North Africa, Hong Kong, Singapore, and was all too aware that this situation was viewed by the Americans as military weakness. The American press had raised the issue of 'Defensive England', and Churchill's own public and the House of Commons were raising questions for him to answer. It even seemed to Churchill that his own military experts appeared to be lacking initiative, referring to them as 'the do-nothing policy of faint-hearted obstructionists'.[3] The

Americans continued to argue for a direct attack into France, and Stalin remained provocative on the subject. As noted above, in February 1942 Stalin had suggested a willingness to negotiate with the Germans, which, if it became a reality would have been an all-round disaster. Churchill needed a success to illustrate British aggression, and he had flown from Cairo to Teheran to Moscow in order to explain to Stalin why there could not be a Second Front, but 'was infuriated by Soviet accusations of British cowardice'.[4]

The Allies were struggling for a strategy, with America still persisting for a direct attack into France, suggesting Operation *Sledgehammer*, which involved occupying Cherbourg or Brest, and it was understandably encouraged by Stalin. Various forms of commando attacks had been instigated against coastal towns and ports, the most successful had been blowing up the huge dry-docks in Saint-Nazaire, stopping German warships utilising the place. This came under the umbrella of COHQ (Combined Operations Headquarters) under the command of Mountbatten who had succeeded Admiral Keyes, the latter had long been exploring the possibility of an assault to procure some form of lodgement on the French coast.[5] It should be noted at this point that while some of the commando type raids had been successful some had been disastrous, with the traditional military commanders being somewhat cynical about COHQ, and not always appreciative of Keyes, and especially lacking trust in his successor Mountbatten. There were many sub-committees and staff looking into the various possibilities of attack, and later the Chief of Combined Operations (now Mountbatten) frequently joined such critical meetings. Mountbatten's inclusion in the Chiefs of Staff (COS) was not welcomed by the other members, and Pound wrote of his objections to the Prime Minister.[6] Brooke was not pleased with the arrival of Mountbatten as head of Combined Operations, because the COS as a body did precisely the work which Brooke thought should be done by the army. Brooke did not even like the title since he believed operations should always be regarded as combined. Mountbatten was to attend only a couple of times a week when larger problems were being discussed. Brooke found Mountbatten good social company, but in terms

## 42 Major Blunders of the Second World War

of military professionalism he believed Mountbatten 'frequently wasted both his time and ours'.[7] Brooke later wrote of Mountbatten that 'he is quite irresponsible, suffers from the most desperate illogical brains, always producing red herrings.'[8] Brooke never changed his views on this royal military commander.

Later, when the Dieppe raid was being discussed as a possibility, Brooke was somewhat concerned that Mountbatten and Churchill were showing too much optimism by discussing lodgements along the French coast; both men, Brooke felt, seemed to be underestimating the power of the potential German reaction. Every time Brooke discussed this issue with Churchill, he seemed to understand what Brooke was trying to say, but he kept returning to other attacks which the realistic Brooke thought were mere mad ideas, and it is little wonder that Brooke felt so frustrated at times, or in his words, 'liverish'.

However, the pressure on Churchill and his government was intense. Molotov had visited London but had no success in persuading the British for a second front, and consequently travelled to Washington. He was supported by the Americans, and Molotov returned to London to try and persuade the British to use *Sledgehammer* as a possible second front. The British argued that it was too soon, not least because air-cover would be limited as would be all the necessary resources: in this they were right, but their persistence in fighting in North Africa often struck the Americans as Churchill's empire ambitions. It was against this political background that the British thought some form of raid on the French coast might be regarded as an opportunity to divert attention from the fraught issue of the second front, and so a raid on Dieppe emerged as a form of replacement for *Sledgehammer*, first and foremost as a political appeasement to the growing criticism of their allies.


### A Plan to ease Political Pressures

The Joint Planning Staff had long been consumed with various studies ready to present to the Imperial Chiefs of Staff, but always hoping the Germans would collapse on the Eastern Front, which at this time in the war seemed unlikely. The Cherbourg Peninsula was the first idea to be considered, based on the theory that a portion of French land could be taken, held, and used later for a major invasion force. As noted above viable aircover was difficult if not impossible at this stage, not least because Bomber Harris had little time for such operations, as he believed bombing German cities and industrial sites was more productive for victory. Although the plan looked hopeful, it was overly ambitious, and the more level-headed knew it could not work at that time when resources and manpower were limited, fearing it would probably result in another Dunkirk. As such *Sledgehammer* was put aside and a study known as *Imperator* was pursued, which was intended to destroy the Luftwaffe facilities and encourage an air battle. Most of the plans were far too ambitious, especially the projected idea which was based on a scheme to land troops in France and head directly towards Paris, destroy German headquarters and race back to the coast. At this stage the British army was still in a defensive position and again the more reliable top military commanders knew it could never work. The British had launched a few smaller commando raids across the channel, killed a few Germans, sometimes gained some important information and intelligence equipment, but these new schemes were demanding too much against an enemy which remained strong despite losses on the Eastern Front. It was suggested that frequent small commando raids would be more useful, but there seemed little point in risking lives without a specific military target and killing a few German sentries.

When the possibility of occupying Dieppe was raised the same questions would be asked. Churchill's well-known 'punch on the snout' was a mere irritant to the Germans, and although at times useful was not meeting Russian and American hopes and suggestions. A major raiding force appeared necessary for these political reasons, but the questions of its viability would not go away. There is little or no evidence that such questions of whether it could be a success under the circumstances of the day were not raised or answered, but a major raid on the coast might ameliorate the political pressures of which the Combined Chiefs of Staff were well briefed.

44   Major Blunders of the Second World War

It is generally assumed that the chair of the Planning Committee, the senior naval officer Captain John Hughes-Hallett was the individual who first suggested Dieppe, but this remains speculative. One aspect was clear, Dieppe served no serious military target. Although it was a small fishing port it could not even cope with U-boats, and such an attack was hardly likely to have the German High Command (OKW) send troops from the Eastern front to defend such an insignificant fishing and holiday port. Even if the port were totally destroyed it would not have hindered German military strength enough to cause them serious concern. The belief that the Germans would send troops from the Eastern Front or even from elsewhere to defend such an insignificant port, demonstrated a self-confidence and lack of overall strategic oversight by the planners. The port of Dieppe was insignificant and hardly the best terrain for a major landing, it was no Cherbourg or Antwerp, and should have raised the question as to whether it was substantial enough to risk men's lives and invaluable resources. On the other hand, the crossing could be made at night and was within easier range for the RAF. The potential military targets in Dieppe were limited, though it was noted that there were some invasion barges in the inner harbour for the potential *Sealion* invasion of Britain. It was believed they could be towed back, but even if it were successful, they were not the best of craft for a channel crossing, and it may have made more sense to sink them at their moorings if the opportunity arose. The plan was fraught with doubts but gathered some momentum when the Russian Ambassador in London, Ivan Maisky continued to exert pressure for something to happen, undoubtedly influenced by Stalin. There was a feeling that something had to be done and Mountbatten regarded it as a critical step in the right direction.

## Town of Dieppe

As the Allies were to learn in Italy some types of terrain made defence easier and attack more difficult. This was a lesson learnt at Dieppe but probably forgotten in the haste of war. The very nature of the town made it easier to defend than occupy, as it was set in a surrounding of steep chalk cliffs as may be found on the Kent coast. The cliffs provided natural lookout points and gave the traditional military demand for dominating heights, not least for firepower but also provided many natural concealed areas. All the German defensive commanders had to do was utilise the natural geographical setting to their own advantage. Machine gun posts and even artillery could be hidden from being spotted by even the most experienced aircraft pilots. Even the caves within the cliff concealed weaponry just as Admiral Ramsay had utilised Dover's cliffs for his headquarters and hidden gun emplacements, though this possible comparison appeared to have escaped the attention of the British planners. Again, like many English Channel seaside towns on the coast, Dieppe had extensive pebbled beaches with the background of a seawall which made it unsafe for tanks to land safely, and, as later at Omaha Beach in 1944, dangerous for men crossing a beach from their landing craft.

Dieppe was a popular holiday resort with a casino, hotels and some rich residents who had chosen to live there, including artists, well-off pensioners and had a small fishing industry. There were some French resistance members, especially communists who tended to come from the working classes and who worked in the small docks, but at this stage it was more a paper resistance of distributing pamphlets and other written material. Politically the town was neither strongly right nor left-wing and very much a small working town and holiday resort, somewhat impoverished by the war.

## Operation *Rutter*

As soon as Dieppe was pinpointed for action, the locals, and more to the point the local German command were not slow to notice the increased amount of aerial activity by the RAF, not just flying overhead, but tending to circle or return quickly. It did not take a genius to wonder why the sudden interest in the small port, especially as all German coastal units were all too aware of commando type raids. The defences were given more attention and the locals noted the influx of foreign labour teams equipped to build and cover concrete gun sites. At the top-end of the

## 46    Major Blunders of the Second World War

German command in France, the aging Field Marshal von Rundstedt was aware of the dangers of coastal attacks or even a coastal invasion, and he had ordered all areas to check and tighten their defence lines.

In the planning of Operation *Rutter*, the code name for the attack on Dieppe, the town and its hinterland were studied with a view of attacking at first light. As noted above they had to be aware that the beaches were pebble with stone walls, that the cliff tops and gullies could have weapons hidden and yet trained with enfilade potential covering both the beaches and other landing sites. It would be like trying to invade the British port of Dover, which also had overlooking cliffs with concealed guns, and a pebbled beach with a seawall promenade which no tank could mount without having ramps in place, even if they managed to make it up a steeply inclined pebbled beach. On Dover's eastern flank, hidden on a beach known as Dead-man's Gulch are old hidden gun emplacements which are almost impossible to spot when approaching from the sea, and they cannot be seen by aircraft.

In Dieppe they had, as in Dover, high cliff tops giving not just a total overview of all sea approaches, but easily concealed weapons and forces for a counterattack. They were high steep chalk cliffs and scaling them, as often seen in popular war films, was in this case mainly out of the question. Later, in the battle for Italy a few Spandau machines guns (MG34s) hidden in high mountains surrounding the valley approach could hold back even a few battalions of the approaching enemy, and enfilade fire adjusted for the beaches of Dieppe would be just as devastating. The cliff tops provided a wide view for batteries overlooking the approaches which could endanger vessels hovering too close to the coastline, to which there was also the threat of Luftwaffe attack despite the RAF cover. There were two possible flank landing beaches pinpointed either side of Dieppe, but the Germans had long recognised this danger and they were well defended. In short, before Dieppe was attacked the Germans had long organised their defence system with views from the beaches and out into the channel, watched by observers in the well-covered gun and artillery emplacements. The German soldiers had several states of readiness, depending on weather, tides, and Intelligence information,

The most important aspect of planning *Rutter* was to study the setting of Dieppe within its natural geographical setting, paying attention not just to the maps of the town, but the topography and possible defence systems which could be deployed. It should have been understood that aerial photographs could not necessarily spot camouflaged gun sites, especially as the Germans were well aware of enemy aircraft equipped with cameras. The RAF's photographic unit improved during the war, but it took considerable expertise by those examining the photographs to pinpoint cleverly concealed sites. Even tyre tracks to a thicket of trees or a cluster of bushes could be noted by a clever photograph reader. The cliffs, the gullies, the casting shadows made the task difficult, and they could rarely spot concealed weapons which were hidden in innocent looking buildings, but which could be wheeled out for action. At one time the idea of capturing a local Dieppe fisherman for information was raised, but at this stage information from inside sources were equally difficult to obtain. Many of the Dieppe population had left, and few would want to attract German attention by looking too closely at their defence systems. The French resistance was yet to reach a stage of development by which it could be effective, especially in small towns. The possibility of gleaning inside information was impossible, and secreting men ashore to investigate ran immense risks if they were captured.

This was going to be the largest operation ever made by Combined Operations, and it demanded a greater armada of transport and naval vessels than ever before, and naturally involved all the military services. They also had no doubt that because of the commando raids the Germans were constantly expecting some form of incursion or attack along the coast, especially in an area which the Germans knew could be provided with British air cover. Knowing the Germans would have been fully aware of a potential coastal attack was sheer common sense, and despite the channel, it was regarded as a frontline position, as was the shelled Kent coastline, especially Dover whose inhabitants were all too well aware. As such, a strategic surprise was possible, but highly unlikely without major

48 Major Blunders of the Second World War

preparations including deceit. This worked in a much later operation called *Mincemeat* with a prepared corpse washed up on the south Spanish coast. The body had an attached brief case with documents intimating that the Allies would attack elsewhere but not Sicily which was the Allied intention. It did not fool Mussolini nor Kesselring, but Hitler and the German High Command were taken in. Before D-Day Normandy Patton and a false army were placed in East Anglia, with other deceits which were carried out to make the Germans think the Calais area was the target, and it generally worked. None of this was given much thought, although later it would be claimed that it was a lesson learnt at Dieppe, but more as an excuse to explain the failure.

Operation *Rutter* was explored but it involved many differences of opinion, with the army questioning whether the proposed attacks on the flanks of Dieppe could work, while also preparing for a straightforward frontal attack on the port. Attacking on the flanks presented problems of river crossings and ensuring the necessary bridges were protected. It was reported that the German defences were manned by low quality troops, but it is unfathomable how this estimation was arrived at, and its reliability was somewhat dubious. The army was represented by Montgomery who, as was his habit, tended to dominate those with whom he worked. He was already a controversial figure something like the modern 'marmite man', either despised or admired. None of their discussions were helped with memories of Norway and Dunkirk always red-raw in the memories of recent months and years. Many were aware of the lack of harmony, but Mountbatten, admired by Churchill and the Americans because of his charm and royal background still held sway. Even the noted Anglophobe the American General Wedemeyer felt Mountbatten was the best man for the task, as did Eisenhower, and Mountbatten always enjoyed this international praise and acceptance, which was all too human. Mountbatten always regarded *Rutter* as a replacement for the projected and unrealistic Operation *Sledgehammer*, intimating that it was fundamentally a political driving force to please the Americans and therefore making Churchill feel content.

The Dieppe Disaster    49

It was not only an inter-Allied political problem but there was a lack of harmony on the home front. The Chiefs of Staff did not have the same certainty of Mountbatten as the Americans. They had not welcomed Mountbatten to their meetings, and there was a degree of animosity for this captain of destroyers who had commanded and lost three ships, but in a twinkle of an eye he held three commissions as Vice-Admiral, Lieutenant-General and Air Marshal when he had replaced Admiral Sir Roger Keyes in Combined Operations. Admiral Keyes had felt the frustration of the Chiefs of Staff holding back his aggressive enterprises, and when Churchill explained to him that public policy demanded agreement, Keyes wrote 'eight pages of foolscap' arguing the case.[9] Churchill dismissed him, but the same problems were to engage Mountbatten, but without the same consequences. Mountbatten had powerful supporters in Churchill, Beaverbrook (for a time) and of course he was King George VI's cousin. Perhaps, more pertinently, he had travelled to America and with his easy social manner had won the Americans to himself, helped by Roosevelt's well-known weakness for European royalty. He had managed to help talk the Americans away from *Sledgehammer*, but despite this valuable help, the Chiefs of Staff were wary of him, especially the navy and even Alan Brooke who was growing in importance and influence. Mountbatten was demanding that his organisation (COHQ) was in charge, or at least deserved a privileged position, which was more to do with his sense of prestige than military necessity. It was necessary for him to point out that *Rutter* was not a commando punch on the snout, but much more significant, which pleased Churchill and the Allies in America and the Soviet Union, where Stalin certainly wanted an attack which would divert troops from Russia which a commando raid would not.

The question of air support was raised, the RAF was already committed to act as cover, but naval gunfire against the coast was another matter. For this there would need to be significant war ships with better calibre guns, which meant battleships. This was out of the question because of their manoeuvrability and being prone to air attack, which left only the accompanying destroyers whose guns would not be powerful enough to

50   Major Blunders of the Second World War

destroy the concrete bunkers enclosing enemy guns, and the blockhouses. The destroyers only had four-inch guns whereas battleships had fourteen-inch shells, but they could not risk the possible sacrifice of such critical vessels. Raeder held the same views in relation to Operation *Sea Lion* arguing that large battleships did not have the space for manoeuvring off the coast, and they were prone to air attack.

### Canadians

Since the Canadians had arrived in Britain they had trained and carried out exercises but had not seen any action. It was even suggested they were suffering from a lack of morale and felt sidelined and had become more like home garrison troops. How far this was true that the individual soldier was seeking to fight will never be known, but again politics was always the lurking factor. The Canadian government wanted its men to be used but not, in their opinion, in faraway battles in North Africa, probably sharing some American views that Churchill was empire building. A direct attack across the channel to German-occupied France sounded preferrable. The Canadian military leaders were Generals Andrew McNaughton and Harry Crerar, and the Canadian government relied on them for on-the-spot guidance. The Canadian prime minister was Mackenzie King, who had been unsure about sending his people to fight yet again in war torn Europe, but he was reliant on his generals for political guidance. The formidable Brooke was critical of the Canadian top military command, especially McNaughton, not as people, but because of their lack of military ability. When McNaughton later returned to Canada, Brooke wrote in his diary 'I am afraid that I have lost a very good friend in the shape of Andy McNaughton. I only hope that he may be able to realise the true situation to rise high enough for me not to lose his friendship'.[10] For Brooke, military strategy and tactics came before relationships, as he was always highly professional. It was for many Canadians a fraught situation because their troops would be under British control, and this tension was felt between the Canadian and the British command. The Canadians had sent soldiers, but America with its vast resources was the major consideration as far as the British were concerned.

As noted, Brooke had often made it clear in his diary that he was not happy with the Canadian generals, but the politics could not be ignored. However, it was probably General Crerar's wish to be involved which not only influenced the Canadian government but also the organisers for *Rutter*. It was helped by Montgomery who had already had the Canadians under him in various exercises while in the South-East home defence command. It is thought that it was Montgomery who persuaded his mentor Brooke as Chief of the Imperial General Staff to agree that the Canadians should be utilised. Later, despite claims made by others, Montgomery denied any involvement in having the Canadian forces involved. Given the eventual disaster it is easy to understand Montgomery's wish to stand apart, and while Dieppe for him was a passing phase, there is no question that he presided over many of the meetings. There were further problems in using Canadians, who although fit and trained were in battle terms inexperienced, but America and Stalin were demanding action. Churchill was eager for success, wishing to demonstrate that the British could still win, and the use of Canadians seemed to fit the bill. It was helped by General Crerar being all too eager for his men to see action.

Everything was kept secret for fear of spies, but Crerar received the message that Montgomery was the senior man involved in the planning, namely the British were in charge and the Canadians were subordinate to this command. Slowly but surely Canadians gathered in force in the southern parts of England, especially in the Isle of Wight, which was seen as an excellent training ground, where they were known as the *Simmerforce*. Their presence with heavy machines such as tanks would have caused local rumours despite the need for secrecy. The tanks were tested on the shingle beaches of Dungeness, where it was noted that it was far from ideal for such tracked vehicles unless moving in a straight line. The Germans had not prepared anti-tank defences at Dieppe because they had already estimated that tanks would flounder on the pebbled beach. On the Isle of Wight, the tanks used firm sandy beaches whereas Dover or Folkestone would have been better places for such experiments, apart from being more easily observable by Luftwaffe pilots. Such was

## 52   Major Blunders of the Second World War

the optimism it was suggested that the force could race to Paris, and quickly return to the coast, but even an amateur strategist would see that this would hardly work, not least because of fuel problems, and the possible loss of men and resources. It was inane and could not have been taken seriously.

### Committee Work

On 5 June a major meeting was held by the planners to finally try and put the jigsaw of various plans and ideas together. Mountbatten was in Washington doing what he was good at in charming the Americans to the British way of thinking, which was always of political value to Churchill. Montgomery, as more often than not chaired the meeting, trying to control a debate raised by Leigh-Mallory the RAF Air Vice-Marshal, who raised the question of the proposed bombing of Dieppe during the night before the assault. Leigh-Mallory argued that unless the raid were not totally devastating it was far too risky as it would alert the Germans as to the proposed area of attack. This was a sound argument as surprise was essential. Later in Italy, Kesselring was caught unaware of the Anzio beach landing, but being a professional military commander, he had plans in hand for such an event (Operation *Richard*), and he had assembled defence troops overnight. On D-Day Normandy allied bombers concentrated in the Calais area on the grounds of diverting attention from Normandy. However, others have since argued that the coastal towns had suffered air attacks and it might not have raised too many alarms.

The hope for battleships having been ruled out, it was agreed on RAF advice that bombing the port would be counter-productive, which left the bulk of the Canadian forces unsupported. There were naturally political and moral problems with bombing French towns and cities, but the committee meanderings appeared to accept the naval and air force's lack of cooperation. There was some dissension caused by fear of a frontal attack without such appropriate support, and it started to raise doubts about the viability of *Rutter*. For his part there were indications that Montgomery was having cold feet, and later he would claim that he

The Dieppe Disaster 53

had disagreed with dropping the aerial bombing from the operation, yet he was the chairman of the committee which made the decision.

An exercise for the operation took part in Dorset which transpired to be a virtual failure, casting further doubt on the feasibility of such a major attack. It was clear to many witnesses that *Rutter* needed further work and more precise planning, but the Canadians remained, according to many sources, all too keen. The question of German defence was discussed, and it was acknowledged that in military matters the Germans were highly professional and astute to potential dangers. It was correctly believed they would be aware of the critical times for attack, mainly the tidal surges and moonlight when they would be more on their guard.

Churchill was aware of the problems but remained politically sensitive to American and Russian demands, and was not helped by it being a difficult period of time for him as prime minister. He needed some form of success, and even a minor victory of a productive blow against the Nazi regime, which hope was constantly at the top of his priority list. He had been with the American President when news was brought to him and Brooke that Tobruk had fallen, and on his return home he called Mountbatten and demanded another perusal of the operation. Mountbatten was later to claim that both Churchill and Brooke were supportive and keen for the operation to go ahead, but the evidence for this is difficult to find. In Brooke's diary which was openly frank about what he felt, and at times embarrassingly honest, Brooke never raised the issue.

On the first day of July the Canadian troops started to embark, believing it was another exercise, and there was considerable activity along the coast from Yarmouth waters down to the south. It was soon announced that the target was Dieppe, but then followed a long delay which must have been tantalisingly frustrating for the embarked soldiers. What they did not know were problems raised by the parachutists who were facing strong winds which made a drop untenable, and then intelligence reported that a German Panzer Division had moved to nearby Amiens. The confusion was added to by the sudden need to adjust timing, leaving only a one tide option. There was also little doubt that the Luftwaffe were aware of the various gathering ships from Yarmouth to the south, as

## 54  Major Blunders of the Second World War

they ran constant reconnaissance flights for such possible developments. This message came home when boats off Yarmouth found themselves attacked by German bombers. They did not create too much damage, but it acted as a warning that the preparations had been noticed. *Rutter* had to be cancelled, and the men went back ashore having been instructed to keep the revealed target of Dieppe a secret, as it may be reinvigorated later. This was an impossible demand, and because many believed the operation to be dead in the water, the information spread by word and mouth and letters home. Montgomery argued that it was off for all times under the circumstances which made sound common sense, and he was probably pleased it was finished.

### *Rutter* becomes *Jubilee*

As far as the COHQ were concerned cancelling *Rutter* was a disaster, and the closure had barely been announced before Mountbatten led a discussion, supposed to be a post mortem, but it was evidently more than a closing of the file, because the corpse was still considered to have some life left. The Canadian commanders were also disappointed because they had been seeking an opportunity for their men to have some action against the enemy. They contacted Hughes-Hallet who, as the chief planner was amongst the disappointed, and the RAF's Leigh-Mallory who had been optimistic that the raid would encourage the Luftwaffe off the ground so they could be destroyed. However, by most accounts the main impetus for bringing the *Rutter* corpse back to life came primarily if not forcibly from Mountbatten, who felt his central role had been cast aside. It is believed that *Rutter* came to official life less than a fortnight later on 11 July, but as far as is known nothing was put into writing, although it was claimed that Pug Ismay, Churchill's Chief of Staff, had informed Churchill and the Chiefs of Staff who responded with a verbal agreement, and it is known that King George VI had been told by Mountbatten.[11] It has been claimed Mountbatten had a degree of sympathy from Churchill and the Chiefs of Staff, so long as it was launched at the right time. The Biblical expression 'in spring, the time when kings go out to war' (II Samuel 11, v1) was applied in so far that crossing the channel prone to coastal winds could only be done when it was safe, which was limited.

However, there remained the question of how far the potential raid was already known or speculated about by German intelligence. Not all were happy, and the highly respected Admiral Ramsay had expressed doubts about cross-channel raids, pertinently pointing out that for those who argued it was a good way of training troops for a serious invasion, should also remember that it was good training for the German defenders. At one stage he all but pleaded with Mountbatten to shelve the whole operation, but despite his experience and success at Dunkirk he was ignored. The choice of potential raiding areas would be of constant attention by the German coastal defence team. The new operation was coded Operation *Jubilee*, and it was given more of a boost when the Americans expressed the views it should still happen while there was time. The American team met General Brooke who had never been favourable in the first place, and he had always been sceptical of COHQ, Mountbatten, and even the commandoes. Eventually the Americans were persuaded about the North African Operation *Torch*, and they agreed to go ahead, but insisted on the proviso that they needed the British to find a date for a cross-channel invasion. By this they meant a major invasion as in D-Day Normandy, and Churchill hoped that a Dieppe operation would indicate British willingness to attack across the channel. Churchill was relieved because he regarded Operation *Torch* as essential, but like Brooke, knew it would be a serious error of judgment to attempt a major cross-channel invasion too early.

The problem with the *Rutter/Jubilee* plans was that it entailed more than a quick commando raid with a small group of well-trained soldiers adept at sudden attacks, and yet this could not be large enough for holding a bridgehead for a major invasion. It is easy to gain the impression that this plan evolved around the political machinations to keep the Americans happy, and to show Stalin and the public that British military success was possible. Churchill was happy, the Americans placated because they had an agreement for a major invasion, but they still wanted some form

## 56   Major Blunders of the Second World War

of cross-channel attack. A constant factor was the intense public pressure for a second front to support the Russians, and in America and Britain many wondered whether North Africa constituted a second front. In the Anglo-American political arena, the possibility of a Dieppe Raid had become an inducement, a carrot, to encourage the Russians and many of the cynical American military commanders to see Britain as pro-active. It is a curious feature of Operation *Jubilee* almost instantly replacing *Rutter*, that there was never found any written evidence that it was signed off as a possible operation.

The major problem for the planners in rethinking the operation was the need for total secrecy. There was always the possibility of spies, of letters written by soldiers who thought *Rutter* had been abandoned, and the surveillance by the Luftwaffe. It was generally agreed that the *Jubilee* operation would go forward under a refreshed command plan, and this time the Canadian commanders were given more room space, previously occupied by the dominating Montgomery.

Again, there were political sensitivities involved, not least that the success or failure of the operation would be scrutinised by their Allies the Russians and Americans. Britain had to prove after years of defence and failure that their country could eventually have a military victory. The Germans were equally inquisitive and concerned about the possibility of crushing any form of cross-channel incursion. At one of the preliminary plannings Leigh-Mallory was asked about bombing again, but once more he argued that bomb-aiming devices had not improved, and it was still out of the question. The raiders would have, as in *Rutter*, to rely on the successful flank attacks and the shells from offshore destroyers. This debate continued to the final days. A known issue was that it was understood the Germans had laid sea-mines across the swathes of water which the approaching armada would have to manoeuvre. It was believed that even if one vessel were sunk the raid would have to be aborted. Minesweepers could do the work at night, and the RAF helped with a technical system used by their bomber fleet (known as *Gee*) which guided the vessels to their destinations, and the lead vessels could utilise this navigational advantage to keep them on track through the cleared paths made by the minesweepers. It was believed that if everything went to plan, Dieppe would be occupied within a matter of a few hours and a bridgehead some four to five miles inland would be established. This would, it was proposed, allow time to destroy German resources and snatch material, even top-level information relating to the Enigma coding system. It was known that the Enigma machine relating to sea codes had an extra wheel attached to the coding system, which had complicated matters at Bletchley where the decoding took place, and such a discovery would have been highly useful.

However, doubts were expressed, not least the reliability of small craft committed to such a long journey. Some of the commando team officers were sceptical about the use of untested Canadians making this type of raid in such massive numbers. The RAF had continued its own surveillance of the Dieppe land space, and they had noted the Germans were preparing new defence systems, with aerial photography noting new gun emplacements which were also spotted on the seafront. Even their activity in the skies above must have been noted by the watching Germans. The German coastal commanders had already been warned to be on high alert at high tides by all being prepared and dressed for battle, the Luftwaffe had spotted the buildup of craft off the English coast and there were discussions on likely spots for a possible incursion. The Germans also appeared to understand that such an attack was likely, speculating the political pressure Churchill was under from Stalin as well as possibly the Americans. The whole venture was based on tactical surprise which the more astute would have guessed was evaporating. The central headquarters were based in one of the underground type-forts overlooking Portsmouth harbour, and Mountbatten toured the various forces wishing them well.

### *Jubilee* Battle

Despite all the warnings and misgivings, the operation was launched at 5.00 am on 19 August 1942. It involved over 6,000 soldiers, a huge number of Royal Navy vessels, and a substantial contribution by fighter

## 58   Major Blunders of the Second World War

squadrons. It was to fall apart the moment it started, not helped by the problem that major batteries were not captured or silenced first, as landing craft were hit by shells as soon as they approached the shoreline. The convoy had also been interrupted and confronted by some small German escort vessels (armed trawlers) assisting a small convoy which stumbled across the attack. The signs and sounds of this gunfire put the coastal defence on immediate alert, although because of the tide and moonlight they were already in position, though they may have assumed it was just another local offshore conflict.

The Dieppe Raid was planned with a frontal attack, but the flank problems were a serious criticism at the time, and the front needed to be shattered before the troops arrived. Air Marshal Portal could offer no serious bomber support since Bomber Harris point-blank refused, seeing it only as a mere sideshow, and dangerous for French civilians, claiming Mountbatten always kept demanding bombers for all his wild ideas. Portal took the opportunity to use Dieppe as a means of destroying the Luftwaffe, and he used sixty-six squadrons of 730 single-seat fighters: they flew 2,111 sorties making it the largest air battle in history, but it was hardly a success. As such, although Portal could not provide the necessary bombers, he was happy for the air-battle, and later wrote that he understood there was no effort made to cancel the raid. Another issue, unlike the aerial battles over Britain, it was the RAF and not the Luftwaffe that were fighting at a significant distance from their bases. What the reconnaissance aircraft could not easily pinpoint was that many of the coastal gullies were strewn with barbed wire traps making access dangerous. There was a small success when a major battery known as Hess was put out of action by some commandoes.

The main focus point of the attack was landing the Canadian force and putting them ashore ready to fight, which was the critical and main thrust of the attack. The beach was well prepared by the Germans with gun sites able to sweep the area, strong barbed wire defences and crowned, like many seaside resorts, with a huge stone wall typical of a promenade as in Dover. Their hidden gun positions were established to enable them to see every point on the beach which would account for many of

The Dieppe Disaster 59

the Canadian casualties. Making their way over the beach through the barbed wire defences against carefully placed machine guns was virtually impossible. This was code-named *Blue* Beach and only one unit made it through the defences. It was immediately apparent that the seawall was too high, and there were soon requests for boats to retrieve the casualties which were building up well beyond expectations. In all this confusion some of the air-attacks were killing their own troops in what is often misleadingly dubbed 'friendly fire'. It also came to light that some of the troops had been landed in the wrong places. The week before the Germans had been preparing for an attack and had demolished some houses for gun sweeps of the beach area, using others as strongpoints, but the French inhabitants were caught unawares.

Where German prisoners were taken, they were tied up somewhat brutally, some were shot, and this caused German outrage. In the planning stages the idea of tying up German prisoners was objected to but apparently over-ruled by Mountbatten, and this was later to cause considerable anger on the German side with threats of reprisals, which for a time were carried out by chaining prisoners.

Landing tanks and armoured vehicles on enemy pebbled beaches was at this stage an untried effort, safe in rehearsal, but very different when under serious enemy counterattack. Setting them down in the right places was confusing when under constant gunfire. It was not an easy task traversing pebble beaches as noted above, and only some 20 to 30 tanks made it ashore, with only a few making it over the seawalls, but they were then subject to attack from gun emplacements in the cliff's tunnels. In the planning stages these tunnels were known about, but it had been unbelievably assumed they were only used for storage. As it transpired most men and vehicles were simply pinned down by guns so well placed, they could observe every spot which could be utilised by an attacking force. The old saying of 'putting one's head above the parapet' had a powerful and deadly meaning for the allied soldiers on the Dieppe beaches. The code word for evacuation was *Vanquish*, but it would become a dangerous and difficult episode which was raised not long after 9.00 the same morning, a mere five to six hours after the attack had started. Not

## 60 Major Blunders of the Second World War

least it had proved impossible for the RAF to reduce the active German guns, but they managed to give some cover to the offshore naval vessels.

The attack had been a complete failure, not because of the fighting men, but by poor planning, lack of intelligence of the area's German defences, underestimating the professional military standards of the enemy, by launching an attack whose aims were minimal, and probably mainly due to political pressures and personal ambitions. The attack had no real purpose, and it resulted not just in loss of face and equipment, but in the many lives, injuries, and captured soldiers. The destruction of a battery, a radio station, an arms dump was not worth the sacrifice.

The Canadians constituted the bulk of the fighting men, and out of 6,086 men a total of 3,623 were killed, wounded, or captured, a staggering 60 per cent. 'It was the sort of event that on the Eastern Front was a daily occurrence', but in the West was unacceptable.[12] Later Beaverbrook attacked Mountbatten for using *his* Canadians, simply because his newspapers were calling for a Second Front, but this was a criticism which revealed more about an angry Beaverbrook. However, it later caused some unpleasant moments in the Canadian relationships with Britain, especially when the casualty lists appeared, indicating the loss of over 60 per cent. This alone may well have deterred many potential volunteers and certainly angered Canadian politicians. The 'Germans suffered 591 ground casualties', which was light compared to the Allied Canadian losses.[13] It was during this raid that the 'first United States soldier was killed in France, Lieutenant V. Loustalot'.[14] The Royal Navy lost at least thirty-three landing-craft and a destroyer, but more significantly the RAF lost 106 aircraft to the Luftwaffe's loss of forty-eight, in what was the largest air battle in history. It was a total disaster and many books have been written on the subject in an attempt to understand what and why it happened, often underlining some myths, and verging on conspiracy theories.

### First Post Mortem

In the immediate post mortem discussions, it was clear that those at home appeared to know little about what had actually happened, and details would take time to surface and years of historical research to find the essential facts. Accusations were raised against the lack of necessary Intelligence and even asked whether there had been a leak. Mountbatten swiftly corrected this by stating 'tide and moon' was a time when the German defence would have been on high alert, begging the unraised question as to how, therefore, they could have hoped for a surprise raid which was an essential ingredient in the planning. It was as early as these initial meetings that the argument that Dieppe was an experiment or learning exercise for a major operation such as D-Day Normandy was raised. Using soldiers as guinea pigs, as was later done in nuclear explosions, was hardly moral or legal. It may well have arisen, not only as an excuse for Mountbatten and his team, but public opinion also needed to be placated. It was argued that it was a reconnaissance force which had little depth as an excuse, as such expeditions were raised to reconnoitre, noting the landscape and enemy dispositions, not to fight on arrival. For the rest of his life Mountbatten and others used the excuse and explanation of the Dieppe disaster as a 'practice run' for greater things to come, but both his contemporaries and most since have found this difficult to believe.

The first rounds of the postmortem finished in embarrassment and almost silence, but such was the defeat and loss of mainly Canadian lives in the futile attack on Dieppe, it smouldered on for years and remains of interest to many historians. Montgomery may well have been right when he wrote in his memoirs that there 'were too many authorities with a hand in it; there was no one single operational commander who was responsible for the operation'.[15] However, the main impetus and thrust came from Mountbatten who many believe was ultimately responsible.

### Further Ramifications

The Dieppe fiasco soured relationships with Russia and America, but most especially with Canada. As noted, it gave rise to a series of myths, left strained relationships between high-ranking commanders, and a vendetta between Mountbatten and Beaverbrook which rumbled on for years. 'Some reputable historians have suggested that Combined Operations' efforts in this period reflected a psychopath at work', which was highly critical but nevertheless pinpointed Mountbatten as the principal author of this disaster.[16] One of the flimsiest myths which comes and goes in credibility is that the Germans were deliberately tipped off because of the need to prove the second front was impossible. However, the Germans, albeit despised for many years, were no fools, and knew a cross-channel crossing was viable, and it was known that they were always on the alert by 'moon and tide' and were constantly preparing and enhancing their French coastal defences.

It has also been suggested that the Canadians and others were deliberately sacrificed to make the Soviets aware that the British had serious intentions about creating mayhem for the Germans, if only to draw pressure away from the Eastern Front. The demanding and obdurate Stalin would have realised that even a large coastal attack would not draw German troops away, this would need a full-scale invasion. More to the point, whatever the criticisms, it cannot be suggested that the planners had not anticipated success, and the idea of a deliberate sacrifice was highly unlikely. However, the political arguments that Churchill and his fellow war leaders wanted to encourage the Russians to keep fighting, and to impress the Americans, may hold some water, but only in anticipation that the raid would be successful. Some have argued that the Americans (and Stalin) wanted a Second Front in France, so Dieppe was utilised to demonstrate that it could not work, which again, as above, implies a deliberate sacrifice of lives. However, not even a war-torn Churchill and Chiefs of Staff would have considered losing thousands of men in a sacrificial disaster to prove it was too early. Looking for motives in this haphazard and emotive way gives rise to conspiracy theories which almost follow naturally from such claims. These myths arise because there is still no substantive evidence as to the raid's objectives and who gave it the final authorization. The whole Dieppe fiasco has triggered its own library, film documentaries, and still raises the temperature, especially in Canada. The question remains as to who actually authorised the raid, and for what purpose, but it can be taken for granted that failure was not the intention.

## The Focus on Mountbatten

In this ongoing dilemma of trying to understand the motives behind the raid and the fiasco which followed, the insights needed should not be based on the unlikely and mainly speculative cynical views that disaster was intended, but what some of the major guiding figures involved were thinking.

An interesting background figure was the Chief of the Imperial General Staff (CIGS) General Alan Brooke, who was a man known for his meticulous procedures and determined professional approach in all military matters. His contempt for American military ability was well known, and he was capable of ignoring American and Soviet pressure. Stalin even awarded him a Soviet medal mainly because he admired his tough approach, and the Americans, although they might not have liked the way he lectured them at their combined meetings, soon respected and many even liked him. General Omar Bradley was American through and through, and he had disagreements with Brooke over strategy, but Bradley admired Brooke, liked his company, while detesting Montgomery. He wrote that 'despite our differences in strategic outlook, I developed a deep admiration for Alan Brooke. He had a truly brilliant global mind... with an equal facility and a hard-nosed grasp of realities and political realities'.[17] Bradley was aware that Brooke and Churchill had opposed the timing of the American plans for *Overlord*, preferring the 'British strategy in the Mediterranean campaign, the indirect approach to the heart of Germany through the soft underbelly'.[18] Later however, he had the grace to realise that Brooke had been absolutely right. As noted in the opening section Bradley wrote that 'I came to the conclusion that it was fortunate that the British view prevailed, that the US Army first met the enemy on the periphery, in Africa rather than on the beaches of France. In Africa we learnt to crawl, to walk and then run. Had that learning process been launched in France it would surely have, as Alan Brooke argued, resulted in an unthinkable disaster'.[19] Unlike the American team Brooke had already fought the Germans in the field of combat in the Second World War, and knew that they were in the senior class when

## 64   Major Blunders of the Second World War

it came to military proficiency, that training, experience, and equipped with massive resources were the only means to defeat them.

Brooke believed that North Africa was the way forward, and the Second Front had to be delayed until there was a real possibility of success. The summer of 1942 was depressing, Sebastopol and Vornezh had fallen, and the American and British press claimed Hitler was winning. Brooke did not authorise or support Operation *Jubilee*, and was away at the time, but he may have seen it as a diversion to take the American and Soviet mind away from *Sledgehammer*. In his personal diary he only mentions Operation *Rutter* but shows no surprise at *Jubilee's* failure. When the news of *Jubilee* reached Brooke in Egypt, he said to Sir Charles Wilson 'it is a lesson to the people who are clamouring for the invasion of France'.[20] This statement was Brooke drawing his own conclusions, as his diaries reveal he was a highly moral and principled man. Brooke would not have sacrificed soldiers and others as a demonstration for politicians and critics of British efforts.

Therefore, it was no surprise that when the facts of the total failure and losses were digested, Brooke was angry and blamed Mountbatten for poor preparation and acting without authorisation. Brooke, who had fought with the Canadians at Vimy Ridge (April 1917), recognised it as an appalling disaster, and its only real lesson as far as Brooke was concerned was that this tragedy acted as a warning against crossing the Channel without appropriate and major preparation. When sometime later Brooke was sharply critical of Mountbatten's planning at Chequers, it led to a confrontation with Mountbatten who was furious, and he wrote to Brooke that he wanted an investigation. This never happened, and Mountbatten's official biographer believed Brooke 'mollified' his subject 'and there is no trace of a written reply'.[21] Unlike Mountbatten, Brooke was a highly professional military man with considerable experience, a high respect for the German military, and a realist who often had to cope with some of Churchill's more outlandish ideas. It had been Churchill who thought of constructing ice-made aircraft carriers, but it was Mountbatten who took it on with some fervour. Some of Churchill's ideas were good and worked, and Brooke recognised Churchill's leadership qualities, but he had no time for Mountbatten and probably dropped the Dieppe argument

## The Dieppe Disaster   65

rather than quarrel with Churchill's favourite royal. Later in the war, when Mountbatten was appointed Supreme-Commander in South-East Asia, Brooke instructed General Pownall to report directly to Brooke because Mountbatten was capable of acting without authority. However, the question remains that although Brooke never authorised Operation *Jubilee*, he never seemed to have cancelled the operation. He may well have regarded it as a diversionary tactic while he was more occupied with what he considered to be more important strategic priorities in North Africa. In his personal diaries he admitted to enjoying Mountbatten's social company, but found his military contributions badly informed, noting on 8 January 1943 that he had attended 'one of those awful COS meetings where Mountbatten and Dudley Pound drive me completely to desperation. The former is quite irresponsible, suffers from the most desperate illogical brain, always producing red herrings, …'.[22]

Mountbatten was not well-liked or appreciated by the senior military chiefs, and the leading Admiral Dudley Pound the Naval Chief, strongly objected to Mountbatten's appointment causing Churchill to force the situation in Mountbatten's favour.[23] Pound and Churchill were not on the best of terms since the saga of the battleship *Bismarck*, this had been followed by Churchill forcing Pound to send the *Prince of Wales* and the *Repulse* to Malaya where they were promptly sunk. In addition to all these problems it was suspected that Pound had given the fateful order for the PQ17 convoy to disperse, costing considerable loss of life and tonnage. Pound was under extreme pressure and was obliged to resist sending battleships to support Dieppe knowing it would put major vessels in extreme risk. A frontal attack on Dieppe demanded that German artillery power had to be crushed, and although British battleships could have done the job, they themselves would be in too much peril because of air attack and lack of manoeuvrability. Such were the pressures on Pound that, like Brooke, he did not authorise *Jubilee*, but nor is there any evidence that he challenged the operation. It would appear that Brooke, Pound, and Portal had acquiesced and not made any objections, and yet there were occasions when the operation could have been stopped. First there was the time when the Chiefs of Staff enquired about the dangers on

## 66   Major Blunders of the Second World War

security grounds, because too many people knew what was being planned; nor did it appear that British Intelligence were entirely in the picture. In December 1942 the Chiefs of Staff had expressed their shock that Mountbatten appeared to have by-passed security experts, and even the role of British Intelligence came under historical suspicion.

As the debate unfolded the general tendency was to blame Mountbatten and the arguments although strong, were not always watertight, but they should be explored. When, postwar, Churchill was preparing his own personal history of this period he had to confront, or rather come to terms with the major loss of Canadian troops in an exercise which seemed to have contained few appropriate objectives. Curiously, following the Dieppe raid, German officers had interrogated prisoners, mainly because they were equally unable to understand the purpose of the attack, and they were baffled by its performance. Dieppe and its environs were too small to capture and hold any form of bridgehead or lodgement, there was little information to be found by the venture, and it was too major an exercise just to irritate the enemy as with commando raids. The loss of so many troops, tanks, landing craft, a destroyer and aircraft did not make any sense, even to the enemy.

Churchill knew and agreed that Operation *Rutter* had been stood down, and after the war asked General Ismay (Pug) to find out who had given the actual order. There was no evidence that the War Cabinet had given authorisation, nor the Chiefs of Staff. Slowly but surely the conclusion was reached that the head of CO (Combined Operations) Mountbatten had taken the decision alone on 31 July; an accusation he hotly contested right up to his death. According to Field Marshal Alan Brooke's diary, he and Churchill, along with Mountbatten, had discussed the raid on Dieppe much earlier on 30 June ready for its launch the following Saturday.[24] On 19 August Alan Brooke's diary included the entry that he was reading telegrams about Dieppe, and on 1 September he was struck by the size of the Allied causalities.[25] Later in the same diary Alan Brooke refers to visiting Mountbatten's Dieppe room; it is not a mystery that Mountbatten was deeply involved in the Dieppe raid, but whether he was authorised to make such major decisions is another matter.[26] Churchill's letter to Ismay seemed to indicate he was totally ignorant about the decision making; he wrote: *'Who made them? Who approved them? What was General Montgomery's part in it? And General McNaughton's part? What is the opinion about the Canadian generals selected by General McNaughton? Did the General staff check the plans? At what point was VCIG* [Vice-Chief of Imperial General Staff] *informed in CIGS's absence?'*[27] Churchill knew that he and Brooke were deeply immersed in military command problems in a visit to Egypt and safely well away from the scenarios surrounding Dieppe.

According to Nigel Knight, one of Churchill's severest critics, after the war Churchill tried to cover up mistakes, including his refusal to acknowledge the fiasco of Dieppe While it is possible that the disaster resulted from Mountbatten's poor planning and over-enthusiasm, it is less certain as to how far Churchill was aware of the operation which had previously been cancelled. This critic claimed that Churchill had been told by Pug that he had recalled Churchill's knowing about the raid, but he was ignored, and Churchill drafted his own version.[28] Whether this was true or not is difficult to ascertain, but either way it is certain that Pug would have stood by Churchill whom he virtually adored. There is no question that the failure at Dieppe pre-occupied Churchill's mind, and following the embarrassing and difficult episode at Chequers with the bitter argument between Brooke and Mountbatten it was probably Pug who tried to mollify the anger, then and later. Even in other people's bitter contentions Pug tried to smooth the way.[29] When after the war Pug had hoped to retire to his Jersey cows and live the 'good life', he continued to serve his country, and when Churchill was again elected to be prime minister, he called the reluctant Pug back to help him, amongst other matters in writing his history of the war.

As early as 1950 Churchill was demanding results to explain the Dieppe raid for his history, and Pug was obliged to write to 'My dear Dickie' [Mountbatten] explaining Winston's request to know why there was so much secrecy over Operation *Jubilee* when its predecessor *Rutter* had been cancelled.[30] The basic question was who gave the orders? When Mountbatten replied he was evasive, seeking information from

68 Major Blunders of the Second World War

his then naval planner and his Chief of Staff, and shifting the blame onto Churchill by claiming he was following his orders.[31] Pug had already warned Mountbatten that Brooke had encouraged Churchill to delve further into the reasons why the Dieppe raid had failed, and he expected Mountbatten to deal with the situation. It is noteworthy that 'Back in 1995 Ziegler [Mountbatten's official biographer] refused to accept that Churchill had signed off the brief, blame-free narrative of the Dieppe raid that appears in *The Hinge of Fate*, the fourth volume of his war memoirs… it seemed unbelievable that, through 'Pug' Ismay…Mountbatten could have convinced 'the old man' to endorse a version of events which was at best highly contentious, and at worst, manifestly false'.

On the occasion at the dining table at Chequers, when Field Marshal Alan Brooke had openly attacked Mountbatten for the debacle in Dieppe, Brooke did not follow the argument through because Mountbatten threatened counteraction. Churchill persisted in his research, but his letter to Ismay on 2 August 1950 brought few answers. Ismay found Mountbatten somewhat evasive, and General Archibald Nye, who stood in during Alan Brooke's absence in Egypt with Churchill, recalled being furious because he did not know the raid was happening until it had started. This factor relating to Nye at not knowing *Jubilee* was happening is a major factor in determining that Mountbatten appeared to have acted alone on his own responsibility. Nye was Brooke's vice-chairman while he was absent, and he held the post for the duration of the war, and like Brooke, was known for his integrity. Had he or the Chiefs of Staff known, there is no question that a man like Nye would not have denied knowledge or lied. Churchill knew that in the December of 1942 he had written a memo asking why the raid had taken place, because he felt that the 'underlying object was never sufficiently defined'.[32]

Churchill expressed serious doubts at No 10, and he was evidently searching for the cancellation orders. He noted that one of the Canadian commanders, General Roberts of the Canadian 2nd Division had expressed serious doubts. Above all, the code breakers at Bletchley had discovered that there was a German naval patrol out of Dieppe, which, according to Andrew Roberts in his book *Eminent Churchillians*, both Hughes-

Hallett and Mountbatten chose to ignore. These opportunities were missed, probably because Mountbatten and his chief planner Captain Hughes-Hallett had been working on *Jubilee* from the minute *Rutter* was cancelled. The Luftwaffe had attacked the landing craft moored in the Yarmouth Roads on 7 July which must have indicated their awareness of some attack, and consequently Montgomery's superior, General Paget, had urged its cancellation. Admiral Ramsay, responsible for all cross-channel activities wrote on 25 July urging that the raid be given up. Leigh-Mallory noted the critical point that there had been no letters of appreciation. These aspects seemed to have been taken by Mountbatten as the formal agreement that the plans had been looked at by services and agreement reached. However, they were highly critical of any such enterprise, not least a major operation such as Dieppe. Mountbatten remained evasive, and he claimed that the Chiefs of Staff had agreed. He managed to convince Churchill of this in 1950, but there was no paper-trail evidence, and when 'Mountbatten was made Fourth Sea Lord, Admiralty histories were revised to include a claim that the Chiefs had agreed'.[33] Churchill never pursued this line of enquiry, probably because first, he had always been Mountbatten's supporter; secondly, Mountbatten had probably persuaded him otherwise; finally, it was not a good idea to upset Canada once more. The most extraordinary aspect of this sorry affair was the complete lack of a proper paper trail for such a major undertaking.

Before further exploring the responsibility for the raid, it is possible that the Chiefs of Staff did not object too strongly because Canadian troops were pressing to be used. Canadian Prime Minister Mackenzie King had refused to allow Canadian troops to fight in North Africa, and they had become garrison troops in Britain. There was a high degree of political opposition to this passivity, and the commander of the Canadian troops, General McNaughton had claimed that the Canadian corps was a dagger pointed at the heart of Berlin. The Canadian soldiers and their public wanted a more vigorous prosecution of the war, and the Canadian Cabinet relented in allowing the Canadians on the Spitsbergen raid where there were no losses because no Germans were present. This encouraged the politicians to give McNaughton more leeway: his deputy Crerar was busy

70  Major Blunders of the Second World War

complaining to Montgomery that the Canadians were not being used, and also making the same complaint to Brooke. It would appear that the Canadian complaints arose at the right time for the planners of Dieppe.

The crux of the problem tends to focus upon Mountbatten. He had powerful supporters in Churchill and King George VI, and had pandered to the Americans in the hope that he would possibly be a future Supreme Commander; as already noted Roosevelt was impressed, and so were many others who saw Britain's military as a bunch of Colonel Blimps.[34] Mountbatten, had taken over as CO from Admiral Sir Roger Keyes who had operated with a staff of some twenty-three, but under Mountbatten and 'within six months the staff of COHQ grew to over four hundred'.[35] Even Mountbatten's official biographer wrote that this 'disregard of expense and the innate urge to build an empire led to over-staffing and the invention of superfluous functions'.[36]

Mountbatten always demanded good public-relations, and he included Hollywood stars such as Douglas Fairbanks Jr. and some of Samuel Goldwyn's assistants; he also ensured he had the ear of those journalists who could turn an article into a book. Incredible as it may seem, during the July when the Dieppe Operation plans were in reaching a critical point in the planning, Mountbatten spent considerable time with Noël Coward advising on the film *In Which we Serve*, which was supposedly based on his last destroyer. He took time to show the King and Queen around the set, and while 'all this was going on…Mountbatten was complaining that he was overworked'.[37] The film was good for public morale, but most knew that it gave Mountbatten a chance to glorify himself: 'no other general, not even Montgomery or MacArthur showed quite such poor judgement (not to say bad taste) during the war.'[38] Mountbatten had lost all his three ships, and had asked the Duke of Kent and others to persuade the Admiralty to award him a DSO; they refused because there was no evidence that he had ever sunk the two U-boats he claimed, and the loss of the *Kelly* 'was his own fault'.[39] Mountbatten may have been admired by many, including Churchill, but the upper reaches of the armed forces were never happy with him as a military commander.

One of Mountbatten's most critical errors was not involving the Intelligence Services, and authorising an operation for which he had no

## The Dieppe Disaster   71

authority, and in doing this he misled or kept in the dark his own staff. His chief-planner Hughes-Hallett was always under the impression the Chiefs of Staff had agreed. The whole question of Intelligence is highly charged; some historians have argued that the Germans were deliberately informed (the official Canadian historian C. P. Stacey denied this possibility) and generally this line of thinking was discredited; it re-surfaced when the German historian Günther Peis claimed to have found evidence the Germans had been informed. The Germans knew from the landing craft in the Yarmouth Roads something was afoot, and Mountbatten refused to heed the advice that Operation *Rutter* was cancelled because too many people knew what was proposed. British Intelligence history indicates that no Intelligence Chief was informed by Mountbatten of Dieppe, and this was an outrageously dangerous flaw in the preparation.

Operation *Rutter* should have been the end of the Dieppe raid, but when it was revised as *Jubilee*, those who could have stopped it failed, leaving Mountbatten to push forward with willing Canadian troops in a plan that was fatally flawed in its execution, suspect in matters of Intelligence, unsupported by heavy Naval guns and RAF bombers, and finally given the go ahead without appropriate authorisation. 'Nigel Hamilton has described him [Mountbatten] in his role as CCO as a master of intrigue, jealousy, and ineptitude, who like a spoilt child, toyed with men's lives'.[40]

In later years Mountbatten remained evasive, changed his tunes, and manipulated answers to avoid the main issue, namely his own role. Even in the late-1970s, on a Canadian documentary just before he was killed, he stated that 'the Canadians go around apologetically saying we were let down...it's a self-inflicted wound...I do not understand why they wish to go on revelling in the wound...they like to be told they were sold to the Germans, they were murdered. I don't know what the Canadians want...they just want to revel in their misery'.[41] This statement came from a man who once said, 'it is a curious thing, but a fact, that I have been right in everything I have done and said in my life'.[42]

The lessons learned from Dieppe were listed again and again to help provide a reason for the loss of so many lives, mainly consisting of the argument that it was a preparation for D-Day Normandy. The need for

## 72   Major Blunders of the Second World War

aerial bombardment and naval artillery support was well understood long before Dieppe was ever conceived. The need for surprise was known could be taken for granted in any form of attack. The need for intelligence on the place of attack was common sense, but Intelligence was not approached. The dangers of a purely frontal attack had already been noted by Montgomery and others, and there was no appropriate means of retreat, no provision for proper re-embarkation craft which caused the deaths of so many. 'Sheer common sense ought to have told the Combined Chiefs of Staff that Mountbatten's plan was misconceived from the outset', the so-called lessons learned for future operations were already known.[43]

Mountbatten as a person is revered by many people and with his royal connections has frequently been seen as untouchable. Many historians gloss over his contribution in the Dieppe Raid, some suspicious of his involvement, some seeing him as the fall-guy, a view first proposed by Lord Lovat, a prominent commando leader, who described Mountbatten as a lightweight cork tossed along on a sea of events. Anthony Eden called him a 'congenital liar'.[44] Field Marshal Sir Gerald Templar told Mountbatten directly in the 1960s 'You're so crooked, Dicky, if you swallowed a nail you'd shit a corkscrew'.[45] Most telling is the summary by Andrew Roberts who describes Mountbatten as a 'mendacious, intellectually limited hustler, whose negligence and incompetence resulted in many unnecessary deaths…the numbers of which increased exponentially as his meteoric career progressed'.[46] Even his official biographer wrote at the end of his work that Mountbatten's 'vanity, though child-like, was monstrous, his ambition unbridled. The truth in his hands was swiftly converted from what it was to what it should have been'.[47] The verdicts of most contemporaries and historians weigh heavily against Mountbatten and with considerable justification, based on his ambitious personality, but always lurking in the background are the political issues and pressures.

### Political Driving Forces

Even in this cynical or realistic age in which we live, it seems improbable that such a massive sacrifice of men would have been made to strengthen

The Dieppe Disaster    73

a political drive or make a point about strategy, yet this possibility must be explored. A raid by the British might be regarded as an opportunity to divert attention from a Second Front and appease the Allied critics. However, having seen Operation *Rutter* cancelled it seems unlikely, given the security risk, that Churchill would have risked the operation just for the sake of public relations; or did he? If he had been responsible, he would have probably either covered the mission in glory, or swept it under the carpet: as it happened, he pursued Ismay for answers until accepting Mountbatten's version of events. Mountbatten's account was clear, he had the agreement of the Chiefs of Staff – or did he?

There is no doubt that *Rutter*, the original plan for Dieppe was conceived because Britain needed, as noted earlier, to convince the major partners of America and the Soviet Union that Britain could achieve a victory. Hitherto, the British had painted the retreat from Dunkirk, as a form of victory for propaganda to boost public morale. In North Africa Rommel's military activities were causing embarrassment to the British, and when *Jubilee* occurred Churchill and General Brooke were in Egypt trying to resolve leadership problems in that area of conflict. The only effective offensive Britain had to offer at this time were its bombing raids, and the occasional commando raid 'to punch the enemy on the snout'. Politically the British were faced with a possible dilemma; the fear that Stalin might possibly seek some form of peace agreement with Hitler, because the Eastern Front was costly in lives and materials, and there appeared little substantial fighting help from the Western Allies. Commando raids across the channel and chasing around the North African deserts did little to help the Soviets. Stalin, like the Americans were pressing the British to start a second front, not in Africa but in Europe with France as the obvious starting point. Every time Churchill started or thought about an attack on Norway, he was always greeted with delight by Stalin, because this was closer to the Soviet front door. Churchill never received the same support from Brooke and his Chiefs of Staff who saw it as a needless risk in terms of life and resources, and they were proved right.

74 Major Blunders of the Second World War

The Americans, equally conscious of the need to keep Stalin fighting and self-aware of their industrial strength, wanted the immediate strategy of crossing the English Channel, making a direct thrust to Berlin. Anglo-American discussions on this issue were fraught, as Churchill and Brooke both knew that at this stage the Americans lacked the experience, did not understand the highly professional status of the German military, and had not realised the dangers of the English Channel which was not a mere large river. The American Admiral King and others wanted to leave Europe to sort out its own mess, crushing the Japanese who had attacked America directly. Many Americans were deeply suspicious of the British, some were deeply Anglophobic, and even Roosevelt suspected Churchill of being driven by traditional British colonial attitudes, especially with Churchill's apparent obsession with North Africa, the Balkans, and the Middle East. Churchill had manipulated Roosevelt into a personal discussion and persuaded him that American soldiers had to meet their German opponents first, and Roosevelt eventually agreed that North Africa would be the best area for his fighting troops to be 'blooded', but first a date for crossing the Channel had to be settled.

It was a serious political dilemma for Churchill as he knew that without American and Russian support the British and Commonwealth forces could not win against Germany. America's military, industrial and financial support were not just useful, but an essential life-saving support for Britain's survival. It is just possible that Churchill, speculatively, knew that if America stayed out of the European conflict, Germany might succeed. He may have also considered that if Russia succeeded against the Nazi onslaught there might be another dilemma. Because Churchill had a more realistic appraisal of Stalin than most, the Soviets might sweep through Germany in the years to come on the pretext of freeing Europe from the Nazi threat, reaching the channel coast. Whatever happened, Churchill knew he had to keep the Americans onside, use Russia to help crush the Nazi regime, and try and maintain not only Britain's survival but traditional place on the world stage as he perceived it should be.

The Americans had to be persuaded at all costs to be a British ally, and there were many well-known conferences when the future strategies were discussed, often leading to cantankerous moments. General Brooke, not always liked by the Americans but respected because of his experience, used all his authoritative ways of lecturing, and painted the future picture of crossing the channel, but only when the Allies were totally prepared, and having weakened the German military in North Africa. As Churchill managed to persuade Roosevelt, Brooke started to make sense of some of the American commanders. Thus, the North African Operation *Torch* was agreed, but with the promise of a cross-channel invasion. As a placatory effort the British had produced the plans for *Rutter* against Dieppe as an alternative to the less realistic *Sledgehammer* operation.

Mountbatten was utilised by Churchill in the American political arena for two reasons. Roosevelt may have been anti-British colonialism, but he enjoyed the dignity and picturesque Royal Family to which Mountbatten belonged. The second reason was that unlike Brooke, Mountbatten could be so socially attractive he nearly always won the affection of the Americans who admired his charming manners.

In many ways Mountbatten's personality and royal background made him the best public relationships man with the Americans, and Churchill exploited this to the full. Later Mountbatten was given permission to explain to the Americans the idea of an aircraft carrier made from ice; only Mountbatten with his charm would have had any success. At the last moment Mountbatten asked if he could demonstrate his project *Habbakuk* which was the idea of ice-built ships.* They agreed, probably because to the Americans Mountbatten was 'a royal' and popular with them. He had already prepared for two types of blocks of ice to be put in the room explaining one was pure ice, but the other was chemically treated, and when hit by gunfire would not splinter. He then pulled out a gun to everyone's astonishment, so the observers quickly moved behind him as they were hit by ice fragments, then he shot at the treated ice where the bullet bounced off and 'whistled' between their legs. Brooke amusingly observed that the people outside the room waiting to re-join

---

\* The inventor of a floating island or ship which was believed to be unsinkable was a Geoffrey Pyke; they were intended to be large floating ice islands rather than aircraft carriers.

76   Major Blunders of the Second World War

the closed session must have wondered whether the arguments had become so intense, they had resorted to their weapons, but only a man like Mountbatten could 'get away' with what most saw as a ridiculous farce.

Mountbatten was well aware of his natural ability to win over support, and he would have felt that Dieppe was an important political factor and, even after it was initially cancelled, resurrected it for political and ambitious reasons. He must have known that a raid on Dieppe would have given few outstanding results, but if it worked then it would not only increase his and British stature but politically would be a success.

The fact that when the disaster occurred and the news reached Churchill and Brooke there were no expressions of surprise that the raid had taken place, but only anger at the loss. He and Churchill may not have signed for *Jubilee* to go ahead, but Brooke's silence in his usually very honest diary entries, seems to indicate that by his lack of surprise both he and Churchill possibly knew it was happening, and at this stage Churchill in particular undoubtedly had hoped for a positive outcome for the political outcome outlined above.

The confusion as to who gave the order for *Jubilee* to start has remained a mystery, whether Churchill's postwar historical research was him trying to cover his own involvement or was genuine will be long debated. Brooke was more decisive on the matter with an open argument with Mountbatten, but that may possibly have been more to do with what Brooke regarded as poor planning, which would have more meaning for a man like Brooke than the political ramifications. General Nye's anger at not being told about *Jubilee* until it was underway, seems to indicate that Mountbatten was more the source of this dilemma than the politically minded Churchill.

There is no easy conclusion to the Dieppe debate. There is no doubt that the Dieppe operation had its basic impetus based on the outlined political motives, but after *Rutter* was put on the shelf this became less significant. After *Jubilee* it became a political embarrassment which could not so easily be placed on the shelf alongside *Rutter*. There seems no question that although political threads were evident, the gross error was bringing *Rutter* back to life: its resurrection, poor planning, and the whole disaster must be placed at the feet of Mountbatten, whose royal prestige appeared to save him from any accountability at the time. Despite Ismay looking for evidence of who authorised *Jubilee*, personnel, and dates, he found nothing, while Mountbatten shifted the responsibility from one person to the next. Political reasons had propelled the initial operation *Rutter*, may have influenced *Jubilee*, but revitalising it and with all the available evidence, the poor planning seems to be the responsibility of Mountbatten. The greatest error was the assumption it would succeed, when at this stage only the Germans could have won. There were demanding political reasons, the public demand for action, Churchill's need for a victory to convince Russia and America that Britain was not just self-defensive, but this still did not justify such an enormous sacrifice of lives. Had *Jubilee* succeeded, even with its own limitations, Mountbatten would have had a pedestal to stand on and the political motives may have felt acceptable, but it failed and served no political aims or military justification. The Dieppe raid taught the lesson of bad planning and inadequate preparation, but few took Mountbatten's persistent argument that it was in preparation for D-Day Normandy seriously , except for one person, Pug Ismay, his friend and a person always prone to calming troubled waters. Mountbatten had been slightly involved in some discussions on Operation *Overlord*, but very much on the periphery. Nevertheless, Pug wrote his congratulations to Mountbatten: 'If anyone had told us two years ago that we could throw ashore a million men, two hundred thousand vehicles, then three-quarters of a million tons of stores, across open beaches, in none too favourable weather, in thirty days, we would have dubbed him mad. So that's a great feather in your cap, Dickie.'[48] The implication appeared to be that Mountbatten's senseless operation *Jubilee* had paved the way for success in Normandy. Mountbatten's biographer Philip Ziegler believed this note was sincere, and Mountbatten found it the nicest communication he had ever received.

It may seem easy to sit at a library desk nearly eighty years later and write a critical appraisal of events fraught with anxiety and fear, but too many men died, were wounded, or captured, and this needs to be underlined. As one intellectual, Arthur Schlesinger later wrote, 'it was

## 78  Major Blunders of the Second World War

I suppose a Good War. But like all wars, our war was accompanied by atrocity and sadism, by stupidities and lies, pomposity and chicken shit. War remains hell, but few wars have been driven by decent purposes and produced beneficial results'.[49] Dieppe was not just a serious miscalculation, it was an appalling misjudgement brought about by a series of complex events and 'office commanders' under stress, which left the planning and authorization in irresponsible hands. What can never be forgotten is that the Canadians sustained 60 per cent casualties, but it should also be a cause of reflection that 'it was the sort of event that on the Eastern Front was a daily occurrence'.[50]

Dieppe is often treated in the same way as Arnhem, a drastic defeat which caused massive loss of life because of poor command decisions, but it is often glossed over in the mythology of epic heroic conduct so giving justified credit to the foot-soldier, while carefully placing in the bin of amnesia those responsible for the disaster. *Rutter* had been cancelled for good reasons, but the resurrected *Jubilee* was a serious misjudgement stemming from the highest levels. It was not just a misjudgement of poor planning, weak Intelligence, inadequate preparation, and no important objectives, but involved other important factors. The political motives behind the raid tended to outweigh the potential loss of life, trying to convince Stalin and Roosevelt the British could fight, but it ought not to have implied it would be done at any cost when it came to soldiers' lives. There is no question that Mountbatten carried considerable responsibility for his determination to stop *Rutter* being cancelled, and there are many questions which still lurk below the surface as to his questionable motives. However, the misjudgement was also higher up the rungs than even a Royal Family member when it came to military matters, as he was allowed too much freedom in this sphere when he lacked real professional abilities. Churchill and others may have found him a useful diplomatic relations officer stationed in Washington, with his charm and pleasant nature, but he was misplaced as a military leader, so his misjudgements were fortified by those who had elevated him.

# Chapter Three

# Edward VIII, A Judas?

## Author's Notes

For a period for most of the last Millenium the British monarchy has ruled but then transformed into a constitutional monarchy in recent centuries. It took time for some monarchs to accept that they could not influence the political views of politicians in a democratic state, but the system works, and the monarchy is held in the highest regard by the vast population of the British Isles, the Commonwealth and even by other countries. The rule is that the Royal family abstains from politics and always follow the advice of the elected government of the day. They are often seen as ambassadors for the country, and they are always a focus of popular attention and often admiration. Even their family life remains of considerable public interest as seen with the death of Princess Diana hitting worldwide headlines, and the polemics surrounding Prince Harry continuing to this day. When they express views it attracts immediate attention, and they know that political comments are a highly dangerous minefield, but their views and comments immediately attract headlines.

When King Edward VIII abdicated in 1936 it caused tidal waves of opinions, unsettled the country at a time when Europe was beginning to realise that it faced an uncertain future. This chapter focuses on this king and his later role as the Duke of Windsor, and it raises the vexed and difficult question that if he were a traitor to his country, whether this was legally valid, or just rumour. It will ask questions of blunders, mistakes, indiscretions, not only in his behaviour given the status he held, but it will raise the issue of misjudgements in the way the situation was handled.

This study tries to pinpoint the essential features of the Duke of Windsor crisis shrouded in a mixture of gossip, speculations, and political machinations. With his wife Wallis, he left a legacy of scandals and provided material for

# 80　Major Blunders of the Second World War

*conspiratorial theorists. Whether he was a traitor by intention, sheer naivety, or stupidity has never been resolved. One thing is certain: he created intense friction during the war years from which the government felt the need to protect the rest of the Royal Family. Many books have been written condemning him as a traitor, others have questioned this approach, and it is up to the reader to make his or her own judgement based on the known facts. It is clearly evident that the literature surrounding Edward VIII is generally biased against him, much of it vitriolic. This chapter is an attempt to find a more balanced view if it exists, but it first provides a survey of the modern monarchy from Queen Victoria to provide a background context. How far he was legally a traitor or simply out of his depth is the point of this study.*

*As the book swiftly explores his life he had many titles, Prince, Prince of Wales, King, and Duke. His family knew him as David, but it felt right to give him his appropriate titles as his life unfolded, which make the text somewhat confusing. The author decided to use the title prince until he became King, then Duke of Windsor or ex-king following his abdication. Where it is a general observation Edward alone is sometime used.*

## Introduction

There are volumes of novels, dramas, and history books about the life of King Edward VIII who abdicated on Friday 11 December 1936. Some of these accounts can be grossly exaggerated and feel as if they verge on conspiracy theories. Much of the popular interest revolves around Mrs Wallis Simpson his future wife, but of greater interest to historians was the crisis of the abdication on the eve of the Second World War, and the ongoing debate as to how far the abdicated king and his wife related to Nazi Germany, and whether he was as many have claimed a traitor. It is, historically a minefield in terms of evaluating reliable evidence, because even the most reliable people of the day had their own agendas and views, and it involved issues of growing importance on the international front, occurring at the time when warning bells were beginning to sound from Nazi Germany through to the pivotal moments of the battle of France. Before looking at the nature of this crisis it seemed sensible to take a brief look at Edward's royal background of which he would have been fully aware and undoubtedly had considerable influence on him.

## An Overview of Modern Monarchy

It has been said that at the end of time there will be only five monarchs left, Diamonds, Spades, Clubs, Hearts, and England. It is a constitutional monarchy and exists in a country without a written constitution.* The modern British monarch is the head of state but does not govern, a task which falls to the elected prime minister and his party, and when the monarch gives the annual speech to parliament it is written by the prime minister of the day, with the monarch saying, 'my government has decided...'. Nevertheless, the monarch remains critically important to the British way of life, and by common consent remains in an elevated position as head of the state. Monarchs of the modern era have been generally popular, and many leading politicians observe with a degree of nervousness what 'royals' maybe thinking when they meet, and especially when it involves foreign policy.

Throughout the history of the British monarchy there have been family or political problems of one degree or another, and in the modern era from the reign of Queen Victoria to today there have been domestic embarrassments often reflecting the human condition. Often the problems associated with each monarch cannot be ascertained with certainty, as royalty is the constant subject of rumour, and a popular target for conspiracy theorists. Being a constitutional monarchy, their private lives are often veiled from public view because they are protected by their governments who could often influence the press by requesting their silence, and when rumours spread, they could be simply denied. This is not so easily accomplished today, because the press is less likely to heed governmental advice, and the use of modern technology has increased their investigative skills by probing royal privacy. As in any family there will always be what can be described as dysfunctional members and even

---

\* The only other country without a written constitution is Israel.

82  Major Blunders of the Second World War

moments, and times change, as once divorce was totally unacceptable, yet mistresses were taken for granted, whereas a generation later divorce was almost a norm and lovers less so. Because the royal family is often subject to conspiracy theories, this chapter will try and keep to the known facts.

**Victoria** was born of Edward, Duke of Kent and Strathearn the fourth son of George III. Because of family deaths, she soon became the heir apparent and turned 18 years of age just on time to avoid a regency. It was an escape for her, because up to this point she had been under the almost iron grip of her mother and her comptroller John Conroy, alleged to be lovers, but it was probably just a rumour, the nightmare of royal families. In 1840, Victoria married Prince Albert of Saxe-Coburg and Gotha. It was no surprise given that the Hanoverian monarchy started with George I, who it was rumoured hardly spoke English, and that the British monarchy had many German relationships. This family connection with Germany was to create problems deep into the next century. Victoria often tried to influence the political policies, but she had also acted as a royal ambassador, the first monarch to visit France since Henry VIII in an attempt to sooth diplomatic relationships after centuries of antagonism. The gossip circuit was chattering about an affair their son Albert Edward, Prince of Wales, had enjoyed while in Ireland, and Albert went to see him in Cambridge about the scandal, as he and Victoria were strict moralists in such matters. When he returned from questioning Edward, Albert died from typhoid fever which Victoria blamed on her recalcitrant son, and she appeared to go into mourning for decades, becoming known as the 'widow of Windsor'. However, during the 1860s there were rumours of her having a romantic attachment with a servant called John Brown, and films are still made of this so-called affair to this day. She probably did enjoy his company but there was no evidence of any romantic attachment which was highly unlikely, but royalty always attracts rumours, a concern of which most royal family members are all too acutely aware.

She was sometimes called the grandmother of Europe, her daughter Victoria marrying Fredrick, later German Emperor and King of Prussia, who amongst her offspring produced not only Queen Sophia of Greece, but Wilhelm II the German Emperor. She had 42 grandchildren of which 34 survived to be adults, and they included members of the royal families of Europe not just in Germany and Spain, but Russia, Romania, and Sweden.

Apart from Victoria's prodigious family output, she left as part of her legacy a high moral standard which she expected society and especially her own family to follow. Although she had tried to influence politicians, she had eventually been obliged to accept that they played the main role in government. She had been prepared to serve the nation in an ambassadorial way, but always tinged with the sense of the importance and grandeur of the Royal Household. Her legacy has been passed on, emphasised in some places, but also challenged in others.

In 1901 her eldest son succeeded her using his second name as Edward VII. He had been the heir-apparent for nearly 60 years but kept out of politics by his mother, and used for ceremonial duties and diplomatic visiting abroad at which he was successful, especially in North America and India. He had also fostered improved relationships with France and is often seen as the instigator of the Triple Entente between Britain, France, Russia, and occasionally praised as the peacemaker. He was known for his sense of fashion which the gentry soon followed. He was married to Alexandra of Denmark on the 10 March 1863.

It was well-known that he had many affairs and he liked 'socialising' with prominent society ladies, whose names ranged from the famous actress Lillie Langtry to Lady Randolph Churchill, and it has been suggested there were over 50 such liaisons, and his wife seemed to accept this as the norm. There were rumours that the current Queen Camilla's grandmother was one of his lovers, but rumour and fact are difficult to ascertain and is not that relevant in the course of history. He was threatened to be named in a divorce case in 1869 by the MP Sir Charles Mordaunt, but it never materialised and instead he appeared as a witness. Twenty years later in 1891 it was revealed he played in what was then an illegal card game, and he had to appear as a court witness again in what has been dubbed the royal baccarat scandal.

84   Major Blunders of the Second World War

As was the case in nearly every royal family in many countries, and is equally true in most everyday families, there were moments of friction when the social and moral norms of the day were fractured, attracting more attention when associated with royalty. He had a better grip on the nature of constitutional monarchy than his mother, but tended to be conservative, being against the vote for women and opposing Irish Home Rule. His views were widely known in the so-called upper crust of social circles. In the final months of his reign, he became somewhat entangled in a major constitutional crisis, when the conservative party in the House of Lords refused to pass the budget proposed in the House of Commons. It was eventually resolved in 1911 with the Parliament Act, a year after Edward died, which restricted the powers of the House of Lords in financial matters.

As his mother had been known as 'the grandmother' of Europe, Edward VII was often called 'the uncle'. The German Emperor Wilhelm II and Emperor Nicholas II were his nephews, and he had family relations in nearly every European royal family of the day. More of interest than the occurring scandal was his relationship with Kaiser Wilhelm II, and despite the superficial exchanges (Edward VII was an honorary German Field Marshal) it was abundantly clear that Edward disliked his German nephew, always concerned that he would cause a war in Europe. He was the first British monarch to visit the Russian Empire (1906) and as noted had helped form the *entente cordiale* between France and Britain with Russia a friendly partner. There were some who blamed Edward VII for creating a paranoia about Germany which helped create the tensions erupting in the Great War, but his perceptions about his German nephew were probably more correct with the benefit of hindsight.

Edward VII, despite the scandals associated with his life, remained a popular monarch, and the position of a royal king held firm although there were the occasional hiccups. He recognised the role of a monarchy within the British system, with the power of rule invested in elected politicians. His travels abroad had been an important role for the British State both in Europe and in the empire. He also imparted his understanding of his role as monarch to his eldest surviving son who would be George V, even

USS Navy Destroyer *William D. Porter* in Massacre Bay, June 1944. (*Photographer unknown. Naval History and Heritage Command ID NH 97804*)

General George Patton. (*US Army*)

Bombing of town and monastery of Monte Cassino. (*IWM*)

The battle scene. (*Jacques Mulard*)

Bari Harbour attack. (*Source unknown, possibly military photographer*)

Memorial to Canadian forces in Dieppe. (*Geograph.org.uk, photographer Mickie Collins*)

Cliffs of Dieppe today. (*Photographer W. Bulach*)

There were many concealed gun sites prepared long before the attack. (*Bundesarchiv, Image 1011-291-1213-4, photographer Karl Müller*)

The steep pebbled beach at Dieppe. (*Bundesarchiv, Image 1011-362-2211*)

The disaster of not understanding pebbled beaches. (*Bundesarchiv, Image 1011-362-211-05*)

Edward VIII.

As Prince of Wales, 1919. (*Press Illustration Service*)

Freda Dudley Ward, 1919.
(The Tatler, *6 December 1922, credited to Bassano*)

Prince Edward and Wallis on holiday, 1935. (Life Magazine, *14 December 1936, p.37*)

Thelma Furness with Prince Edward, 1932. (Life Magazine, *29 April 1932, photographer unknown*)

With his mother Queen Mary on Remembrance Day, 11 November 1936. The last picture of the King at an official function. (*Photographer unknown*)

Meeting Hitler at the Berghof, his home in Berchtesgaden. (*Photographer unknown. Source Bibliothèque nationale de France*)

In the company of Robert Ley (far left), the Duke of Windsor inspects German troops, 13 October 1937. (*Bundesarchiv, Bild 102-17964/Georg Pahl/CC-BY-SA 3.0*)

Their love of meeting important people (President Nixon). (*Photographer Jack E. Kightlinger*)

U-boat snorkel.
(*Photographer, Tormentor4555*)

Living inside a submerged machine. (*Source Flickr by Reminiscencerestore*)

U-boat crew; men and officers happily mixed. (*Source Flickr by Reminiscencerestore*)

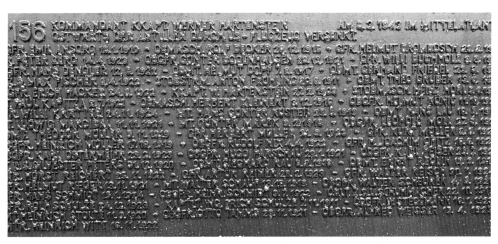
Plaque commemorating Hartenstein and crews of *U-156*. (*Source MisterBee1966*)

Karl Dönitz. (*IWM A 14899*)

Dönitz as watch officer on *U–39*, First World War. (*Source: unknown Kaiserliche Marine Serviceman*)

Dönitz made a habit of always greeting U-boat crews. (*Photographer Wächter, Bundesarchiv, Picture 101II-MW-5564-25*)

Depth charges straddling Type VIIC *U-266*, 15 March 1943. (*Photographer Royal Navy. Source IWM C3575*)

Dönitz, Speer and Jodl taken prisoner. (*Photographer Captain E.G. Malindine, US Army Photograph Unit (IWM)*)

People paying tribute to the navy and Dönitz having helped them to escape to the West. (*Photographer Friedrich Magnussen, permission by CC BY-SA 3.0 DE*)

sharing with him the political papers with which he would one day have to read. Edward VII even arranged for George to have academic lessons on the constitutional monarchy which was far-sighted.

George V was crowned in May 1910 because the heir-apparent, his brother Albert Victor had died young from influenza. As the second son, his father had placed George in the Royal Navy for training, which was abruptly halted with his brother's unexpected death. George, as the new King, experienced a world which was undergoing dramatic changes with the appearance of Irish republicanism, India demanding independence, a stronger form of socialism, as well as fascism and communism all changing the political backdrop to the future world and the British Empire. As a younger man George, while serving in the navy, had fallen in love with his cousin the Princess Marie of Edinburgh, and while most of the family saw it as an appropriate match, both mothers of the two candidates disagreed, significantly on the grounds that her side of the family was considered too Germanic. Marie later married the future king of Romania. George eventually married the fiancée of his deceased brother, Princess Victoria Mary of Teck, known as May within the family, with which Queen Victoria agreed. It transpired to be a stable marriage.

George, unlike his father, never led a socially scandalous life, and he valued his wife Mary, with whom he shared his political views, and she often helped him with speeches. They were often claimed to have been overly strict parents behaving more like tough schoolteachers rather than parents, but again rumour's tentacles stretch far and wide, and more likely typified the ethos of that day. It is known that George V was constantly worried about his eldest son the future Edward VIII, warning him that smoking was potentially dangerous, and that he had to eat more and take less exercise, which amounted to sensible if not kindly advise.[1] This was ongoing as the king continued to worry about his son's behaviour, and he talked to him about how the public loved him, but this would change if all his sexual affairs and his private life became public.[2] (This writer's father, born in 1904, used to explain how tough parents could be in those days as he let the writer off his many youthful misdemeanours.) They lived in Sandringham for much of their domestic life, but not in a

## 86  Major Blunders of the Second World War

palatial setting but in York Cottage, living more like a family from the middle-classes. George's main enjoyment was stamp collecting, which over the years accumulated to be world famous. He also enjoyed big game hunting when doing his international tours of the Empire, which would upset the current day public. When he had visited India in 1905 the racial discrimination caused him to be critical of the state of affairs, and it was a sign of a humane character that this had disturbed him. He was from his early times moving away from some of the old traditional values, and prior to his accession had insisted that the anti-Roman Catholic wording of the Accession Act had to be changed which was duly done.

He had barely been on the throne a few years before the Great War exploded across Europe, based on powerful nationalistic impulses, generating much hatred towards Germans. He recognised that the royal family all had Germanic names, his paternal grandfather had been Prince Albert of Saxe-Coburg and Gotha, and many other German names associated with the family. Following advice from his advisors, he changed the name to Windsor which was very English. His cousin Prince Louis of Battenberg also replaced his name with Mountbatten having been sacked as First Sea Lord because of his Germanic name. This international time of turmoil led to an embarrassing moment when his cousin Tsar Nicholas II of Russia sought help during the Bolshevik Revolution. George, despite pleas from Prime Minister Lloyd George refused on the grounds that the British Royal Family could not be tainted by foreigners, and they were murdered. Lloyd George took the blame at the time, and later surviving members were scurried out of Crimea by the Royal Navy.

The Great War was quickly followed by the Irish fight for independence, and George was horrified by the killing carried out by British troops more accustomed to the carnage of Flanders. He appealed for some form of reconciliation and a truce was signed, and by 1922 Ireland was partitioned. He was able to use his influence without interfering in the democratic process, and the nature of royal influence has lessened, but probably still persists to this day. He was concerned about the growth of socialism, but he made a point of knowing the leading Labour politicians, and during the global financial crisis encouraged the formation of a National Government in 1931. Interestingly, he expressed concerns about the rise of Nazism in Germany, which indicated he was astute in political matters. In 1932 he gave the first ever Christmas address over the radio, somewhat reluctantly, but was told that his people would appreciate the effort.

His lifestyle was also much more acceptable to the wider community than that of his father, but as always, his children caused him problems. He had four sons, John who died tragically young at the age of 13, Prince George the Duke of Kent who had for a time drug addiction problems and enjoyed 'night life', Prince Henry Duke of Gloucester who had to be convinced not to marry while abroad. More seriously Edward, the heir-apparent, was surrounded by rumours and complaints of his seemingly unending affairs with married women. George V was so distraught by Edward's behaviour he was convinced he would not be his successor, and with astute perception predicted his failure as a king. He was fond of his second son who had a stable marriage, children, and a loving wife, and who would later become George VI.

His legacy was different from his predecessors. He and his wife Queen Mary upheld family values, and tried to establish a better relationship between the royalty and other classes in British society, and not just keeping in touch with aristocratic friends. He worked well through social problems, dealt with the Great War crisis, the Irish revolt and made a point of meeting the socialists, even though by nature he was a strong conservative and traditionalist. It has been suggested that he tried to influence politicians more than a constitutional monarch should, but again it is more rumour than proven fact. His only problem, which could not be resolved before his death, was the personality and behaviour of the heir apparent Edward at a time with Nazi Germany was on the rise and stability was required.

## Early Life of Edward VIII

As was the situation in most royal and aristocratic homes Prince Edward (he was known within his family as David) was brought up by professional

88    Major Blunders of the Second World War

nannies, one of whom had tended to be cruel and was promptly sacked, crushing the rumour that his parents were not caring. Although George V had the reputation of being a disciplinarian, it was apparent from many accounts that he and his wife Mary were affectionate towards their children. Prince Edward was tutored by a man called Hansell who taught him German and French, and then, following his father's love of seamanship, he started a course at the Royal Naval College at Osborne in 1907. He did not enjoy the experience, but he continued with another two years at the Royal Naval College at Dartmouth.

When his father was crowned, he was in the traditional way created the Duke of Cornwall, Duke of Rothesay, and soon after Prince of Wales and Earl of Chester, he then went to Magdalen College, Oxford, where he had his *en suite* rooms, probably the first undergraduate to have this luxury. He became a member of the notorious Bullingdon club where he was known for being excessive with his enjoyment of smoking, drinking and pranks. He left after eight terms with no degree as he was not intellectually gifted, nor interested in any form of study even in a moderate way. In 1913 Prince Edward travelled to Germany to meet relatives, improved his language skills and describing the Germans as 'a vigorous people whose blood flows so strongly in my veins'.[3] He always spoke German fluently, but he made little effort with French, although later living in that country for many years. When the First World War started the following year he joined the Grenadier Guards in June 1914, but as the heir-apparent Lord Kitchener as Secretary of State for War stopped him serving on the front lines, although Edward always claimed he was willing. He visited the frontlines, when possible, which gave him some popularity amongst the soldiers and veterans after the war. At the end of the war in 1918 he also gained his pilot's licence. He was awarded the Military Cross which he did not appreciate, honest enough to know he had not deserved the medal.

After the war in 1919 he became the honorary president of the British Empire Exhibition at Wembley Park, suggesting it should be a national sports arena which it eventually became. He travelled extensively on a global basis representing his father, became known for his fashionable dressing like his grandfather Edward VII and was a celebrity for photographers. Between 1919 and 1935 it is estimated he did some 16 major tours. While in Canada he acquired a ranch in Alberta (£12,000) as an investment, but it later lost him $100,000. He also avoided injury travelling on a derailed train in Australia.

## Character, as revealed in private love letters

By the final stages of the First World War, he was 25 years old, and his character or personality traits were becoming embedded as they do with most people. It was well-known that he was drawn to attractive married women and enjoyed his social life, and some sports. He had a long-term mistress, a married woman called Mrs Freda Dudley Ward who remained his number one mistress from during the First World War until the mid-1930s when Wallis Simpson caught his attention. This is mentioned at this stage because he wrote hundreds of letters to Freda between 1918–1921 which have since come to light by pure chance and were published in 1998. The book is a 500-page volume which is unbelievably tedious to read unless the reader is trying to understand Edward's nature.[4] This writer, having first glanced through it decided to read it in detail, because it suddenly became clear that these letters give a full indisputable picture of the man who wrote them, and much more reliable than the gossip and rumour circuits. His views on others and his attitudes are made crystal clear, and they demonstrate and explain some of the later issues which became of international interest and concern. The very fact that he could write what he did in these letters was a signal of his indiscretion and lack of thought. Many people are just as guilty of this, but as the heir-apparent he should have thought twice, and perhaps asked Freda to destroy them once read. The letters are inundated with spelling errors, childish code words, swear words and blasphemies, but reveal his obsession with women. He addresses Freda like a young teenager trying to impress his girlfriend: 'Ah Sweetheart, My Angel, My own Darling, My Darling Girl, My Precious little Fredie Wedie, My vewy vewy own

90   Major Blunders of the Second World War

darling beloved', are but a few of his opening lines. On occasions he wrote every other day, often between midnight and four in the morning.

(*Author's note: rather than use endless endnotes any direct quotes from the letters which follow are numbered in the text*)

He wrote from Canada that 'I shall miss my very own beloved little mummie [sic] so terribly and I miss all her comfort and advice', (p.208) which offers evidence of what was later called his mother syndrome. This was when he needed to be dominated by people like Freda and later Wallis Simpson. It was his desire to be dominated by women, not necessarily as often impugned that he was bullied by them. Later Wallis Simpson would be accused of dominating Edward but there is no real evidence that he enjoyed this type of relationship. It was also evident that he did not enjoy the immense travelling and meetings he was asked to do on behalf of the royal family and government as heir apparent. When he described these tours to Freda, the words, and phrases, 'dull, bored, tedious, dullest weekend on record' were regularly used to describe how he felt. Time and time again when he met people who had come to greet him, plant trees, unveil plaques, both at official and unofficial level, he always referred to them as 'stunts' as if he were a royal performer for public consumption.

It was evident from these personal letters that he did not enjoy the nature of his work, he saw it as an imposed duty which he would rather not do. He wrote to Freda that 'Christ I am fed up with the job of P. of W, it's such a hopelessly thankless one, though I am never rewarded for all the misery of it'. (p.258.) This attitude remained a constant theme when he later wrote 'this ghastly existence of mine really seems to get more intolerably strenuous and difficult each day'. (p.386.) However, his doctors were worried about his stress. Nevertheless, most people would have loved to have seen the world, be treated as royalty and be rich, but Edward admitted to Freda that 'I do get bad fits of depression' (p.114.), a condition which often haunted him for the rest of his life. He would rather have been playing golf or one of his other sports, surrounded by doting women whose husbands appeared acquiescent.

It was fortunate that his views on his hosts wherever he visited, be it the commonwealth or elsewhere were hidden in these love letters and not disclosed until long after his death. Unlike his father who had been disturbed by racial discrimination in India, he was strongly opposed to any form of Indian independence, but this may have been more political than racial.[5] He described the indigenous Australian as 'the most revolting form of living creatures I've ever seen!! They are the lowest form of human beings and are the nearest thing to monkeys'(p 433), in the same letter describing them as 'filthy nauseating creatures' (p.434). He regarded 'Italian military parades like pantomimes' (p.75) and having lunched with an Italian general he noted 'they are indeed repulsive natives these dagoes, both the men and the women' (p.101). Later he added the 'The Belges [Belgium], I hate them as much as the Dagoes' (p.145), described the Germans as Huns having 'revolting women, (p.155) and the men as 'thick skinned' (p.157). The French whom he had been with during the Great War he described as 'dirty little Frenchmen' (p.375). When in Canada he wrote to Freda that 'I am fond of the Canadians but get rather bored with them, (p.108), later adding that the French Canadians 'are a rotten narrow-minded touchy crowd who haven't played the game at all during the war and never do!' (p.216). He thought the Hawaiian women 'were very fat and such legs and ankles, though they knew how to waggle their fat b*ms', p.334). When in New Zealand he described the Maori ceremonies as 'dolled up in mats while inane Maoris danced and made weird noises at me!' (p.359). His allotted task was to bring the British and royal friendship overseas which was why he was tasked to travel so much. However, his stunts were obviously well prepared because he was seen as a popular visitor, but his inner thinking shared with Freda revealed his public appearances were a show (stunts in his words) and exposed a self-centred person. This feature of his character created considerable problems which in the pre-Second Word War years became a major issue.

His social views were little better, mentioning that he had heard fearful rumours of church worship the next day and 'I shall have to be British and do my best' (p.142). He described the Bishop of Exeter as looking 'quite mad and is anyway revolting with a scraggy beard' (p.186), and a general in the

92  Major Blunders of the Second World War

First World War as 'one of those people who take life fearfully seriously', (p.146). When as a guest of the Butes [Baron Cardiff], he wrote to Freda that they were 'a vewy [sic] weird couple, both rather mad and religious, and she breeds like a rabbit', ( p.189). He tended to refer to women as 'bits', writing 'there was quite an attractive bit in the leading woman's part', (p.467). His father was a traditionally inclined conservative, but he had at least tried to meet socialists and listened to their point of view. When Prince Edward had been in Australia, he had found the mining villages difficult because of having the 'red flag element' (p.433).

Nor did his family evade his cynical approach, referring to his father the king as 'my bloody father' (p.470), and later 'Christ! What I think of him [the king] and my contempt for him increases daily', (p.399). Nor did his brother Bertie, later King George VI escape his views, referring to Bertie's flirtation with Sheila, Lady Loughborough (p.182) when Edward lured her husband away to play golf to give Bertie time with her', (p.184). He later wrote to Freda that Bertie 'was getting it in the neck' about Sheila from George V, (p.373) noting later that 'personally I think [Bertie] is an ass to accept the title' [Duke of York], (p.395).

Nearly every normal human being has ups and downs with parents, but by Edward's age there seems to have been a distinct lack of maturity, not least by sharing his views in writing to his mistress. It appeared she could be trusted, another may have made a fortune from this inside knowledge, but she kept the letters safe but had no control of them after death. His social views and racially inclined nationalistic view of foreigners were cynical in the extreme for a person in his position. Later the government would be concerned that he was indiscreet with government papers, too much of a chatterbox on sensitive matters; had they seen these letters it could have meant he would have been asked to abdicate to avoid putting the constitutional monarchy at risk.

### The Interbellum Years

Prince Edward's early life as the heir apparent to the throne had been one of social frivolity even when on official tours for the crown. Early signs of his love for women were demonstrated when on leave in the Great War, living it up in Paris where he became infatuated with a Parisian courtesan, a polite word for prostitute. This led to early scandal rumouring, and he had to finish the affair. Wherever he travelled there were tales of his various liaisons, mainly with married women, some books offering great detail, but such was the quiet nature and discretion by others it is impossible to say whether they were all affairs in terms of sexual relationships, or just frivolous flirtations. It can only be speculation and the only thing which can be confirmed historically is the reputation he acquired of being a womaniser with other men's wives. Later there would be questions as to how many illegitimate children he had fathered. This was soon known about in the royal household, as were scandals associated with his brother George, the Duke of Kent, who frequently joined him in the pursuit of hedonistic pleasures. George became a drug addict but Prince Edward in his home Fort Belvedere locked him away, curing him of the problem, one deed which pleased his father.

However, his propensity for attractive women was only known in the social circuits in which he mixed, and he was always popular in the public eye as he always appeared as a charming personality. This was mainly because he showed interest in housing conditions and the problems brought about by poverty in the post Great War era. In 1928 he became the patron of the National Council of Social Services, but it was mainly him gathering popularity, as was suggested in a letter he wrote to his friend Godfrey Thomas, when he referred to his social activities as 'stunting', or putting on a show, as confirmed by his letters to Freda.[6] The Prime Minister of the day Baldwin was concerned at his general behaviour, as was Tommy Lascelles, who had been his assistant Private Secretary since 1921, when Edward's title in those early days was Prince of Wales. Lascelles stayed with Edward for eight years then resigned because of his behaviour. He travelled with him across Canada twice, Central Africa, writing that 'I saw him sober and often as near drunk as doesn't matter', but by 1927 'my idol had feet and more than feet, of clay'.[7] It should be noted that despite Edward's behaviour many of the officials he greeted on his tours found him charming and with a vivacity

94   Major Blunders of the Second World War

they admired. However, Lascelles watched him in his early life in his 'unbridled pursuit of wine and women' and decided he was not fit to wear the crown. The crunch for Lascelles came during a visit through Kenya and Uganda when Baldwin had asked for Prince Edward to return to England as George V was seriously ill. To Lascelles' annoyance Edward claimed it was just an election dodge by the prime minister, ignored Lascelles, 'and spent the remainder of the evening in the successful seduction of a Mrs Barnes, wife of the local commissioner. He told me so himself, next morning'.[8] Lascelles was so shocked with his behaviour he formally resigned his post in 1929, and thereafter remained one of Edward's harshest critics. Curiously Lascelles was asked in 1935 to serve George V as one of his private secretaries, and at first, he refused on the grounds that he might well have to serve Prince Edward again if the king died. George V's sudden death in 1936 caught everyone by surprise, but by this time the rumours of Edward's obsession with the divorced and re-married American Wallis Simpson dominated the thoughts of all those who were aware, namely the upper social classes. In his diaries Lascelles speculated that Edward had already decided he did not want to inherit the throne. There may have been some truth in this perception, as it was abundantly clear that Edward needed the freedom if he were to enjoy his life of fun and frivolity. Lascelles was close to the unfolding drama and wrote that in his opinion because of Edward's character no one could have persuaded him otherwise. Lascelles knew Edward was self-centred, rich in money and wanting to accrue more, writing that in his own opinion Edward had 'no comprehension of the ordinary axioms of rational, or ethical behaviour; fundamental ideas of duty, dignity and self-sacrifice had no meaning for him, and so isolated was he in the world of his own desires that I do not think he ever felt affection…for any living being, not excluding the members of his own family'.[9]

Lascelles was highly critical of the heir apparent quoting various opinions that suggested some form of psychological or even hereditary problems which stopped any possible maturing after adolescence, implying that he never stopped being a teenager, even down to the detail that he did not have to shave on a regular basis.[10] Lascelles in his diary often noted the signs of immaturity, not least his lack of education, once being given the famous novel *Jane Eyre* of which he had never heard. He was well known for his liaisons with a variety of women, had a long-time affair with Mrs Freda Dudley Ward mentioned above, whom he had met in 1918, she was good looking and intelligent but with a husband some 16 years older than herself.

## Wallis Simpson

Wallis Simpson, his latest and last female obsession, was to become an ongoing contentious issue resulting in him abdicating the throne. Wallis had married a US Naval pilot called Earl Winfield Spencer when she was aged twenty, but he was purportedly an alcoholic and the marriage did not last long. Like most families they were horrified at a divorce, but it happened. It had not been a happy marriage, and when Wallis had visited Paris and China, she had discovered that the last straw was her husband drinking before breakfast. All sorts of claims were later made against her arising from her time in China. Later, there were accusations of sexual adventures in what was called the Chinese file or dossier, often claimed that this arose because of investigations by the British Secret Service, but the file and its contents were highly unlikely, either a rumour or a fabrication to dishonour her. In an effort to defame her, she was accused of an endless list of traditional sins, of being a lesbian, nymphomaniac, Nazi spy, worked for the NKVD, Ribbentrop's mistress, and had learnt techniques in Chinese brothels for which there is no real evidence. There were rumours that she had biological sexual problems, and similar issues were sometimes hinted at regarding Edward, all without evidence and undoubtedly generated by the powerful feelings aroused by their eventual union. It was all dressed up with accusations of being affected by various 'syndromes' which had little to no substance apart from angry bigotry. Some have suggested Edward was bi-sexual and needed Wallis's expert sexual knowledge, others that Edward never passed the age of puberty and many other opinions have been expressed. Many books dwell on these matters but they can be nothing else than speculations which

## 96   Major Blunders of the Second World War

readers enjoy while providing no concrete evidence. If she had not been totally normal it would have been unlikely that the traditional Ernest Simpson, her second husband, would have fallen in love with her. He offered her both financial and social security following the nightmare of her first marriage.

A few years later, living with Ernest in London she met Prince Edward who was immediately drawn to her. Many far-reaching reasons have been projected as to this mutual attraction, some of them products of rumour and sheer speculation. Suggestions have been made that she enjoyed regal company and its attendant high society, and he enjoyed her American forthright views and wit, others it was purely sexual attraction, and while some may hold water, few have the expertise to identify what attracts two people together. Ernest at first was pleased that his wife drew Edward's attention, and it was generally understood that if royalty had some form of affection for another's wife this was for most husbands socially acceptable. Dudley Ward, his longest-term mistress, confirmed this to be true in her case, but it was not a tradition acceptable to everyone, and Ernest later had a change of mind but always retained his gentlemanly approach in this matter. Prior to Wallis, Edward's latest mistress had been a Thelma Furness whose husband decided to divorce her in 1933, a year before Edward put her aside for Wallis. Thelma was the twin sister of Gloria Vanderbilt who had asked Wallis to look after Edward while on a trip to America, which she did all too well.

This relationship rapidly developed, receiving widespread interest in American newspapers, but by agreement with the government the British press remained silent, so the British public tended to remain oblivious to the developing crisis when George V died. Politicians were divided, the established Church opposed, and the royal family deeply upset by his relationships. His brother Albert George and his wife Elizabeth were worried at the prospect of abdication, and Elizabeth, popularly known to the current generation before she died (2002) as the 'Queen Mother', made no bones about how she felt about Edward's latest mistress. Stanley Baldwin, the prime minister at the time, even asked the British intelligence agencies to research Mrs Simpson. As the years have passed the debate evolved around Edward and Wallis as to who was to blame. One tendency was to blame Edward's self-centred attitude of demanding what he wanted and always having his own way, on the other hand Mrs Simpson was blamed for leading him astray. It will always be a contentious and enigmatic issue as to who controlled who in this relationship between Edward and Wallis. It seemed to this author that it was more Prince Edward's fixation for her company which carried the most weight. As the years passed, he would become obsessed with her company, and all kinds of slurs of sexual proclivity were laid at her feet. One writer made the more astute observation that 'it was her personality more than her looks and sex which dominated him'.[11]

The information gleaned by the secret service, although somewhat suspect, was utilised to build up a bank of hostility towards the twice divorced American, and generally over time she gathered considerable public hostility. Some of the accusations were evidently false, not least that while with Edward she was having an affair with a car salesman from Fords [not even Rolls Royce]. Other, probably false insinuations were that she was having an affair with the German Ambassador Ribbentrop. That they had met was true, but in the company of Churchill, and that they had an affair was unlikely. As far as it is possible to ascertain she only met Ribbentrop twice, and it was well-known that he was always trying to work his way into British high society. It was even suggested that she was pro-Nazi. A recent writer and researcher, Anna Pasternak, has produced a book on Wallis Simpson which paints a very different picture of the detested woman, clearly indicating that she did her very best to stop Edward abdicating as the crisis developed, right up to the last moment when it was too late.[12] Anna Pasternak rightly stated that 'we have been overfed a diet of fantastical slander: that Wallis was really a man; that she had a perverse psycho-sexual hold over the prince; that she used manipulation and feminine wiles to lure him into abdicating; that she was ruthless, a cold ambitious bitch, who schemed from the start to be Queen of England'.[13] She was seen as producing a constitutional crisis and was regarded almost as an enemy of the state. Some of the attacks delivered against Wallis Simpson were the machinations of the secret

## 98   Major Blunders of the Second World War

services, others trying to defend the hopeless Prince Edward, and some emanated from those who enjoy scandal. In attempting to understand the dilemma it is necessary to try and keep a measured but honest approach, and it may be necessary to see Wallis Simpson as more of a victim than the wicked witch. She may not have been everyone's cup of tea, her lifestyle, and habits many people today would find obnoxious, but often prejudice runs deep and has to be explored with care.

Despite the many photographs she was a small woman at five-foot-five, but Prince Edward was only two inches taller. Both Wallis and Edward enjoyed the high life of dinner parties, dressing well, and creating a sense of luxurious taste in their many homes. He showered gifts of jewellery on her, much of it claimed to be part of the royal family assets, which by today's financial value would be in the millions. His father objected to her presence at social or formal meetings, the Duke of York and his wife were cold towards her, only his other brothers, Henry and George appeared to accept her company. The British world of politics, Church, and high society were divided on Edward's lifestyle with some fearful of future consequences. Mountbatten (Earl Mountbatten of Burma) who had a lifelong hobby of family genealogy even prepared an extensive list of potentially suitable brides for Prince Edward from the European royal families, but as King George V had slowly begun to realise, Edward had a mind of his own and Wallis was the only priority.

It was widely known amongst the more elite circles that Prince Edward held pro-German views, was highly critical of anti-German attitudes which did little to help his situation as far as the government was concerned. Despite King George V's efforts to train him as a young man he lacked constitutional propriety, which he exhibited on many occasions. He had made his views clear in 1933, when he told Prince Louis Ferdinand of Prussia that 'it was no business of ours to interfere in Germany's internal affairs either Jews or anything else', adding that 'dictators were very popular these days and that we might want one in England before long'.[14] His social life, obsession with Wallis, his pro-German views and political forthrightness started to make abdication welcome to some politicians and others. It was all contained in the higher echelons of society and unknown to the wider public in Britain, although the American press had no restraints and made him at times their headlines.

## The Divisions at Abdication

The crisis reached its apex on the death of George V, not least because many were all too aware that the heir-apparent was known for making choices and expressing opinions from the acceptable norms of the day, especially with his association with people like Diana Mitford and her lover Sir Oswald Mosley. This situation raised questions about his political views, not least his apparent support for Germany now under Hitler, usually expressed through idle gossip. This caused many to wonder whether the crown would be able to maintain its essential stance of political impartiality. It has also been alleged that it was his relationship with Wallis which was causing Edward to be so indiscreet in his opinions, but already a general disliking of her was growing because it was rumoured that she held too much influence over the heir apparent.

Those who were aware of the situation were sharply divided. In the royal family King George V and his second son the Duke of York with their wives had constantly deplored the relationship. His father George V had expressed doubts about his potential as a monarch, and although there were political concerns over his apparent support of pro-Nazi Germany and his personal lifestyle, he also had many supporters and was popular. This popularity rose and fell which is normal for a person in the public eyes. Much later George VI's wife Elizabeth made an interesting comment when in conversation with Eric Anderson (Headmaster of Eton College) she explained, 'I don't think he ever wanted to be King. I don't think he thought of it as something he ought to do. Very odd people do change in a strange way. He had extraordinary charm and then it all disappeared'.[15] She was a lifelong critic of Edward VIII but close to the truth. During the 1920s Edward and his brother Albert (George VI) had been good friends and during these days Elizabeth had been very fond of him, but from many sources it was clear that during the 1930s his lifestyle started to change her views.

## 100   Major Blunders of the Second World War

His brother who was to replace him as George VI was unhappy at the thought of being king, because of the burden of office and his speech stammer which made public speaking a nightmare for him, and he thought this should exclude him from this major role. His other brothers George and Henry tended to be supportive of Edward VIII. This was especially true of George, the Duke of Kent who was especially sad, as he was rumoured (and only rumour) to have had a reputation for homosexuality which in those days was a criminal offence. Prince Edward had several times rescued him from embarrassing situations and also weaned him off cocaine and morphine addiction.[16]

In the outside world Prime Minister Baldwin was strongly opposed to the marital match and several times tried to talk the king round to his point of view. The Archbishop Cosmo Lang represented the Church of England's opposition, pointing out that the monarch was the defender of the faith. He argued that the king, if he continued down this road, could hardly hold that role by marrying a divorced woman which was in those days against the rules of the Church. In high society divorce was seen as a scandal whereas having an affair was regarded as quite natural so long as it was discreet. The Archbishop of Canterbury preached a sermon which virtually condemned the King, stating that he had been 'ruined by his disastrous liking for vulgar society, and by his infatuation for this Mrs Simpson'.[17] For the senior Primate to be so forthright in condemning a member of the Royal Family indicated the heat of the feelings at this time. Edward remained popular with many people, and the archbishop received some angry letters. It was an ironic twist of history that the Church of England came into being because the monarch Henry VIII needed a divorce.

In the pro-king camp was Chips Channon, people like Cecil Beaton, the news magnate Max Beaverbrook who followed most of Edward's requests, and most importantly Winston Churchill.* It was even rumoured that Churchill would go so far as to initiate a King's Party, which never happened though it gave Edward some hope. There had been concerns

---

\* Max Beaverbrook, once on his way to America, promptly returned at Edward's request.

in the higher reaches of society that even after a civil wedding her appropriateness for being a Queen of England was in serious doubt. It was also believed or rumoured that she had some sympathies for the Nazi movement, which at this time was a growing concern in terms of national security. As noted above, it has often been stated that Edward VIII never wanted to be king, that he wanted to be free of such burdens, and his relationship with Mrs Wallis Simpson provided him with the excuse.

None of this anxious controversy was resolved, and Edward VIII decided to take a holiday in the Mediterranean, hoping to start in Venice, but with the Foreign Office warning of the dangers of Italy under Mussolini and the start of the Spanish Civil War. Edward was irritated but started elsewhere with Royal Naval destroyers acting as his protection. Today there would have been sharp criticism if a royal family member insisted on taking a holiday in a potential war area and expected the taxpayer to pay for Royal Navy protection. Later, in early 1939 when George VI and the Queen took a trip to America, he refused to travel in HMS *Repulse* in case war started.

The American press had a field day, but this expensive holiday did King Edward's position no good. He was portrayed as enjoying an expensive holiday with high society friends while there was a crisis at home over the coronation, as well as events in Europe, especially in Germany, Italy, and Spain, which were growing decidedly uncomfortable. Wallis was on a shopping tour in Paris where she read the newspapers' criticisms of the holiday, and she tried at this stage to encourage her lover, now the king, from avoiding abdication. This may explain why on his return, King Edward VIII did a well-publicised tour of the Welsh coal valleys where unemployment and poverty were all too characteristic of the British landscape at this time, hoping the image of the People's Prince could be restored.

However, the public were now more aware of what was happening, and Wallis started to receive hate mail, having to abandon her home when she came under abusive attack. It appeared to King Edward that whenever he made a public presence he was popular and it would seem he wanted Baldwin to understand this fact. Ernest Simpson's divorce

## 102    Major Blunders of the Second World War

was now taking place, with Ernest taking the blame as a thoroughly old-fashioned gentleman. Edward simply could not understand why he could not marry Wallis, even with the prime minister and the archbishop of the established Church disagreeing.

In all this mayhem of conflicting views Wallis appeared to be making the greatest effort to stop him abdicating. She had clearly picked up the sheer determination of the establishment that there could be no marriage: she wrote and spoke directly, imploring him to release her, threatened to leave him and return to America. This has been known for years, but the recent book by Anna Pasternak offers overwhelming evidence that Wallis made a determined effort to encourage Edward to leave her and not renounce the throne.[18] Despite her efforts he remained obdurate and gave the well-known abdication address through a radio broadcast. His infatuation with Wallis, which generations of writers have tried to understand, caused this momentous upheaval in royal and British history. It was his decision and despite the claims still frequently made, it was not Wallis who stole the king from the throne, but the king who made the choice against her advice.

The major factor creating this national dilemma was a self-centred personality behaving like an over-indulged spoilt child always wanting his way. His early life with his social behaviour had already intimated his propensity for wanting his own way and seeking his own pleasures. He had been brought up by strict and moralistic parents, but as in many families not all the children go down the anticipated path planned for them. His over-indulgence in the more hedonistic pleasures of life had happened before with his grandfather Edward VII, and it is a feature of most human families, including royalty. Because of his position as heir-apparent he had been given adulation and respect merely because he was the future king by accident of birth, not because of his qualities.

When as King Edward VIII he gave his abdication speech, which Churchill helped him prepare, it was the first time in British history that a monarch had voluntarily left the throne, as it was passed to his brother George VI with the subscript that no progeny of Edward would be an heir to the throne. Knowing that Baldwin would also have to

# Edward VIII, A Judas?    103

make a speech, the king asked him to accentuate that the royal brothers were on the best of terms, and that Wallis had tried to dissuade him. Baldwin mentioned the first request which as a truth was questionable, but omitted the point about Wallis which had some veracity. Now as the Duke of Windsor, he was shut out, not only by the government but by the Royal Family: he was to become an outsider. Wallis still received angry letters as it was assumed she had influenced Edward, and in the famous Madame Tussauds her effigy was not placed amongst the royals, and it was almost an insulting effigy in its modelled appearance. At this stage the Duke and Wallis were apart, and they remained so for twenty weeks for legal reasons as her divorce with Mr Simpson was taking place. Edward spent time in Austria, often on the phone to his brother the King making all kinds of demands, ranging from the need to grant the HRH title to Wallis, demands for money, and offering advice which was often contrary to what the government was proposing. Even Ribbentrop capitalised on the abdication, telling Hitler that the abdication was a plot by the British government to rid themselves of a king who held favourable views on Germany.[19]

Their marriage took place in France at a chateau in the Touraine region at a place owned by Charles Bedaux. He was a French American millionaire who had worked with the Nazi government in America, as he saw their type of leadership as the future. It was an inappropriate connection for Edward because of his host's various machinations, of which Edward had become one. Bedaux was painted as a German agent but there is no substantive evidence. Edward had anticipated or at least hoped some of his family would attend, but even Mountbatten replied in the negative. It was considered too damaging for any of the royal family to attend, and even Churchill agreed with this view. The Duke of Windsor was now the outsider even to the family, and it was further aggravated when he heard Wallis would not receive the HRH title. This would aggravate Edward for the rest of his life, making him paranoid on the issue. As he had been awarded the title of Duke of Windsor it would have been normal practice for his wife to be HRH. Just as irritating was that even old friends started to keep a distance, only a few arrived. An imported and somewhat obscure Anglican cleric called the Reverend Anderson Jardine arrived. He ignored the Church rules and presided over the service, later he felt that he had to resign his post and moved to America, later Mexico, then South Africa, before returning to Britain where he died in 1950 with no known marked grave. He showed his true colours when he promptly toured the USA giving talks on the wedding offering the so-called inside story.

The date of the wedding was 3 June which happened to be George V's birthday, which did not go unnoticed by Queen Mary. Because of the paucity of attenders Edward asked his old equerry Major Edward Dudley Metcalfe, better known as Fruity to be his best man. Meanwhile, Beaverbrook ran a newspaper campaign for them to return to Britain, but it failed.[20] Beaverbrook was one of his strongest advocates and supporters, knowing that Edward feared the *Times* newspaper because of its national and international reputation, and Beaverbrook even went as far as accusing Dawson, the *Times* editor, of driving Edward to abdication. All this underlined the serious divisions the royal marriage created in Britain, at the very time when international friction was becoming potentially dangerous.

They honeymooned in Austria, and they borrowed a mock castle, the home of Count Paul Münster who was associated with Mosley. They wondered where they would live in future, he preferred the countryside, but Wallis the cities with her love of shopping, especially Paris where she had the same hairdresser for thirty years.

From the various accounts written at the time and by historians since, it appears that although Windsor had established his long desired private life with the woman he loved, there was a feeling that he regretted not being so important. His opinions on matters at home and abroad, on the domestic and international scene became a feature of social gossip. He spoke freely to the hundreds of guests attending their dinner parties, entertained in a variety of luxurious homes they were either offered or rented, and his political attitudes became of interest in governmental circles in Britain, Germany, America and elsewhere. His views were often in demand, and he often spoke without reference to the government.

## Edward VIII, A Judas? 105

While George VI was visiting the USA with the Queen, Edward gave a broadcast from Verdun appealing for peace. There was nothing wrong in asking for peace, but sound political sense should have warned him to talk to the government first. He considered himself a private man but despite abdication he remained, for the public and world at large, a representative of the constitutional monarchy, which fact raised his level of significance in British history. He may have explained he wanted to be a private man, but he always wanted to be in the limelight and recognised as part of the royal family. When his brother King George VI and the Queen visited France, Edward expected to meet him as part of the formal meetings which was ignored.[21]

His obsession for money and possessions, living the grand life, mixing with the perceived important people, high society, and being seen as important were well known, well documented, and remain a feature of most histories relating to him. His need for wealth was widely commented on, and came to light when in his father's will, his siblings were given money and he was given nothing, on the grounds that the Duchy of Cornwall would furnish him with all his needs. He was angry and walked out from the meeting.[22]

However, his verbal indiscretions were becoming politically dangerous and cast a darkening shadow over his history. Instead of becoming a mere aging dilettante of high society social life of little consequence, he became a political embarrassment on an international basis. At social functions he enjoyed dominating the conversation, expressing his views all too easily while enjoying being the centre of attention and seeming reverence for what he had to say. This would have been fine if it had been mere social chatter or local gossip, but he showed a high degree of indiscretion, not only in what he said, but with whom he mixed.

This was a time of growing tension especially with the growth and perceived threats from Nazi Germany, and he was making it clear to his dinner and luncheon guests that, perhaps admirably, he did not want war. Appeasement should not be seen as a 'dirty word' as peace is always preferable to war, but events were unfolding in Germany, which to the more astute intimated imminent serious dangers, and were quickly

## 106   Major Blunders of the Second World War

perceived by his political supporter Churchill. However, it was not just appeasement, but he voiced opinions on Hitler being the right leader for Germany, and he often liked to speak and sing in German on social occasions. He may not have thought that his social chatter was of interest outside his dining room, but it soon spread, illustrating his sheer naivety. His self-opinionated views which he confided to his so-called friends demonstrated a gullibility which was almost dangerous.

### Nazi Sympathiser or Traitor?

It was known that the Duke loved reminding everyone that he had German blood in his veins, but even Wallis, probably inadvertently had employed a lawyer called Armand Gregoire, who acted for many leading Nazi leaders, and he advised those whom he helped to provide the British fascist leader Mosley with funds from Mussolini.[23] This may have been sheer innocence, but it promptly attracted official attention, not least when it became known that Ribbentrop had associated with the Windsors. There were fears at the governmental level that Wallis was pro-German, and when King, Edward had been far too careless with the official papers he received.[24]

At this stage there was no war and for the Windsors, Ribbentrop as the German Ambassador would have been seen as an important society guest. Even some of his friends and supporters such as Chips Channon wondered whether Edward was turning too pro-German. It is tempting to speculate that the ex-king resented the way his home government had rebuffed his wishes, while his German lineage appeared to have some sympathy for him. Many suspected that Wallis was the schemer behind this tendency to look so favourably on the Nazi regime, but it probably originated from the traditional British need to protect the British Royal Family. Although no longer king, his views and actions could unsettle public opinion about 'royals' in general. It was suggested by some that the Duke of Windsor was contemplating returning as king, a suggestion which would re-surface from time to time in the following years, and just possibly a rumour with some possible justification. He had always been spoilt and was behaving like a boy who had regretted giving away his toy castle.

In October 1937, the Windsors, without seeking advice, did the unimaginable by visiting Germany, even though they must have known about the growing international tensions, arriving to a mixture of Union Jack flags flying amongst the swastikas. The ostensible reason for the visit was for Windsor to visit the homes of the working class as he had done in Britain to show he cared. The visit had been arranged once again through Charles Bedaux, and for many this venture proved that Windsor was pro-German if not pro-Nazi. Others have argued he saw himself as in a third-party role trying to establish peace, and it had also been suggested he made the trip only to give Wallis the sense of feeling important in an overseas state visit; opinion was divided then and remains so. The Germans offered them two servants, but the British protection officer believed they were spies and reported this suspicion back to London. They were shown around Germany as tourists visiting the better sites as well as German industry, and knowing his supposed interest in working-class homes visited such areas. They were taken by Robert Ley (later a defendant at the Nuremberg Trial) who loved his alcohol too much, and once with his royal guests on board crashed the car into a gate post. They met Göring and played with his model railway, and Windsor saw pinned to Göring's wall a map of Europe with the intended *Anschluss* planned by the map colours. Göring later significantly observed that 'they could work with such a man'.[25]

It was probably Windsor's motivation, as mentioned above, to impress Wallis with a state visit, demonstrating how important he was, and show her the exhilaration of such treatment. They were treated as heads of state, Wallis was always addressed as HRH, and they met Adolf Hitler who according to some impressed Wallis, and on saying goodbye to the dictator they shook hands, and Hitler proffered the Nazi salute to which the duke promptly replied in kind. Once again it has been suggested by some that the duke was only waving farewell and not saluting, but probably best described by the Duke of Windsor's official biographer as a 'half-aborted Nazi salute', probably being overly polite. It was known

## 108 Major Blunders of the Second World War

that Edward was a strong appeaser, but the visit gave the Germans the impression they had a member of the royal family in their support. Windsor was not alone, it should be recalled that there were many in Britain who thought it possible that Britain could work with the new German regime, believing Russian communism to be the real threat.

However, while the Germans were pleased with the visit it was not viewed in the same way in the west. Even Charles Bedaux was becoming recognised as a Nazi sympathiser (which was a better assessment than being a Nazi agent) and he was not made so welcome in his adopted home of America, where the American side of his industry wanted him ousted. As noted, Bedaux had substantial business interests and was probably driven by mere capitalistic instinct, and there is little evidence that he was a German agent in the normal sense of the word, only pleasing his financial investors. This claim of the ex-king's acquaintances being Nazi agents is frequently raised, especially in the more conspiratorial accounts.

More to the point, this visit did the Windsors little good in Britain or America, and a modicum of common sense would have warned them of this outcome. What they did was ill-advised, arousing major criticism in America, and embarrassment in Britain. The world of journalism on both sides of the Atlantic was not impressed, but it seemed to have little impact on the Windsors. It appeared that Edward was more interested in creating his own stage where he held a central place. However, he was now being regarded as pro-Nazi and therefore a risk factor, and Wallis was also being criticised for supporting the Nazis, but it has also been suggested that in reality she was indifferent to politics. She liked those who offered her respect which the Germans managed in abundance, and disliked those who criticised her husband. Whether she had strong or any views on politics remains speculative.

However, such was the animosity that Windsor cancelled a visit to America announcing he was just a private man and not a public figure. This did not stop people being suspicious of his motives, but he was more concerned about his financial wealth and not having to pay tax. Nevertheless, none of this stopped him expressing political views, and when the question of the Sudetenland and Czechoslovakia was the issue of the day, he argued that 'it was a ridiculous country, just look at it, how could anyone go to war for that'.[26] He said this is in private, too naïve to grasp the fact that his views would be repeated, and demonstrated with this comment a rather perverse attitude towards international understanding. He later suggested that had he been on the throne the occupation of Austria would not have happened. Another over-dinner view he expressed was that he thought he would have made a better king than his brother, but thereby clearly indicating that he had failed to understand the nature of a constitutional monarchy, where leadership arises from the elected politicians of the day. It was during these months that the Windsors were being watched but feeling more and more isolated, and certainly not trusted by their hosts the French. It was reported when on the verge of war that Windsor, according to a Special Branch Report, was considering talking to newspaper magnates about his return with Wallis to Britain.[27] Whether this was to return to the relative safety of the British Isles or to try and be influential can only be speculation, but it was immediately clear he was not welcome. Various reports were heard that Windsor was gaining a reputation for letting his views be known, that he hated communism and tended to support Hitler. He caused annoyance in Britain by broadcasting a talk to America to maintain the peace, claiming he was speaking as a private person and a soldier of the last war. He was more interested in a book on the abdication in which he was helping, again a form of excuse or explanation as to why he had taken a course which he may have regretted in more private moments. One thing was already clear: that Baldwin and others may have been right, as Windsor was far too outspoken on political matters and appeared to favour the potential enemy. Many thought he was far too dangerous because he was too much of a chatterbox on the wrong subjects. George VI was already offering stability to the monarchy and heeding the advice of the government.

## The Second World War

When the Duke heard that war had been declared he said that this would open the way to world communism, which was his only comment before

## 110  Major Blunders of the Second World War

he went for a swim. There had been an initial offer that he could return to Britain, but this was withdrawn when he insisted that he should stay at Windsor Castle and Wallis must be given the title of HRH. In a time of national crisis these demands were hardly welcome. Perhaps the strongest opponent was Queen Elizabeth who had written to Queen Mary that 'I haven't heard a word about Mrs Simpson ... I trust that she will soon return to France and STAY THERE. I am sure that she hates this dear country, and therefore she should not be here in war time'.[28] It will be long debated how influential Queen Elisabeth's role was in keeping the Windsors out of Britain. Even his friend Fruity Metcalfe, criticised Windsor for being so demanding and failing to understand the nature of what was happening in Europe. When his legal friend Walter Monckton arrived by plane to take them to the safety of the south of France, he was refused because the Windsors had too much luggage and Wallis did not like flying. Their luggage took lorries to accommodate their belongings.

The British government were becoming concerned as what to do with the ex-king, various posts of a safe nature were considered, but George VI was determined he should not be allowed back into the country. A gallop-poll in 1939 had indicated that 61 per cent of the British population wanted Edward back, 16 per cent objected, and 23 per cent did not know.[29] It was known that the ex-king was popular amongst soldiers, and both George VI and the government in these pivotal times needed stability. What to do with him remained a problem, but they eventually arrived on British shores on board Mountbatten's vessel HMS *Kelly*. The Windsors stayed in the Metcalfe home as they were not offered any royal accommodation. The ex-king had hoped for a post in Britain, even as a Regional Commissioner for Wales, offered on the terms they stayed in Wales, but eventually he was given a liaison role with the French and granted the honorary rank of major general, and not his former status of being a field marshal. It was a post which was intended to keep him out of harm's way and might possibly help the British military have a better understanding of the French defence system, especially regarding the Maginot Line. It was well-known that the French were reluctant to share their military defence system and strategy even with their allies.

# Edward VIII, A Judas? 111

There were, however, concerns not so much about his security, but that he might be a risk because it was known he shared everything with Wallis, and both were ceaseless gossips, often intended to impress their visitors.

This new post created major tensions, best expressed by the historian Weinberg, writing that 'although the evidence is not entirely clear, there seems to have been a German agent in the Duke's immediate entourage, with or without the Duke's knowledge, and during the first months of the war important information passed from his blabbering through the agent to the Germans'... later adding ... 'when the couple went to Madrid where the British ambassador, Sir Samuel Hoare...tried to get him off the continent as quickly as possible'.[30] Weinberg further noted that it was a possibility, concerning the duke, that 'the evidence is clear that he seriously considered working with the Germans, and in fact, remained in contact with them for some time after going to the Bahamas'.[31] When later in the Bahamas it appears he contacted the Germans, but probably relying on his old friendship with them to look after his property and belongings in France. Others have suggested that information was deliberately passed on, and that evidence was found in 1945 Berlin of the Duke's observations on the weak points in the French system. According to this historian it had been transmitted by the German Ambassador in the Netherlands by Charles Bedaux regarded as a Nazi agent.[32] Bedaux and his wife had made firm friends with the Windsors by helping them, but how aware Edward was of their Nazi background remains controversial, and it has to be proved that Bedaux, though a Nazi sympathiser was not necessarily an agent. Some writers have not hesitated to regard this as an act of sheer treachery whether Edward knew or not the nature of this contact.[33] Others have suggested Edward was deliberately supplying this information.[34] Edward had been trusted by the French, inspected parts of the Maginot Line, and wrote about the various weaknesses he perceived which, notably, were later utilised by the Germans in their attack.

Such are the conflicting views, opinions, and evidence it remains an embarrassing and contentious enigma. There seems little doubt that Windsor was surrounded by German infiltration, but how far he was aware that his information was passed on remains speculative, but there

112 Major Blunders of the Second World War

is little question that he behaved irresponsibly given his position of trust, and it raised the question as to how far pro-Nazi he had become. He was far too free with whom he spoke, expressed his views too often in public, and it may have been better had he been allowed back to Britain where he could be restrained and monitored. It could be argued that Edward was treacherous, because of his freely expressed views with high society friends without knowing who they were. For some it was his naivety, for others his stupidity brought about by his self-centred approach which created traitorous action whether he knew it or not.

The problem was that Windsor could produce the popular touch, especially with soldiers, and King George VI even asked that he should be kept away from British soldiers when he was wandering around in France. It had been noted that when he had visited British troops, he was indiscreet when he took the salute of the troops before Lord Gort and even his brothers who were senior in rank; this behaviour did not look promising for the future. The Windsors could have been isolated in some luxurious castle in Scotland and kept on the estate on the excuse of their own safety, while monitoring those who visited. Later Churchill would try and managed this by giving him a post in the Bahamas. The ex-king had considered the problem, one time writing to his friend Monckton asking to return to London because 'of a network of intrigue against me'.[35] Again, even this request was self-centred as 'against me' implied he was in potential danger, not that he was the cause of the problem.

He was soon bored with his new post thinking his work was not appreciated, spending more time in his hobbies of golf, and enjoying his tapestry work. In January he flew to London to discuss the issue of meeting British troops, but he spent most of his limited time trying to convince everyone to avoid war by talking to the Germans. He was speaking out behind government backs which itself was wrong and there were growing suspicions about his intentions. It was known that his relationship with Bedaux was ongoing, and this man was watched as he was seen as a possible German spy or feeder of information from the Windsors.

Edward VIII, A Judas? 113

When war started against France on 10 May 1940, the German success was so rapid that Windsor sent his wife Wallis to the top hotel in Biarritz (southwest France) while he stayed behind burning his private papers. There was anxiety about his papers as the British were concerned about Wallis having them because of her perceived alliance with Ribbentrop, but this had been overly exaggerated. Such was the concern it was decided that no military information should be sent or given to the ex-king.

In the meantime, in late May he set off early one morning to catch up with Wallis at Biarritz without telling his friend Edward Metcalfe (Fruity), even though he had been his constant companion and friend always close by. Fruity realised he had not been a friend, but he was now an unneeded accoutrement rejected after 20 years of friendship, and the ex-king's treatment of this close friend lacked any conscience. Many thought, probably correctly, that as he held a military position he should have stayed with his unit and not fled to his wife, which could have amounted to a serious breach of military code.

It was arranged by the British consulate in Nice for them to travel to neutral (technically) Spain, but they refused to go by boat because their luggage would be limited and insisted on a car accompanied by a lorry. Given the thousands of refugees struggling to escape the same fighting, and only with what they could carry or fit in a pram or wheelbarrow, made this demand feel somewhat obnoxious as it was too selfish for words. This relatively unimportant aside is mentioned because it demonstrated their main weakness of only thinking about their own welfare and perceived importance. For the same reasons of comfort relating to their status the ambassadorial residence was considered unfit for the royal presence, and they were placed in the Ritz, the finest hotel in Madrid, known to be packed with spies and international busybodies, where private conversations could be easily overheard if not monitored. It was also critical for German intelligence who were welcome guests under Franco. Germany and Italy had assisted Franco to win the civil war and had his support, but he stayed neutral probably for two reasons, Spain was exhausted from her internal conflict, and secondly if the British Royal

## 114    Major Blunders of the Second World War

Navy blockaded Spanish ports the consequences would have been serious. The next step was to be Lisbon, but the Duke of Kent was visiting, and the decision was made to keep the Windsors in Madrid since it was considered unwise for the brothers to meet.

The ex-king was anxious to return to Britain which he considered the next step, but under no circumstances did he want to appear as if he were running home. Once again he was speaking too freely and it was soon heard that he was against the war, casting the blame on Anthony Eden, the Jews, the communists, and adding the devastating lines that if England were bombed it would soon bring peace.[36] He claimed he wanted peace but the suggestion that England, if bombed, would seek peace was a slur on the British people who grew more resistant and belligerent when bombing happened. This statement about bombing Britian could be regarded as traitorous by suggesting a method of defeating his home country. There were even rumours that he was in direct touch with the Germans. The situation in Madrid was proving to be a disaster and hurried discussions were taking place in England with what to do with him, not least the fear the Germans might kidnap him. It also transpired that Windsor was indecisive himself with his various demands, wanting to be given an important position. The gossip was also keeping pace during this mayhem, especially the rumour that Windsor may have been thinking he might return to the throne under German influence. Churchill was perplexed and furious having to worry about what the ex-king was doing with more serious matters occupying him. He went so far to remind the duke in a telegram, that he held a military position, and to break or ignore orders could lead to a court martial. Windsor paid no heed that in London, Churchill, and his ministers, were having to spend too much time on his personal demands when it was the most critical time in British history.

When the Windsors eventually arrived in Lisbon, the situation remained difficult as the anticipated hotel did not have sufficient rooms, so they were placed in a well-situated house nearly twenty miles out of Lisbon, made available by a wealthy banker who was a German agent. It seems almost unbelievable that this could happen, but the war was taking up most of the intelligence work and there was little importance attached

## Edward VIII, A Judas?  115

to Portugal, being Britain's oldest ally. Churchill and the government remained anxious because it was now well-known from his gossip, that Windsor wanted peace at any price, along with the distinct possibility that he favoured the Germans. There was a widely held belief, possibly with some substance that he had allowed himself to become embroiled in some form of intrigue. The traditionally inclined Churchill was concerned that if his worse fears were confirmed, it would be a major embarrassment for the Royal Family in London, undermining their reputation as their German names had done during the Great War. Intelligence reports were flying back and forth, some of them intimating that Wallis was pro-German and causing many of the problems. How far this was true remains speculative, but it may have been a ruse to deflect any damage from the person of the Duke of Windsor. She may well have been involved if only to support her husband, who, she may have thought, was being badly treated by the British, but again this can only be speculation.

The situation was so serious the Windsors were monitored, and it has been claimed that one agent was 'under orders to shoot them if they threatened to fall into German hands during their nightly visits to the casino'.[37] This was not only an indicator of the concern their loose gossip was causing, but it underlined what would be ongoing for the rest of the war and immediate postwar years, namely while the British public was under military attack and suffering from severe rationing, the Windsors continued to live the high life. They ate the best food, played golf, went shopping, swam in the swimming pool, entertained guests when at home, and while others were sick with worry about the future, they were only obsessed with being seen as important and a social centre for those they deemed important.

From the German perspective they tended to view the Windsors as potential for making peace with Germany, that the Churchill group were not having any such nonsense, and for some reason the Nazi leaders thought an ex-king could influence the situation. The historian Henri Michel suggested an interesting insight for the cause of these various machinations. It was about this time that Hitler, with his long-term plans on Russia was seeking some form of peace with the British to avoid a

116   Major Blunders of the Second World War

two-front war. He had tried to use the King of Sweden as an intermediary but was firmly rebuffed. Michel suggested the next move was to drive a wedge between Churchill and his public, by utilising the popular figure of the Duke of Windsor. Some Spanish friends had warned the Duke that Churchill would have him assassinated, which was highly unlikely as it would serve no purpose, was not part of Churchill's character, but despite his misgivings about the war Windsor refused negotiations against the instructions of his government.[38] If Henri Michael's observations are correct it implies that the ex-king had listened and decided he would not contradict Churchill's political demands. However, his propensity for loose chatter and wild political views were well-known. He was supposed to have had a conversation with a junior secretary at the embassy, during which he said the Churchill government would fall, and Labour would negotiate peace with the Germans.[39] It was the ill-advised conversations which caused others to lose faith in him, especially when he claimed that Britain would not cope with bombing raids which would bring the war to a halt.

Meanwhile, the Windsors were more concerned about their belongings in their home in Paris, and asked the Germans if a maid of the Duchess could be given freedom to travel to Paris to collect their luggage before they went to the Bahamas. The Germans were happy with this, holding in their arsenal a member of the royal family who was pleased to have Nazi assistance. The Bahamas was Churchill's ploy to take the Windsors off the continent, but not back to Britain. At one time it was considered whether he should be attached to General Wavell's staff, but this was considered too risky, and the Bahamas seemed the safest place.[40] The only problem with the Bahamas was whether Edward would continue spreading his appeasing and often defeatist views within the close proximity of America. Again, entirely without consideration for what was happening in the wider world, Windsor asked for the return of his valet and chauffeur to go with him to the Bahamas, when both had been called up for service. It was a selfish request as Edward was always stubborn in his demands, by stretching the patience of those like Churchill trying to protect the reputation of the Royal Family as a whole. Before the Duke would agree with Churchill's plans his demands were continuous, not least wanting to

Edward VIII, A Judas? 117

travel to New York on the way while the British government, knowing his pro-German sentiments did not want his views aired in America where isolationism remained strong. Churchill had supported the ex-king during the abdication crisis, and always remained his 'obedient servant', but it would have been interesting to know his inner thoughts about the royal person during the war years. Churchill would have been acutely aware that there were still appeasers in Britain with some regarding him as a dangerous warlord, and he was desperate to keep America on side, knowing their support was essential. It was for Churchill and the government a risky venture to let the ex-king loose in America with his views, comments, and unsafe social gossip. Rumours of the Duke's activities were rife with the Portuguese and other secret services, suggesting that Windsor was active in many meetings and reluctant to leave the country. The German intelligence policeman Walter Schellenberg was sent to Portugal by Heydrich to try and persuade him to work for Germany, purportedly offering him 50 million francs to travel to Switzerland. Windsor, it has been claimed, asked for time to consider the matter. Whether to persuade or kidnap him (known as Operation *Willi*) the Germans appeared extraordinarily determined to hold the duke on side. Later Schellenberg claimed he had looked at the reported conversations and felt they held little or no significance.[41]

The British were aware of the situation, and they sent Walter Monckton with directives from Churchill to the Duke, instructing him that when in the Bahamas, he was to follow government guidelines in matters of policy regarding the war, while making it crystal clear that this was to be his next move, so on 30 July the duke announced his departure in a special press conference, which he duly did on the SS *Excalibur*. It must have felt like trying to convince a recalcitrant schoolboy to do his work and stop trying to play truant.

## Bahamas

When the Windsors travelled to the Bahamas they must have felt that they were being removed like a rugby player into the sin bin. They could

## 118  Major Blunders of the Second World War

only watch what was happening from the safety of the side lines and not, what the ex-king had hoped for, namely a position of importance and not to be exiled. He had been used to social status and yearned for its retrieval. At this time America was still technically neutral which was why the British government feared Windsor demanding appeasement in that country. The new post was not to his liking, and they both found the heat too much. The population of the Bahamas during this period was just above 70,000 the size of a large English town. Over 80 per cent of the population was black and unless they were servants were not allowed through the doors of government house. It had always been this way and the ex-king did nothing to change this, any more than his other racial views by remaining anti-Semitic.

It was rumoured, that even in this remote island in the north Atlantic, he remained in touch with his German connections which for many could have been viewed as treason. When Wallis sent clothes to be carefully laundered in America there were even suspicions, almost paranoid, that she was secreting messages to agents. However, he was closely monitored and causing concern because of the people whom he met, especially a person known as Axel Wenner-Gren. He was a Swedish millionaire who had built himself into the Bahamas, was supposed to be a friend of Göring but had only met him a few times.[42] Edward found him useful for the Bahamas because of the money he fed into the economy, and he liked wealthy people. Wenner-Gren was on the American blacklist, but that did not make him a spy or German agent.

All too typically Windsor demanded money for the redecoration of the official residence and stayed as a guest in the home of Sir Harry Oakes the richest man on the island, who owned huge portions of the land. The ex-king was still hoping to return to Britain for a major post, but his brother George VI blocked every such decision. When the Americans had exchanged 50 old destroyers for British bases, this included the Bahamas which meant that American intelligence was taking an interest in the island. When the Windsors did eventually visit America, apart from people being staggered at the amount of their luggage they were greeted as popular figures. Windsor wanted to be appointed Ambassador to America which, with minimal consideration could never happen, revealing his naivety. It was a desperate time and Britain was suffering from the prospect of defeat, and it was not helped that Windsor had expressed his views wanting Roosevelt to demand peace. He had even stated this in a publication (a magazine called *Liberty*) that he thought Britain could not win, and Churchill warned him this was defeatist talk, and this article caused many problems. There was a tendency for the ex-king to think his perceptions were always correct. Churchill was right to point out the danger of defeatist talk not only for the sake of American and British opinion, but in the enemy camp. In Germany, Goebbels wrote in his diary that the duke 'pretty frankly disclaims all chances of an English victory, we decide not to use it for the present, so as to avoid suffocating this tender seedling of reason'.[43] Goebbels also noted that the Italian press had reproduced the article in a 'distorted form', adding 'we shall not use it, so as to avoid discrediting him'.[44] It was apparent from these comments that the Germans saw Windsor as being of use to them, and curiously felt the need to protect him from scandal as much as the British.

Information about his activities and loose chatter was widely known because they were carefully monitored or reported. It was known that at the parochial level he was running up bills with the locals on the grounds it would be later paid by the British government, which was financially struggling. The Windsors, as was their habit, were spending far too much money, usually on things to please themselves and enhance their reputation as the best of hosts. There were suspicions that he was involved with black market currency, which given his lifelong propensity for money was possible. He even wanted to fly to his ranch in Canada where there was a possibility of oil beneath the property, but despite his hopes it gained him nothing but expense. Other rumours were more aggravating as it had been speculated that the Germans, in the event of victory would instal Windsor as king, and that Wallis had an affair with Ribbentrop. This latter rumour was frequent but unproven, and only indicated her unpopularity. Though it was clear, as far as American Intelligence was concerned, that she was anti-British, this was probably

120   Major Blunders of the Second World War

based on her views of a government which had not appreciated the value of her husband.

Nevertheless, when America entered the war, Churchill was concerned that the Germans might try and kidnap Windsor by landing and snatching him away. Edward when at work, was dealing with a landscape ridden by poverty and unemployment, and to keep the balance Wallis worked hard in helping to run a RAF canteen. Her husband however, who wanted a more important status was unhappy and bored in this exile, especially when he heard of the death of his brother George the Duke of Kent who had died in an air crash. He was still bitterly angry with his family and that the HRH title had not been granted to his wife, all of which resulted in excessive smoking and drinking. As the war passed, which the ex-king only gleaned from the headlines, he continued to say things which were, under the circumstances, not only out of line but at times stupid. He was supposed to have stated in one of his many chatterbox sessions that the Labour Party would win and make peace with Germany, that the age of constitutional monarchy had passed, but in the meantime many of his pro-German friends were being rounded up or moved. There were aspects of his life as Governor that he did well. On one occasion while in America he heard there had been riots in the capital of Nassau with looting and buildings burnt down. He flew back at once and resolved the problem by increasing wages to five shillings a day.

Much of his better work was overshadowed by a scandal, which was part of his own making. His friend and supporter Sir Harry Oakes had been battered to death in his bed. The duke demanded a news blackout, decided the local police could not handle such a crime and brought in a squad from Miami, yet there was no need for him to be involved at all. A culprit was pinpointed, the son-in-law Alfred de Marigny whom Windsor thought to be the culprit, but he was later found not guilty by the jury, which was an embarrassment for the duke because he had interfered in the process. Questions were asked as to why the local police had not been allowed to investigate, and his money arrangements with Sir Harry Oakes became a point of unwelcome gossip. This murder would involve journalists and dramatists well into the postwar years, and because he had intervened this did not help his reputation.

He continued to seek popularity in America visiting it for the fourth time in September 1943, and already looking to the postwar years when he hoped to resign. Whenever he travelled observers were bemused by the amount of luggage they carried, on one short visit it amounted to 73 pieces, and it was known they had 118 travel trunks each one numbered.[45] He was continually enjoying life on Palm Beach, playing golf, Wallis' expenditure was watched with horror, while Britain was suffering from war impoverishment, for which he was often criticised.[46]

His position and where to move him was debated by the government all too aware of the risks and harmful gossip surrounding him. One thing was certain because of George VI's views and the reputation of the Royal Household it would not be in Britain. The King stated that he could live in America or France, but never Britain. In desperation South American ambassadorships were suggested, but even this was turned down as too risky given his past, and it became an on-going issue. Eventually Windsor resigned his post on 15 March 1945, still uncertain what to do postwar. He had thought about settling in the USA but demanded an official post to avoid tax, but this was not entertained. France seemed the likely place, but postwar it was politically precarious having trouble with the collaborators and communists, the latter gaining much prominence because of their resistance efforts against the Nazi occupiers.

## Postwar

What the ex-king probably did not know was that in the immediate aftermath of the Nazi defeat thousands of German documents were discovered, including a file on the Duke of Windsor prepared by the State Secretary Ernst von Weizsäcker, which were quickly moved and researched and found to be authentic. Later the infamous spy Blunt would be sent to retrieve others, and they remain mainly hidden, some destroyed, but many writers have claimed they contained material which was embarrassing to the Windsors and therefore the British. Much has

## 122  Major Blunders of the Second World War

been made of these papers as if they revealed appalling possibilities, but Blunt's trip was no secret at the time, and amongst the concerns were the retrieval of some of Queen Victoria's correspondence. The various papers kept returning over the years as haunting ghosts. When Churchill was back in power, he remained concerned about keeping them under wraps. When in 1957 papers relating to the Windsors' stay in Spain were published, the Queen and Queen Mother were warned beforehand. None of this was helped when it seemed to be true that Windsor had applied for a code to stay in touch with the Germans, though possibly this was more to do with his property and belongings left in France. Later, in 1962 more papers surfaced deepening the suggestion that the ex-king had favoured an alliance with Nazi Germany. These later documents were not helpful, because by this stage the full horror of the Holocaust and other massacres had received full publicity revealing the sheer evil of the Nazi regime.

In the meantime, it was rumoured that Windsor, who appeared blissfully unaware of the Nazi atrocities, was wondering whether he might be made Governor General of Canada. He was unlikely to receive any high position simply because there were too many skeletons in his cupboard. At a more personal level he had been upset when his old home of Fort Belvedere had been given to the government and was in a state of decay. He had been granted this Georgian folly by the King in 1929. It was a glamorous looking building at the southern end of Windsor Great Park, which he always thought of as home, not least because it was the antithesis of Windsor Castle. When after the war he saw it up for sale he expressed a desire to purchase the site, but it was swiftly withdrawn from sale. Fort Belvedere had been the place of his dreams and probably represented the happiest times in his life. He even asked permission for a mausoleum to be built there to hold his and Wallis's bodies after they had died. Plans were prepared but then blocked for fear of vandalism. Later Fort Belvedere was sold on a 99-year lease, ironically to a relation of Tommy Lascelles, and today is the home for a wealthy Canadian family.

His life in the postwar years revolved around golf, their various homes, avoiding tax and social entertaining. His one desire was an important role which would never happen, and Wallis spent her time making their various homes look majestic and creating what she saw as appropriate surroundings for the ex-king's court. In October 1946 they had paid a quick visit to Britain with Edward looking for a post from his brother, but they were not well received, and Wallis had some of her jewellery stolen. It hardly made headlines as her jewellery was of little interest in Britain where people were recovering from a major war, with the usual rumours that Wallis overestimated their value for insurance purposes.

This was the start for the Windsors of what might best be described as a social nomadic life, spending most of their time in their various homes in France, holidaying in America, especially Palm Beach, and socialising. When invited to other people's homes they would demand to see the guest list first before accepting the initiation, which some found obnoxious. Socialising and being seen as important, tending to be their central focus in life. At one stage they considered moving to Switzerland because the French government was too left wing for their taste. France as a republic had looked after them, treated them well, even with tax breaks, and finally they decided to stay socialising in France. The French were even generous enough to allow Wallis tax freedom after her husband's death. Despite the previous years of conflict with Nazi Germany, the ex-king's main party piece at various parties was to sing German songs and speak German, which did not always go down well in his host country.

Using a ghost writer the ex-king wrote his book on the abdication, which was published in 1951, mainly to convey and justify his past actions. It was the same year that Wallis had had cancer of the womb, which was successfully treated in New York. The book caused something of a stir in royal palace circles, but it made him some £300,000. They promoted it by travelling around America where they were treated with popular acclaim, but less so the book. One journalist from the *New York Times* wrote that it was a 'character study of a well-meaning, undistinguished individual, destined from birth to a life of monumental artificiality', which would have rung true for many observers then and today.[47] Wallis followed with her account published in 1956 which did not sell so well, and met even more damning reviews.

124  Major Blunders of the Second World War

Their domestic life, like so many others had its ups and downs, and there were reports of Wallis having affairs, the most gossiped was with Jimmy Donahue, the heir to the Woolworth fortune. He was believed to be safe as he was gay, others claiming he was bi-sexual, and he enjoyed the good life to the full. It was even rumoured that Windsor was bi-sexual with suggestions of a *ménage à trois*, followed by more gossip that their fairy-tale marriage was over. Donahue paid for the three of them to take three major cruising holidays in the Mediterranean. The rumoured affair continued over many years probably as late as 1954 when a mutual animosity suddenly developed. When a friend asked Windsor whether he was jealous of the relationship he brushed it aside pointing out that Donahue was a well-known gay; others could see that it distressed Windsor. According to one writer the breakdown of the relationship between Wallis and her so-called lover occurred when Donahue arrived late smelling of garlic.[48] This affair was certainly widely known and gossiped about, but the truth of what happened will never be known, and it is hardly important, no more than the remaining aspects of their lives.

They spent a life of entertaining the celebrities of the day, actors, artists, singers, and anyone who they thought would be either interesting or best to know. Their expenditure on such occasions knew no bounds, often including parties in top restaurants and hotels. It is generally accepted that the ex-king was fastidious in accruing wealth, and they spent money like water from a tap. Whenever they travelled most people were shocked at the amount of luggage they took, often needing a lorry, and every item in their house had to have value. Their wardrobes were extensive, and the duke had over 40 lounge suits alone, and hundreds of pairs of shoes. They lived in many houses, rented, leased, or offered as temporary gifts, but eventually leased a house on the edge of the Bois de Boulogne which was to be their main residence thereafter for the remainder of their days, all duty free and they paid no income tax. It was a beautiful structure, once lived in by the Renault family, and had housed General de Gaulle in the immediate postwar years. They also purchased a country residence, an eighteenth-century watermill in the Chevreuse Valley, which gave

Wallis much happiness in redecorating the building and making it look like a court for a king.

The old problems still emerged from time to with his indiscreet observations on the immediate past, stating views like *if I had been the king there would have been no war*, and blaming the war on Eden for not handling Mussolini appropriately which was sheer nonsense. In 1958 there were personal embarrassments as the question of how he handled and manipulated his financial resources again raised the question of black-market deals.

However, after the war the animosity of the Royal Family continued for a time but later eased. When his brother King George VI had died from lung cancer on 6 February 1952, the ex-king was allowed to attend the funeral but not Wallis, and this was repeated in 1953 when his mother, Queen Mary died. He attended the funeral, but it should have been no surprise that they had not been invited to the marriage of Elizabeth, the future queen, when she married Philip Mountbatten. However, it was noteworthy for him that when he turned 70 in June 1964 the Queen sent him a congratulatory telegram, perhaps an indicator that the new generation of royals were now emerging. This was confirmed when a few years later in June 1967 he was invited to Marlborough House for a plaque to be set up for Queen Mary. He was told the Queen Mother would not attend if Wallis were there, so he refused, but the Queen Mother relented, and for the first time since 1936 the two women met. Even so there was no royal bedchamber for him, and they stayed with Mountbatten at his home in Broadlands, Romsey.

However, it must have felt that doors were opened for them even though it was late in their lives. In January 1970 they were interviewed by the BBC and Prince Charles made a short visit to them in Paris, but by this stage it was clear that the ex-king's health was not that good, as in 1971 he had been diagnosed with throat cancer. In May 1972 the Queen, the Duke of Edinburgh and Prince Charles all paid a visit to see the ex-king, but his health meant once again it was a short visit, the duke at this stage weighing less than six-stone. At least the new monarchy was showing signs of reconciliation. In fact, he was in his final days, and

## 126   Major Blunders of the Second World War

on the 28th day of that same month he died less than a fortnight after the royal visit. His body was flown to England for burial at St George's Chapel, unaccompanied by Wallis who was in serious distress, and she flew in later. For the first time she stayed as a guest at Buckingham Palace and not at Claridge's, and later she stated she was treated very kindly, especially by the Queen. He was buried at Frogmore, and fourteen years later on 24 April 1986 Wallis died, having suffered from dementia, and she was buried alongside her husband. She had not enjoyed her widowhood with frail health, controlled by a French lawyer Maître Suzanne Blum, and with suggestions that she was not only bullied by this person, but pestered by Mountbatten busy trying to retrieve royal belongings back to Britain. It was only in their tombs that they were accepted back into the Royal household.

### Final Observations

When an incident occurs seen by a dozen people, they may well give several different accounts when questioned about what happened. Their observations may vary based on the person who initiated the reported incident. There will be those who regarded the central figure as a friend, a respected figure, or feel sorry for him or her, while others may have disliked or distrusted the person. In any analysis of these events of over 70–80 years ago, they must be treated with caution. There is the additional attentiveness demanded by the issue that social and morality values have changed over the years. In 1936 the Archbishop of Canterbury condemned Edward VIII for wanting to marry an American woman divorced twice, but in 2023 one of his later successors crowned King Charles III and his wife, who was a divorcee, and she became the Queen consort without objection. It could be claimed that Edward VIII was born in the wrong age as he was closer to contemporary society.

One of the main points of contention surrounding the Duke of Windsor was not so much his personal lifestyle habits, but whether he was a traitor or not. The first question which should be considered is what makes a traitor. As within the Cambridge spy ring of the 1930s it could be a matter of principle based on communism being regarded as the best political system. It could be that a traitor emerges on pure greed, offered money by the opposing side. Sometimes it is pure blackmail where a person is caught in a honey-trap usually of a sexual nature, or even hoping to gain power and authority such as Vidkun Quisling in Norway.

In a British court of law there are two critical principles which have to be established. The first is *mens rea* which indicates a guilty state of mind, in other words was it the culprit's deliberate intention to carry out the crime. Secondly *actus reus*, the actual act is committed constituting a crime; in other words, a crime was committed and that was the culprit's intention. As to whether the Duke of Windsor was guilty of this crime or not, remains confusing, but highly unlikely that in a court of law he would have been found guilty. Despite the vast literature and recorded opinions of many people, and references to dossiers and files many of which have never been seen, the evidence for a court case is weak.

There are, however, other elements which need to be considered from the brief garnering of information in this study. From his early youth his social habits of 'wine women and song', a common fault of many people was at times excessive, not least because of his pursuit of married women. His general conduct suggested that at times he was too indiscreet, his behaviour was even by those days questionable, and his selfish egotistical outlook made him unfit to wear the crown. He expressed his opinions often too openly, and his views on other races was often derogatory, stating once that the indigenous Australian was 'the most revolting form of living creatures he had ever seen', and even post Holocaust remained anti-Semitic telling a lady that 'the Jews had Germany in their tentacles. All Hitler had to do was free the tentacles'.[49]

His attitudes towards appeasement were shared by many and after the Great War were understandable, but there came a time when most people recognised the Nazi danger, but the ex-king still spoke too freely even in the safety of the Bahamas. It was soon heard that he was against the war, casting the blame on Anthony Eden, the Jews, and the communists. It had long been understood that Windsor was known to be sympathetic to the newly emerging Germany, something openly admitted by his official

# 128  Major Blunders of the Second World War

biographer. His visit to Germany had been unwise, but most probably to show Wallis their importance as unfavoured and estranged people, more than aligning himself with the Nazi regime, though his liking of the Nazi regime was easily and understandably assumed. From his youth Edward lacked any intellectual depth otherwise he would have thought twice about with whom he associated, and more importantly what he said publicly. His continuous defeatist talk indicating he believed Britian could not win, his suggestion that the government would sue for peace if bombed, the suspicions that he hoped to be returned to the throne if the Germans occupied Britain, all built up a huge prosecution case against him. It has been claimed that the most dangerous indicator was the 15 August 1940 telegram, using a code to stay in touch with Germans. Many suspected he was a traitor, the ex-king, being the type of man he was, may well have been more concerned about his apartment and belongings in Paris.

In British law any person is considered innocent until proved guilty, and Windsor's case would never have proved easy whether guilty or innocent, as proving the issues one way or another probably lacked reliable evidence. However, he was a man who thought only of his own wishes, stole other men's wives, was greedy for money, wanted a recognition for importance he did not deserve, was basically a racist, a snob, intellectually weak, and self-serving. His sense of self-importance and his belief that his views were always correct, meant he made ill-advised and downright foolish comments in public. The growing tensions with Germany and his outspoken views on the Nazi growth, his relationship with the enemy during wartime while in Spain, his criticisms of the British government, his defeatist talk hardly endeared him to his own country, especially as he and Wallis lived the highlife both during the war and in the postwar years when most countries were impoverished, while recovering from a devastating war. Even after years of research by many historians it still seems that it would be difficult to prove intention (*mens rea*) that he proposed to commit treason, or that he actually did (*actus reus*). The central issue seems to be that he was seen as traitorous because a man in his position should not have behaved like a fool by expressing stupid views and associating with the wrong people, and only interested in what was best for him, even a court jester would have had more sense.

In many ways from his youth onwards the ex-king was in a continuous state of misjudgement, but it became a serious situation with the emergence of Nazism and during the Second World War. Because he was an ex-king, he was a problem, he was not just some opinionated neighbour mouthing off in a bar or at some party. Because of his assumed status his views and opinions were not welcomed by the government, and they feared for his influence in America raising the question of whether sending him to the Bahamas was a mistake. For the sake of the Royal Family, they could hardly imprison him, but perhaps he would have been better placed in a more remote place such as the South Island of New Zealand, and closely monitored by wartime regulations on the excuse of his safety. Edward VIII and later as an ex-king was a walking talking misjudgement, and perhaps this was compounded by Churchill being too kind, when he should have been under stricter control, to stop him feeding the Nazi regime that they had a sympathiser in the highest echelons of British society, and also avoid the problem of the ex-king influencing American attitudes.

Chapter Four

# U-Boat War, was Dönitz Guilty?

**Author's notes**

At the Nuremberg Trial after the Second World War various Nazi leaders stood trial, a few were found not guilty, some imprisoned and most hanged. There were four indictments, the first was participation in a common plan or conspiracy for the accomplishment of a crime against peace. Secondly, planning, initiating and waging wars of aggression and other crimes against peace. Thirdly, participating in war crimes, and the fourth was crimes against humanity.

Dönitz had been charged under counts one, two, and three and was convicted under counts two and three. Count one was put aside as he had not been privy to the higher-level discussions relating to any conspiracy to wage aggressive war. As such, count two was something of a surprise in being active in waging aggressive war, because on these grounds all senior military officers could be convicted for following their duties. In the verdicts, Dönitz was given 10 years which was the lightest sentence, with many thinking he should have been acquitted.

This raises the question of whether this was a misjudgement. The Nuremberg Trial has sometimes been claimed to have been Victor's Justice, though such were the crimes committed by the Nazi regime many of the verdicts were correct, if one is inclined to accept capital punishment.

In this chapter the U-boat war will be explored, and the life of Dönitz. This is because the Dönitz case raises the question as to whether he was guilty of war crimes, and initiating and waging a war of aggression, or was this victor's justice because of his leadership of the successful U-boat war, or punishment for Hitler instructing that he take over the leadership following the Führer's suicide. There was a popular feeling prevalent in the postwar years, which continued for many years thereafter, that the U-boats had behaved in an *immoral way. Dönitz and his U-boat war needs reappraising in the cold light of hindsight. This is a complicated issue, but with the question of an international misjudgement regarding Dönitz this demands some attention.*

*It therefore demands some understanding of the nature of Dönitz's war, starting with an exploration of the nature of U-boat warfare as seen by many as unfair and tyrannical, despite the fact it was used by every major combatant nation. It felt important first to start this chapter with an insight into a U-boat's life by <u>very briefly</u> summarising an autobiographical account of a U-Boat ensign and later commander who served for the entire duration of the war. The book is well-worth reading as it provides insight into the nature of this weapon and the men who fought in them. The second stage is to make a brief historical survey of the nature of the U-boat war and its immense ramifications.*

*The third step is to take a brief biographical look at Dönitz, his background, life, and the nature of his role. There were various sources for this information, but the biographer Peter Padfield produced some interesting insights.[1] The fourth stage is to examine his trial at Nuremberg, the arguments of the prosecution and defence, as well as observations made by various people in their different functions at the trial. The final stage is to search the arguments over the years since the trial, as to whether he was guilty, or whether he was condemned on a misjudgement based on wartime bigotry and a sense of revenge.*

## A U-Boat Commander's Autobiography

This writer once boarded a Royal Navy nuclear submarine, allowed to do so because of his son was a member of the crew, a sort of open day. It was many times larger than a Second World War submarine but still felt cramped and claustrophobic, giving the impression of living in a machine without any natural light. In the immediate postwar years, for many people the Royal Navy or American submarines were crewed by heroes prepared to serve their country, whereas the German U-boats were regarded as the wicked enemy who sank innocent merchant ships without mercy. By the 1980s there was a rebalancing of these views helped by a film called *Das Boot* based on a novel by Lothar-Günther Buchheim. The men on

132    Major Blunders of the Second World War

board the U-boat soon gained the sympathy of the English-speaking audience, who hoped the depth-charges missed their one time enemy.

In addition to this was an autobiographical account written in 1969 by Herbert A. Werner, a former U-boat commander entitled *Iron Coffins*.[2] He started as an ensign and rose through the ranks to become a U-boat commander, but rising to this command at a time when the Allied powers were gaining the upper hand in the U-boat war. It is a frank and honest account of his life below water and reflects his feelings and attitudes. He gained immense pleasure from sinking merchantmen vessels, and on one occasion, before America had entered the war, his commander had a clear target view of the American battleship *Texas*, but on the Führer's directives was not allowed to fire on American ships thereby disappointing the young author.[3] Werner was not a Nazi Party member, but he was imbued with the idea he was fighting for his country and the Führer and it must therefore be justifiable. He recalled that 'we had been taught that there was no possibility of Germany living side by side with the Soviet Union and it was clear the British were also the enemy we had to fight'.[4]

He recalled as a junior officer meeting Dönitz who was known as *the Lion*, and then meeting him again near the end of the war when he looked fragile and old, hearing him give instructions which Werner could only interpret 'as a frantic attempt to delay the inevitable defeat. Yet I wished in my heart that I was wrong'.[5] Interestingly, and challenging the U-boat's ruthless reputation, although Werner rejoiced at sinking merchant vessels, when they spotted a naval escort picking up survivors, it was an easy target, but he noted, 'an unwritten law prohibited attacks on ships engaged in rescue operations', which barred attacking them.[6] When this occurred again his commander said 'to hell with these tin-boxes, let's get some freighters' and let the survivors be saved.[7] At this stage the U-boat war was causing devastation, and in March 1943 almost a million tons of shipping was lost, leading to Churchill's statement that the U-boat worried him more than anything else.

As Werner rose in the ranks the U-boats became more vulnerable to attack, not just by naval vessels with better sonar detection, but from planes which seemingly appeared from nowhere. There were desperate bids by the Kriegsmarine for better U-boat equipment, with more powerful anti-aircraft guns attached, more advanced radar equipment, and some of the more sophisticated and recent boats were equipped with schnorkels. These had been invented by the Dutch and allowed a submarine to travel on diesel engines while submerged, making it safer from air-attack.

Only a few of the new U-boats had this valuable equipment and Werner, when a commander in his own right, tried desperately to source one, and when he succeeded, he found it was prone to malfunction causing near fatal moments. Werner also discovered that when returning to his home port it meant running the risk of air-attack which was turning the tide against the Germans. It was, as he noted, no surprise that 'a U-boat man's estimated life span on the front was but six or seven months – no more'.[8] His descriptions of avoiding attacks by naval vessels and air attacks are continuous and terrifying in their descriptions, but he was one of the few commanders to survive the war. He knew from radio broadcasts that the war was turning, startled by the news that Sicily was being invaded, found it difficult to believe Mussolini had been overthrown, noting that 'if the broadcast had not come from a German radio station, we would have derided the report as an enemy lie'.[9] His parents and sister were bombed out of their homes, he witnessed the destruction of Berlin, and was then told his parents and family had been killed in a bombing raid. He hoped the propaganda about new weapons was right, but he was astounded by having some of his senior crew changed and receiving new recruits with no experience. He received instructions for D-Day Normandy with other commanders, namely to fire all of their torpedoes and then finish by ramming an enemy ship, which was, as he noted, a kamikaze order.

Miraculously he survived the war and the first enemy he met was a British Army officer who questioned him about the amount of tonnage he had sunk. When he understandably replied he had no idea, the officer asked, 'Does that mean you hope to disown responsibility for what you've done?'[10] In asking this question was the implication or insinuation of war crimes, which was a commonly held view. It was a theme constantly referred to in the postwar years, not least in the Nuremberg Trial of

## 134  Major Blunders of the Second World War

Dönitz, and will be explored later in the text. Werner also explained he had never been a party member, he had not joined from the Hitler Youth, 'and membership in the Party was not a prerequisite for joining the navy. We had only to meet the sort of qualifications your Navy asks'.[11]

Werner was born in 1920 and in 1939 he was only 19 years of age when he joined the U-boat service, in 1945 at the surrender he was only in his mid-twenties. His survival was brought about by his naval skills, his instincts and good luck. He was awarded the Iron Cross First Class, eventually retiring to Florida in the USA where it is believed he died in 2013. His book has provided invaluable insight into life in U-boats, the dangers of living in these underwater vessels, the nature of their tasks, and how they operated.

### Submarine Warfare in the First World War

In early history it had often been the dream to have a submersible vessel capable of inflicting damage on the much-feared surface vessels capable of conveying armies. As early as the time of Drake and Raleigh a carpenter called William Bourne had produced plans for such a vessel, but he died before it was built.[12] For this to be a realistic possibility the time of combustion engines and electric batteries in the late nineteenth century made it a more realistic possibility. When the Great War 1914–18 started the British Royal Navy appeared as the most powerfully equipped force, with the huge and powerful Dreadnought battleships, but the German response was to use the cunning underwater weapon of the U-boat. U-boat *U-9* under Otto Weddigen in the autumn of 1914 sank three major British warships (*Aboukir*, *Hogue*, and *Cressy*) which changed the nature of naval warfare in this triple blow. Earlier *U-21* had sunk the British light cruiser *Pathfinder*, and the major surface vessels were at risk. In May 1915 *U-20* sank the liner *Lusitania*, killing over 1,000 passengers including over 100 Americans. This caused outrage but this modern war showed no mercy. It was no surprise that in December 1916 Admiral von Holtzendorff announced 'unrestricted U-boat warfare' in the hope that

Britain would run out of food, which was the same policy that the Royal Navy was carrying out against Germany with some success.

When a British coaster *Glitra* was tracked by *U-17* it was stopped, and after a brief chase surrendered, the crew taken off, the ship was sunk, and the crew towed in their lifeboat to within distance of the coast. The sinking of an unarmed merchant ship was deemed uncivilised, but this, under the exigencies of war changed in the blink of an eye, although when a French vessel was sunk without warning there was anger in the Allied camp. The German navy declared the waters surrounding the British Isles were to be declared a War Zone. The British very soon developed the convoy system and the Germans planned ways of attacking the system by the use of U-boats working together. During the Great War it is estimated that the U-boats sank some 11 million tons of shipping, thereby establishing a threat to an island nation dependent upon the sea.[13]

The Great War had brought to light the serious menace of the U-boat because with just one torpedo a huge battleship could be sunk. The Germans had an impressive number of successes by this method, forcing the Royal Navy to find safer harbours for their fleet. The British with their superior surface fleet established a naval blockade of Germany, bringing starvation levels to that country, which was countered by the U-boat effort against the British Isles. The U-boat was also utilised for mine laying, giving the Germans success in both the French and British coastal waters, and causing their enemy to have to work out how the mines had been laid in the first place. The U-boat development had by the end of the war established itself as a major component in naval conflict, involving not just the military but the civilian population in its repercussions.

## Interbellum Years

During the interbellum years the British wanted the submarine outlawed as a weapon of war but were opposed by the Americans and Japanese. However, an international policy was agreed and set down in the London Protocol of 1934 with a set of rules, namely:

# 136  Major Blunders of the Second World War

1. The submarine must surface before attacking.
2. Crews and passengers had to be guaranteed safety. They could not be abandoned in small boats on the high sea. Either they had to be taken aboard the submarine [which was impossible in terms of space], or the submarine captain had to hail a neutral ship to take them aboard [a dangerous policy for any submarine], or the ship had to be let go.
3. Merchant ships were not to be armed.
4. Merchant ships were not to use their radios to call for help or warn other ships at sea about the submarine.

'As these rules were laid down, the most practical of naval authorities knew they were bunk, and that they would never survive the early days of any war', amongst the main sceptics were Dönitz and Churchill.[14] As with the Army and Luftwaffe the Kriegsmarine started to train U-boat men in a clandestine fashion. *U-1* began its first patrol on 28 July 1935, and the rest followed swiftly until the first flotilla of six were up and running, while working on better models which could run faster and over longer distances. Dönitz claimed 'he could assure Germany of a victory over the British, no matter how quickly they implemented their convoy system'.[15] Dönitz kept the service secret, allowing no civilians into the U-boat area, not even Nazi Party members, arguing that combat efficiency was the only priority he recognised. He had wanted at least 250–300 U-boats, but he had little chance in anticipating such numbers with the slow and expensive production problems.

### Submarine Warfare in the Second World War

When war started again in 1939, Dönitz who had served as a U-boat commander in 1914–18, was a supporter of Hitler, and since 1935 Dönitz had been responsible for rebuilding and structuring the U-boat service of the Kriegsmarine. The Versailles Treaty had denied Germany submarines, but through the 1935 Anglo-German Naval Agreement the Germans could rebuild their navy to 35 per cent the size of the Royal Navy, but submarines were granted 45 per cent. By 1939 Dönitz had less than 60 U-boats with about 20 in service, most being the Type VII which could travel on the surface at 17 knots, with a possible range of 8,500 miles. Other more advanced types were built one after the other, but not in the numbers Dönitz wished as the resources were decreasing rapidly during the war years. Later Hitler would be more concerned about defeating the British in North Africa and his failing Operation *Barbarossa*, to appreciate the significance of the economic warfare conducted by the U-boats.

On 1 September 1939, Dönitz realised his part in the war was about to start, and knew his U-boats, albeit limited in number, could surround Britain. He made a point of informing his captains of the Hague Convention and the Naval Treaty. Sea troop transporters and merchant ships could be seized as prizes, enemy warships could be sunk without warning, liners were to be left to their own devices unless carrying military materiel.[16]

On the day war was declared there was the infamous sinking of the liner *Athenia* by *U-30* under the command of Fritz-Julius Lemp. Lemp protested that he had thought it was an armed ship, Goebbels and Hitler blamed it on Churchill trying to induce America into the war, and it took months before the Americans realised and accepted that the *Athenia* was sunk by a U-boat. Lemp's position was complex as his only view was through the murky lens of a periscope, and they had been warned about armed merchant ships, but it was a serious misjudgement which meant that the German political cabal had to cover and forget the incident as fast as possible. Although Hitler wanted Lemp on trial, Dönitz ordered conduct to be more 'gentlemanly…many a British ship was sunk afterward, but, if the sea made it possible, the Germans would surface, talk to the men in the lifeboats, give them provisions and liquor, and directions to the nearest land. A good many British seamen came home from a sinking with a high regard for their enemies'.[17] There were many occasions in the years to come when U-boat commanders, despite changes in orders, often came to the assistance of survivors, which will be explored later in this text. However, Churchill, as First Lord of the Admiralty demanded every merchant ship had to have a radio and if attacked signal SSS indicating an attack by a U-boat. This ruling by the British was soon realised by the Germans, and it was not long before most merchants ships were armed.

The following month in October 1939, following Dönitz's plans, *U-47* under the command of Günther Prien ingeniously navigated its way into the Royal Navy base of Scapa Flow, which had been carefully protected by underwater nets against U-boats, and he managed to sink the major battleship the *Royal Oak*. As in the Great War it was a sharp reminder that a small underwater vessel could sink a capital ship. Prien was seen as a hero, and Goebbels made a point of making U-boat crews the centre of his propaganda. He often sent journalists out with a U-boat to paint a picture of the work they were doing and the courage it called for. When U-boat crews were rescued and interrogated by the British a mixed picture emerged. Some were dedicated Nazis, but many others were just young men who saw themselves as called up to serve their country. It was a picture which was widespread; the enthusiasm of the Hitler Youth was drilled into some, in others less so, and as the war progressed and U-boat crews found their homes bombed and families killed a natural degree of cynicism crept in. However, for a time, Goebbels' propaganda led to higher morale, and as U-boats left their ports and returned there were hero welcomes, high-ranking officers to greet them and parties before and after. When later the war turned, and U-boats were lost in greater numbers this enthusiasm lost its sparkle as seen both in Werner's biographical account and the film *Das Boot*.

When the merchant vessel *Olivegrove* was challenged by *U-33* under Hans-Wilhelm von Dresky it tried to escape but failed, the crew were disembarked, the vessel sunk, and von Dresky radioed help for the crew from an American passenger vessel. Dönitz soon realised that such chivalry took time and increased the risk to the U-boat, so he sent out the order 'Rescue no one and take no one with you. You have no care for the ship's boats. Weather condition and the proximity of land are of no account. Care only for your own boat and strive to achieve the next success as soon as possible. We must be hard in this war. The enemy started the war in order to destroy us. Therefore, nothing else matters'.[18] Dönitz called his

U-boats Wolf Packs after the wolf hunting packs on the prairies who work together to hunt down their victim. It was the start of a bitter war above and beneath the sea lanes.

A major part of the U-boat war raged in the Atlantic as supplies from America grew and then exponentially when America entered the war, known as the Battle of the Atlantic. There were technological advances on both sides of the conflict with the British developing ASDIC and radar, but the convoys remained in serious peril until 1942–3. It was during this year the tide turned with the USA increasing its input and supplies, and the use of aircraft which made the U-boat more vulnerable. The British had discovered the way to interpret the German naval code Enigma, helped by the capture of a U-boat, which meant they could be tracked.

The Germans also made technological advances, with the torpedoes which exploded on impact, or magnetic ones designed for detecting a magnetic field, and later in the war acoustic torpedoes which head towards the largest identified sound. Once the Allies had discovered this device, they countered this with noisy decoys, and the Germans started to develop 'pattern moving torpedoes', which were programmed to move in circles, so when released into a convoy a target was soon found. Most importantly, as mentioned in the opening autobiographical section, the schnorkel, which were attached to later models, allowed a U-boat to travel underwater using its diesel engine. However, this development was late and when resources were reducing rapidly so few were developed, and they tended to be fitted to the new types of U-boats. One of the main problems faced was having a sufficient number of boats and the resources to equip them with the latest developments. Had Dönitz been given the resources for more and better equipped U-boats, the consequences could have been even more serious for the Allies, but while Hitler enjoyed hearing of the sinking of an enemy warship the economic battle against the merchant ships was less attractive. It must have been a frustrating time for Dönitz knowing he was sending his men out with reduced support, especially in support boats and without the latest equipment. It appears 'his men' were important to him. Such was Dönitz's character he knew

140    Major Blunders of the Second World War

all his captains personally, and he rarely left the situation room where the planning and plotting was under constant review.

The Wolf Packs, directed by Dönitz would merge on a convoy and create sheer havoc. In the early years it caused serious damage to supplies for Britain's sustenance, with individual captains reporting sinkings of above 200,000 tons of shipping, and 'Churchill did Dönitz the honour of declaring the U-boat war to be the most vital part of Britain's struggle, and took personal charge of a special cabinet committee devoted to that struggle'.[19] Some of the early star captains were lost with their crews, but were replaced with other up and coming leaders, and in early 1941 the U-boats were causing the most serious damage, but as the British defences improved and new forms of counterattack were used, it remained for a time an up and down war for both sides. The Italians tended to use their submarines in the Mediterranean, but they also took over the West African coast and the South Atlantic, but the German U-boat commanders found it difficult working with their Italian counterparts. Soon the Germans with their longer-range boats moved into the South Atlantic. Dönitz was also obliged to send U-boats north and to the Black Sea once the Russian war had started, but there was little to do at first as there were few convoys from the West to Russia, though this would soon grow.

Dönitz had always insisted that U-boats were not to be captured by the enemy, but *U-570*, led by Captain Rahmlow surrendered after an attack, and the British seized the vessel probably because the crew and officers were new recruits, not expecting the conditions under which they found themselves. The captured U-boat was examined by the British and then used by them as HMS *Graph* sometimes to move quietly into enemy waters. Captain Rahmlow had to be moved to another prison camp, because of the fear that in the naval one to which he had been sent, there were rumours that he might be executed by the other prisoners. Given the use of this captured U-boat by the British it was perhaps understandable for Dönitz's demand of no surrender of the boat.

When Germany declared war on America, Dönitz sent a few U-boats to the American coastline with orders to ignore smaller vessels, and the

## U-Boat War, was Dönitz Guilty? 141

first was sunk outside New York. The American coastline was evidently a massive hunting ground for the Wolf Packs, and the Americans were not prepared for this type of warfare. Hitler remained more interested in European waters, especially regarding the convoys taking supplies to the Russians. By March 1942 both Churchill and the Americans were alarmed at the growing losses caused by U-boats. The French ports for the U-boats became more and more important as they could access the easier hunting grounds of the Atlantic and reach the Caribbean area. Such were the easy pickings off the American coast it felt like a new era, and this possibly induced a degree of overconfidence as new commanders tried to enhance their reputations. The Americans took time to respond to this new danger but eventually, especially with the use of aircraft, started to come to terms with this new form of warfare, helped by British experience.

Dönitz was under pressure from Hitler to concentrate on the convoys to Russia being more concerned about defeating the Russians who were fighting back with greater determination than anticipated. In Britain it was decided to use smaller aircraft carriers and custom-designed hunter-killer escorts, (corvettes) making life for the U-boat more difficult. The attacks still continued with great losses, but the U-boats were finding the situation more and more difficult. Hitler had never grasped the importance of the U-boat service and its ramifications in the economic war, continuing to demand more U-boats in the Mediterranean Sea to end the North African war. Even arriving in the Mediterranean was a dangerous task as it meant passing through the small and well monitored straits between Gibraltar and North Africa. The Mediterranean would have better suited the Italian submarine force, as Dönitz was losing too many of his limited boats in this area. The U-boats were in the wrong place to be effective, and not helped by the failure to be producing new ones in the required number. Donitz 'knew that his boats were being wasted here in an impossible attempt to stem the tide. He protested. The High Command ignored him. On 16 November Raeder ordered Dönitz to replace all the sunk and damaged boats in the Mediterranean and bring down more boats from the North Atlantic'.[20] These demands

142    Major Blunders of the Second World War

from Hitler and the German High Command stretched the U-boat force and made it less effective.

However, the battle still raged in the Atlantic, and in 1942 the U-boat fleet had sunk some 1,160 ships in 1942, with Dönitz still hoping for more boats. Hitler had noticed that the surface warships had not been active and decided the men should be deployed elsewhere, suggesting the battleships be scrapped and their massive guns used on land. Raeder disagreed and resigned, and Dönitz was selected as the leading Admiral. As 1943 started there were 164 U-boats in the Atlantic, 24 in the Mediterranean, 121 tackling the Artic convoys, and only three or four in the Black Sea.[21] The Black Sea was deemed essential to harry Russian supply routes.

During 1942, despite its successes, the growing pressure of enemy counterattacks meant resources were held back for the Army and the Luftwaffe. It reached a point when it became necessary to keep U-boats at sea longer, that a captain could take his anticipated leave, and the U-boat went out again under 'another skipper'.[22] Leave was not always easy and when the Germans utilised French ports for U-boat bases, it could take a year before any leave was granted, it also increased aerial attacks as the French bases were closer to Britain than those in North Germany. U-boat pens were built in many of the French ports and some in Norway. They were built between 1940–1941 in Lorient, La Rochelle, Saint-Nazaire, Brest, Bordeaux, Norwegian ones at Narvik, Trondheim with German bases at Heligoland, Wilhelmshaven, and Kiel. They were massive bunkers, unlike the British who produced small ones in Dover for their motor-torpedo boats. The German pens were made from deep reinforced concrete and were built before the RAF discovered their purpose. They would need very heavy weight designed penetrative bombs with pinpoint accuracy even to damage them.

The use of smaller aircraft carriers meant the Atlantic, normally free of aircraft attack became a danger zone; the Atlantic airgap had disappeared. Many U-boat captains were soon caught by surprise when deep in the Atlantic they suddenly became aware of Allied aircraft zooming in for an attack. It was also clear the British appeared to know their whereabouts (due to the Enigma naval code breached which the Germans did not know until after the war), their radar, Asdic and powerful searchlights had vastly improved. Despite the use of snorkels in some U-boats, equipped with anti-aircraft guns and many other new developments there was a hint that the tide of the naval war was changing, but still the U-boats were proving damaging to the Allies. By the early months of 1943 it was becoming more dangerous to be crew on a U-boat than on a merchantman, not least because the escort naval vessels were growing in number, and their depth charge tactics had improved. It was a matter of Dönitz and his team trying to search for the Allied weak spots. The battle continued, but the U-boat was now at the disadvantage. The main U-boat benefit of the Atlantic was its huge size, but the ports from which they sailed could be easily targeted, making the Bay of Biscay risky for the comings and goings of U-boats. As the Atlantic became more problematic Dönitz sent some U-boats to the Far East to cooperate with the Japanese, who were also wanting to see more of the snorkel. The presence of the U-boats caught the British by surprise as on their trip there and back they sank nearly 60 ships.

### The Crewmen

It was not surprising that the young U-boat crews when in port drank heavily and pursued women and sought a good time. Some senior officers objected, others joined in, and most had to forgive their men because each time they left port they all knew it might be their last time. As in many other submarine services the usual grades of officers, petty officers and seamen was more rank-blurred with living, sleeping, eating together in the same tin box and the officers standing by their men as they were all exposed to the imminent dangers of instant death. It was, on a smaller scale, like the attritional war of the 1914–18 trenches, but this time the commanding officers were in the same trench (or metal corridor) as their men, and not safely ensconced well behind the lines. The intimacy of sharing the fear of death even spread to sharing the same drinking parlours and tables, which would be unheard of on a surface vessel. A

144   Major Blunders of the Second World War

slightly drunk seaman would not dare sit down at the same table or bar as a captain or other officers.

These young men were said to be volunteers, but they were selected after a harsh and robust period of training and told they had volunteered. Their lives were in perpetual danger, and 'their environment was cramped and claustrophobic, insanitary and smelly, but they were bound together by the dangers and the purpose they shared, however ill-conceived that purpose may have been'.[23] As is the case in all wars, one nation's submariners are heroes, while the enemy were dreadful murderers, skulking beneath the waves and behaving against the rules of law and codes of morality. These men had to share bunks and be alert for sudden commands of action stations, or emergencies, watch their food resources diminish and turn rotten, know that they might die from lack of air or drowning while all sharing the same coffin. Under the attack of depth-charges there was no means of defence or retaliation, just a matter of holding tight and wondering whether they would ever draw another breath.

The death toll was high, with the result that new recruits were hurried through, both officer and crew, often lacking experience and unprepared for the sheer brutality of underwater conflict. It is impossible to find accurate figures for the U-boat war, the tonnage estimated by the U-boat commanders could only be speculative, and often the tonnage of many boats was not noted or kept unless they were major vessels under Lloyds type of insurance. It has been suggested that U-boats 'accounted for 69 per cent of the Allies' shipping losses…a U-boat sank a ship for every day of the 68 months that the war lasted in Europe'.[24] The same problem of precise figures occurs when studying U-boat losses. There is a U-boat memorial near Kiel recording the dead amounting to 27,491. It is known there were about 5,000 PoWs from U-boats, and about 39,000 men served in U-boats. Out of the 863 U-boats 754 were lost.[25]

In both wars, especially the Second World War, the fighting at sea was dangerous for both sides, it was bitter, and there was the serious danger that being an island the British could not only lack essential military resources, but the population could suffer from starvation rations, and on the German side few of the U-boat crews survived.

## U-boat Conduct of Warfare

Having explored life in a U-boat, the nature of its warfare, and before examining the life of the German overall commander of the U-boat service, it is necessary to explore the nature of this warfare. Various incidents will be outlined in terms of human reaction and responses to the cruelty of this sea war. Two incidents in particular are important as they were raised at the Nuremberg Trial of Dönitz; namely the *Laconia* incident and the trial of U-boat commander Eck condemned for shooting survivors. The general views of U-boat warfare frequently involve considerable hypocrisy, and experience has demonstrated that wartime propaganda lasts a long time and develops into a myth and unreliable hearsay; the legal profession describes this as 'hearsay within hearsay'. This section draws attention to human conduct, and the way it varies depending on the nature of the commanders and admirals responsible in any given situation.

U-boats were regarded by many in the public arena as villains lurking beneath the water's surface ready to launch unfair attacks on innocent victims. They were also used as a successful means of conveying mines into coastal waters, a tactic which was also considered devious.[26] Allied submarine crews on the other hand were admired by the public as courageous, as were the U-boat crews by the Germans. It was all a matter of propaganda, and the U-boat commanders came with the same heroes and villains as in other aspects of life. The U-boat war waxed and waned, 'from 1939 to 1945 U-boats sank 2,800 Allied ships as well as 148 Allied warships'.[27] Another statistic reveals that during this war Germany 'deployed 896 U-boats, of which 662 were lost to various causes'.[28] In proportional terms the U-boat service lost more men than the other military services. Sea warfare could be brutal from the point of view of the surface ships and U-boats, which often left men burnt, and drowning in water and oil with no hope. For the U-boat crews it was just as dangerous because their chances of survival became minimal as the war continued.

As noted, the sinking of the passenger liner the *Athenia* on 3 September 1939 by Fritz Julius Lemp in *U-30* in the north-western sector of Ireland,

146 Major Blunders of the Second World War

mirrored the sinking of the *Lusitania* on 7 May 1915, when England and Germany tried to stifle one another with economic blockades. The sinking of the *Athenia* on the first day of the European war gave rise to anger amongst the British, and a high degree of embarrassment to the German High Command, with Hitler agreeing with his naval staff 'to deny German responsibility'.[29] Goebbels had noted in his diary that 'Churchill had holes bored in her bottom', which was pure nonsense, but some critics in America wondered whether the Germans were capable of such a blunder, not whether Churchill was that unscrupulous.[30] The theme of incompetence and misjudgement always emerges in times of conflict, as does hearsay and rumour.

It was a frequent rumour that U-boats would surface after the victim ship had been sunk, and the German crew would shoot the victims while they struggled in the water. One of the survivors of the *Laconia*, another passenger ship to be mentioned later, wrote 'we'd been told about the atrocities perpetrated by U-boat crews against survivors of the ships they'd torpedoed. Machine-gunning people while they were still in the water was common; we'd been led to believe. As the U-boat crept towards us, diesel engines rumbling, I wanted to curl up into a ball, but I was frozen solid with fear'.[31]

This opinion is still held by many people to this day. In 1943 a classical war film called *Action in the North Atlantic* depicted such brutality which was more understandable, because it was during the war years and propaganda was stirring up hatred. However, in 1971 in the film *Murphy's War* similar brutality was dramatized, and even in a more recent film screened in 2000 called *U-571* a U-boat commander ordered the execution of unarmed survivors in a lifeboat. The real *U-571* was a Type V11C, which conducted eleven war patrols before being lost with all hands following an attack by an Australian-crewed Sunderland aircraft, west of Ireland. The film was entirely fictional and not based on historical reality. 'According to Dr Lawrence Suid, a noted historian…the Office of War Information (a US governmental propaganda agency) issued orders in late 1943 that the portrayal of enemy atrocities in films would no longer be tolerated…and such films would not be given export licences'.[32]

Much of the fear about German behaviour at sea was due to allied propaganda demonising the enemy. This was a common practice for both sides, and in the aerial warfare some German pilots believed that if they parachuted onto English soil they could well be tortured; there could be no room for any sympathy for the enemy, just hatred and fear.[33] The general impression was that once the ship was sunk the survivors would be killed. There were 'exaggerated dockside rumours, press reports, accusations by leader writers that the enemy often machine-gunned lifeboats, and an alliterative reference by the Prime Minister [Winston Churchill] to "merciless murdering and marauding," all contributed to these fears'.[34]

In 1938 the British Admiralty issued instructions that if a submarine demanded an unarmed merchantman to stop, the Merchant Navy captain was ordered to take every effort to escape. Many merchant navy officers knew that this was a useless and dangerous order. Most U-boats could match the speed of a merchant ship, and their firepower from the 105mm deck gun would be lethal against an unarmed or lightly armed merchant vessel. In March 1942 the cargo vessel SS *Cardonia* tried to escape from *U-126*, under the command of Ernst Bauer, even laying a smoke screen to cover its retreat. The U-boat's deck gun took its toll and eventually the ship surrendered, whereupon the U-boat stopped firing and allowed the surviving crew to abandon ship before it was sunk by a torpedo. This was not a single incident of this type of behaviour, nor was it the pattern of conduct that was widely broadcast under the war propaganda machine. Propaganda painted what it regarded as the necessary pictures to bring the population on side against the enemy.

The public often needed this or an incident to bring them onside. When in September 1941, before war between Germany and the USA had been declared, the USS *Greer*, an old-fashioned destroyer, joined in with a British air-attack against the *U-562*; the submarine was depth charged from the air and the British pilot was guided by the American destroyer. The U-boat retaliated against the destroyer unsuccessfully, but Roosevelt naturally took the opportunity to call this an act of piracy. It could have been called self-defence since the German U-boat was being attacked by what was technically a neutral warship, but this suited

148    Major Blunders of the Second World War

Roosevelt in his attempt to persuade the American people towards war. Propaganda and rumour were useful companions in a war generating hatred based on fear.

Passenger liners in the early stages were viewed with the greatest sensitivity especially after the sinking of the *Athenia*. As early as 7 September 1939, it had been agreed by the German Kriegsmarine command that 'passenger ships should be spared even in convoys... submarines in the Atlantic are to spare passenger ships', and finally the Führer 'approved the proposal that action should be taken without previous warning against armed enemy merchant ships definitely identified as such (with the exception of unmistakable passenger vessels), since it may be assumed they are armed'.[35] War is a brutal environment and especially when the gloves are off and it descends into total war, but even so it was clear from the original intentions that certain humanitarian rules were to be applied. In the same Naval Conference, it was stated that the 'notorious expression of unrestricted submarine warfare is to be avoided'. The German Naval Staff War Diary of 4 October 1939 read 'as far as circumstances permit, measures are to be taken for the rescue of the crews after eliminating possible dangers to the submarine. Passenger boats that are not serving as troop transports, are not, now as before, to be attacked, even when they are armed'. Sadly, the gloves came off as the war became increasingly bitter and unforgiving, and the German rules changed. In a report of 16 October, the Führer's Naval Conference diary noted that 'all merchant ships definitely recognised as enemy can be torpedoed without warning', and 'passenger ships in convoy can be torpedoed a short while after notice has been given of the intention to do so'.[36]

There was only the one verifiable incident of a U-boat Commander firing on survivors; it was not usual despite the rumours. This occasion related to Heinz Wilhelm Eck of *U-852*, when he sank the Greek freighter SS *Peleus* in the South Atlantic. He based his defence on the excuse that he did not want the enemy to find the debris and signs of his whereabouts. However, there were two or three survivors who eventually provided the evidence. After the war Eck protested that he was only destroying the debris. Some crew members pointed out it was dark, and

## U-Boat War, was Dönitz Guilty?    149

they could not see the survivors. The men who did the shooting were a Hans Lenz (engineering officer), Walter Weisspfennig (boat's doctor), the second in command August Hoffmann, and an enlisted engineer called Wolfgang Schwender. This *U-852* was later attacked off the Somali coast; the surviving crew were captured by the Somaliland Camel Corps and sent to prison camps. The U-boat log survived, and this along with the surviving witnesses was enough at the Hamburg War Trials to have Eck Hoffmann and Weisspfennig sentenced to death by shooting at Lüneburg Heath on 30 November 1945; many regarded this as victor's justice. When, for example, some of Patton's soldiers had massacred Italian prisoners in Sicily there were no death sentences and only reprimands.

This was the only recorded and known incident by the German navy in the Second World War, although there had been more ghastly incidents during the Great War as in the case of shooting survivors from the hospital ship HMHS *Llandovery Castle*. There had also been accounts of the British submarine HMS *Torbay* shooting prisoners, and a similar example of the American submarine USS *Wahoo* doing the same. It should also be noted that British destroyers opened fire on some two hundred men in the water following the destruction of the German destroyer *Erich Giese* near Narvik on 13 April 1940.

In the Second World War Eck's behaviour is the only recorded incident of a U-boat killing survivors in the water, and under the excuse of operational necessity. Brutal war is too often a two-way process. In the Japanese war there is overwhelming evidence that Japanese submarine commanders shot survivors in the water, but no records of the Italians doing this, and at times it was noted Italian submarine commanders helped survivors.

The historian James Duffey provides example after example where U-boat commanders knowing they were obliged in their war duty to sink ships and leave men in the water, often did their best to help them survive. As a matter of curiosity this writer knew a Merchant Navy engineer officer called Laurie Edwards, who once said he had rowed to Liberia. He explained he had been torpedoed, watched with trepidation the U-boat surface, only to find they were not machine-gunned, but had

150 Major Blunders of the Second World War

their rowing boat righted, given provisions and a compass and the course towards the African coast. Sadly, the details from this conversation were lost in a stolen laptop, and Laurie has since died.

Within the first week of the war the famous Günther Prien of *U-47*, notorious for torpedoing the battleship *Royal Oak* in Scapa Flow, sank the British cargo ship *Bosnia*. He surfaced and fired at the vessel to stop the radio operator sending out a distress call, and he watched as the crew scrambled to abandon ship, with the lifeboat toppling, and casting the men into the water. He assisted by putting them into the other lifeboat and contacted a passing tanker to rescue them. When this was done, he used a single torpedo to sink the *Bosnia*. When he had sunk the battleship HMS *Royal Oak* hundreds of men lost their lives, which demonstrated the reality of war. He could not put his vessel in danger when he was attacking a Royal Navy ship, and it had to be done in submarine style by silence and stealth. When he sank the *Bosnia*, he tried to save the lives of the crew even before sinking their vessel.

As mentioned above the same pattern of attack was applied by Kapitänleutnant Hans-Wilhelm von Dresky of *U-33*. Having stopped the British merchant ship *Olivegrove* travelling from Cuba to London, the crew climbed into the lifeboat and the *Olivegrove*'s captain was taken on board the U-boat to look at the best routes to safety, then, just before leaving the survivors, the U-boat fired some distress flares to attract a passing liner to come to the rescue. This often happened in the early part of the war.

One U-boat went to extraordinary lengths to save the survivors. A Kapitänleutnant Werner Lott had sunk the Greek ship *Diamantis* just off Land's End near Cornwall, and he ordered the crew into lifeboats which seemed to him unsafe in the weather conditions prevailing at that time. He took the crew close to the southern Irish coast and set them ashore using the U-boat's inflatable craft. This incident was reported in the Irish press and in the *Evening News* in London and became the cover story in an issue of *Life* magazine.[37]

*U-124* was launched in March 1940 under the command of Kapitänleutnant Georg-Wilhelm Schulz, and on her fourth patrol he sank the British steamer *Tweed* along with ten other vessels. After the sinking of the *Tweed* Schulz noted that one of the lifeboats was badly damaged, and while his doctor cared for the wounded, his crew repaired the damaged lifeboat. He stocked the lifeboats with food, water and cigarettes and gave them a course for the African coast. Schulz survived the war, and in 1958 he and his wife were invited to Poole in England to attend a reunion of the survivors to receive their gratitude. He eventually died in Hamburg in 1986. He was one among many German U-boat commanders admired by those under the obligations of war whom he had been obliged to sink. Later in 1994 his autobiographical account was published.

The development of anti-submarine detection and attack started to transform the behaviour of U-boat commanders, but much of their code of conduct changed following the *Laconia* sinking. In this well-known incident, about which films and documentaries have since been made, *U-156*, under the command of Werner Hartenstein, who sank the liner *Laconia*. A fully comprehensive account of this liner and the incident was written by Frederick Grossman in full detail with many witness statements and photographs.[38] Another book was written by a survivor who described the sense of 'overwhelming terror' as 'German sailors emerged from the conning tower', only to help him onboard to save his life.[39]

This 1921 built luxury liner *Laconia* had been converted for war-work, and carried some 2,600 passengers including Italian prisoners, Polish guards, British military personnel, women and children, who were left floundering in the mid-Atlantic near Ascension Island. Its old boilers puffed out an excess of black smoke which made it an easy target as did its huge size. Many such vessels had some armed defences, but like the armed merchant ships they did not have the steel protection of warships, and they were often known as *Admiralty Made Coffins*.

To Hartenstein it may have looked like an armed merchant man because it had an antiquated gun on its rear deck, had it advertised a PoW sign it may possibly have escaped. The *Laconia* held, as noted, many Italian prisoners of war. There has been much discussion of the ill-treatment of

## 152 Major Blunders of the Second World War

these prisoners by the Polish and British guards which was raised with the rescuing German sailors. When another U-boat came to assist, they took on board the Italian prisoners to relieve their tensions with the British.[40]

Hartenstein realised as he drifted through the wreckage the scale of the human disaster, because he was surrounded by hundreds of survivors. He started a rescue procedure to the best of his limited capacity. At one stage he had nearly 200 survivors on the submarine, lifeboats in tow, the wounded received assistance, the rest were given rations and water. He radioed Dönitz for help, and either Hartenstein or Dönitz asked for French Vichy help. It is curious to note in the light of later condemnation that Dönitz responded with sympathetic consideration; 'he understood Hartenstein's reasons for showing a Red Cross Flag, the action of a man prepared for all eventualities, who in good faith believed he could secure similar status to a hospital ship for his submarine'.[41] Dönitz ordered other U-boats in the area to provide assistance, namely *U-156*, *U-506*, and *U-507*. It was *U-506* under the command of Wurdmann and *U-507* under Schact which came to assistance, as did the Italian submarine *Cappellini*. The Vichy French ordered three vessels out, including their cruiser *Gloire* and picked up many survivors; they arrived late but managed to save many.

Meanwhile on Ascension Island the Americans were setting up a secret airbase called *Wideawake* and soon became aware of the situation.* Hartenstein had sent an open message asking for help promising he would not attack any ship which came to assist. A single B-24 Liberator under the control of Lieutenant Harden from Ascension Island passed over *U-156* and saw the Red Cross on the U-boat's deck. He radioed back to Ascension Island for instructions, and a Captain Richardson and a Colonel Ronin ordered the immediate destruction of the U-boat. This was a questionable decision, but in the heat of war and the determination to sink U-boats to avoid further attacks, as well as the need for secrecy of

---

* Ascension Island had become part of the dependency of St Helena (since 1922) another British territory and was mainly important as a linking base for a cable between Africa and South America.

## U-Boat War, was Dönitz Guilty? 153

the American presence on Ascension Island, it was a complicated decision to make on the spot, and too easy to criticise in hindsight.

As the plane re-approached the U-boat with its bomb-doors opening Hartenstein refused his survivors' requests to open fire. His U-boat was not hit but damaged, and he had no choice but to evacuate the survivors and submerge to depart. He left them with directions, food and water and advised them that help should be on the way. Nearly a thousand people survived as a result of his humanitarian actions. Many of the survivors commented on the good nature of the German sailors and the kindness of their commander. A nursing sister called Doris Hawkins wrote that the 'Germans treated us with great kindness and respect the whole time; they were really sorry for our plight. The commandant was particularly charming and helpful; he could scarcely have done more had he been entertaining us in peacetime'.[42]

The immediate result was the *Laconia* Order issued by Dönitz that no U-boat was to risk such action in the future, and having ascertained the necessary information and captured any senior officers such as captains and chief engineers (which would denude the enemy of experienced officers), all U-boats were to depart the scene at once. In terms of explanation Dönitz added that 'rescue runs counter to the most primitive demands of warfare for the destruction of enemy ships and crews', and as his final point added 'Be hard. Remember the enemy has no regard for women and children when he bombs German cities'.[43] This may well have been prompted by his personal anger that his men were attacked when trying to rescue the enemy.

The war changed for the U-boat. It was now considered far too dangerous for a U-boat to be caught on the surface, and the direct order was to depart as soon as possible regardless of the plight of possible survivors. As a matter of interest Hartenstein ignored the order when in September 1942, he sank the cargo vessel *Quebec City,* and surfaced to give the survivors sustenance and directions. In March 1943 Hartenstein and the entire crew of *U-156* were obliterated by aerial depth charges in the West Indies. It was not only the *Laconia* Order which dictated future behaviour by U-boat commanders, but the increasing number of

154   Major Blunders of the Second World War

aircraft capable of flying the oceans increased, as did the Allied technology mentioned earlier.

There has been much heated controversy over Dönitz, some naval historians dismissing him out of hand, claiming he 'had dumped the rule books in deep waters', others taking a more measured approach.[44] Some 67 former U-boat commanders imprisoned in England wrote protest letters on his behalf during his trial. He was charged on various counts, including waging aggressive war by attacking without warning, which will be explored later in this text.

British and American submarines were under the same orders in so far that they were not to leave their vessels at risk by trying to save survivors. Despite the early war propaganda, it is now known that many U-boat commanders often helped survivors, and as noted above some took immense risks to do so. Others submerged and drew away from the scene as fast as possible to avoid detection. It all depended on the man in charge, and there are many examples, too many to list here, when it was apparent that despite the obligation of war to destroy and sink enemy vessels, some U-boat commanders showed extraordinary compassion. As noted, there are records which indicate that Italian submarines rescued survivors when it was safe, the Japanese were entirely different with a history of killing survivors, rather than regarding them as tragic human beings left to their fate.

Very few people gain pleasure from killing other people. Bomber crews often reflected on the fact that at least they could not see the deaths they created, but through the periscope the suffering was horribly visible. The better propensity of human nature to rescue victims was a natural reaction, but the *Laconia* incident underlined the nature of a totally unforgiving war. It was the policy for submarines to move rapidly away from sinking ships and remain hidden for all the national navies involved in the conflict; even as late as the Falklands War this procedure was followed.* It suited national propaganda to paint a picture of a viciously inclined enemy to kill

---

* The Argentinian warship *General Belgrano* was sunk on 2 May 1982, by the Royal Naval submarine *Conqueror* with the loss of 322 lives, just over half of Argentine military deaths in this war.

innocent people from a safely concealed position, and then to compound the overall theme with helpless survivors being machine-gunned. The sadness is that war-time propaganda persists to this day.

These thoughts lead to the man who from long before the Second World War started had been responsible for the German U-boat service, its rebuilding, the types of U-boats and weapons used, and the strategies and tactics deployed.

## Karl Dönitz to 1918

At the funeral of Dönitz in 1980 the pastor explained that Hitler's political successor 'was, for me, one of the most devout Christians I have ever met'. [45] He had been raised in a middle-class Christian family since his birth in 1891. His sense of devotion may have been true of his retirement years, but although as a young man he and his family were staunch Protestants having believed this was the way to raise a family, Dönitz as a young man and father was not known for regular attendance at church, only returning to his Christian faith postwar which was common to many other military men.

He had no military background, loved his father who instilled into him the Prussian traditions of the day, especially those which appertained to the obligations to the state. He did not have to be aristocratic or military to hold Prussian attitudes. He was born at a time when Germany was intent on making itself into a country of significant importance. It was the time of *Weltpolitik* (World policy) which amongst its many other potential implications was the Kaiser's belief that Germany had to have its rightful place on the world stage. Wilhelmine Germany needed to be regarded as important by developing its colonial growth, and these ideals needed a fleet to challenge the dominance of the Royal Navy who appeared to rule the waves. It is not surprising given Dönitz's background environment, along with many others born in this era, that he was by nature nationalistic in outlook, obedient, and put his country first in all matters; it was virtually part of his DNA. He did well at school and although the Army was seen as the senior service (unlike Britain)

## 156   Major Blunders of the Second World War

the German Imperial Navy was highly selective. He had to pass their educational requirements but was then scrutinised on financial and social status background. He was admitted as a sea cadet, and following initial training went to a training cruiser, soon to become a midshipman. After this he became part of the crew of the light cruiser *Breslau*, given the post of signals officer and posted to the Mediterranean. The area of the Balkans prior to the Great War was always sitting on a knife's edge where the *Breslau* travelled. In 1913 he was a sub-lieutenant having received a good report from his captain. His ship was being refitted in Trieste ready to accompany the Kaiser's yacht on holiday when alerts came through about suspicious build-up of arms, with the need for Germany to find an ally in Turkey, and as such Dönitz found himself in the Mediterranean as the Great War exploded across Europe.

The *Breslau* ran into a Russian mine and had to be repaired, during which time Dönitz spent time training as a pilot and served as a gunner and observer. While there he met his future wife Ingeborg who was a nurse, and while on leave married her in Berlin. He was also awarded the Iron Cross and later the Knight's Cross and appeared in the ascendancy. When back on the *Breslau* they ran into conflict with a Russian battleship, and despite using newly devised smoke screens had trouble fleeing from the superior vessel. The captain suggested ramming his ship onto the rocks to save the crew, but Dönitz suggested another smoke screen would help, which it did. It was therefore no surprise that as an Admiral in the next war he ordered that no boat should be surrendered. After this Dönitz was ordered home to train for U-boats. He passed out of the course in mid-January 1917. He was sent back to the Mediterranean area to the Adriatic for a posting on *U-39* under the captaincy of Walter Forstmann.

The *Lusitania* had been sunk, causing widespread embarrassment to the German government which forbade unrestricted warfare by U-boats, mainly for fear of causing trouble with the USA. The navy chiefs were unhappy about this but had to comply. This was later reversed to a degree just as Dönitz was joining his first U-boat, *U-39*. Forstmann and Dönitz were pleased with the policy but then sank two ships, one of which was carrying German civilians fleeing from Egypt and on their way home. Their next victim was a transport ship. While on *U-39* Dönitz also had the experience of being attacked by aircraft, unusual in the Great War but to become a serious danger in the next. Dönitz was soon given command of his own craft, the *UC-25* which was a U-boat designed for laying mines, but also equipped with torpedoes. Setting off in the Adriatic looking for a British repair ship in Port Augusta, he sunk what he thought was the designated ship and then moved to Palermo to lay mines. It was for this effort he received the Knight's Cross, but in fact he had only sunk a coal ship. His reputation grew and he was assigned to a faster vessel, *U-68*, albeit at this stage with an inexperienced crew. Probably as a result of the young rapidly trained crew the U-boat floundered in the midst of a convoy, and Dönitz became a British prisoner, where he came across a British captain whom he thought was honourable. He landed up in a PoW camp near Sheffield, wondering what was happening at home. While as a prisoner, according to some, he feigned madness and was sent to an asylum, but because of this was repatriated home. It will never be known if this were a clever ruse, though a major biographer raises the possibility that events had made him unbalanced.[46]

### Interbellum Years

Germany was in turmoil, mutiny in the High Seas Fleet had been brewing since 1917, Socialists and Communists opposed by Right-Wing elements were causing civil mayhem. There was exceptional unrest caused by the harsh terms of the Versailles Treaty, not only in the guilt clause, but the demands on reducing the military, and the resulting economic ramifications of financial retribution, which impacted Dönitz and his wife having their children during these difficult years. From the beginning the military, the Army, Luftwaffe, and Navy were determined to rebuild their forces in a clandestine fashion. There was anger when the Allies produced a list of war criminals which also included some U-boat commanders. Dönitz from his youth had been a monarchist and the politics of the new era, whether communist or democratic

## 158   Major Blunders of the Second World War

would have felt repugnant to a man brought up as a teenager and young man in the military during the Wilhelmine period. Naval officers were especially traditional in their approach, and it took little time for Dönitz to become a serving officer in command of a torpedo-boat. In all his choices he had the advice of his father-in-law General Weber, a staunch loyal Prussian traditionalist as Dönitz's father had been. He remained with the torpedo-boat flotilla just short of three years, and then he moved to a post in Kiel as an adviser to the Torpedo, Mines, and Intelligence Inspectorate.

In terms of the clandestine redevelopment of the U-boat force it appears that Dönitz was not a critical figure although some have argued otherwise, but all the available evidence indicates this was mere speculation. About 1930 the Germans made use a Finnish submarine training and testing facility, but with the naval men dressed in civilian clothes. As the interbellum years progressed Dönitz found himself with a varied naval career. He had served as the navigator on the cruiser *Nymphe*. At the age of 37 he was promoted to Lieutenant Commander, and he was made chief of the 4th Torpedo Boat Flotilla. A report written about this time commended his work, describing him as a 'very competent staff officer with a thorough knowledge of all spheres', adding that 'his strong temperament and inner verve frequently affected him with restlessness and, for his age, imbalance…he must therefore be brought to take things more calmly and not set exaggerated demands, above all on himself'.[47] Interestingly this report was written by Admiral Wilhelm Canaris the future head of the Abwehr.

In the meantime, Hitler was growing in power and like the monarchy of earlier years saw Germany as the supreme power in the modern world. This made Hitler's connection with the navy that much easier, as that thought process had been the naval thinking since before the Great War. There was much in common between the Nazi and the Imperial thought process, though Hitler was less sophisticated and more brutal. Britain in the mid-1930s was not seen as such an enemy as possibly Russia and France. Although democratic British views regarding Mussolini had indicated to German observers that they preferred dictatorships to communism, they did not have the same interest in Europe as they had in their colonies, though because of their navy the British were always a potential enemy.

As high politics and redevelopment rumbled on Dönitz in 1933 was granted a Hindenburg travel grant, to enlarge his knowledge of the world outside Germany. His reflections on meeting the British in their colonies tended to indicate that although he liked individuals, he was far from being pro-British. He was promoted to Commander and in June 1934 took command of the light cruiser *Emden*. Before taking this command, he had an 'investigative holiday' in England where his hostess looked after him well, even taking him to visit Portsmouth. On his return Hindenburg had died and Hitler fulfilled his role making him the one and only total leader, the Führer. There followed the military oath to Adolf Hitler and the military flags and insignia carried the Party symbol of the swastika. Fermenting in Hitler's mind was the naval pact with Britain (later signed 18 June 1935) indicating Germany's willingness to rebuild her navy but in proposed smaller portions to the Royal Navy. The concept was to keep the British onside and the British were happy thinking that cooperation with the resurrecting Germany was the best way to maintain peace.

After the *Emden* had been refitted and just before Dönitz took the ship out Raeder introduced him to Hitler, which was the first time they had met. What Dönitz thought about him at the time remains unknown, but unquestionably he was attracted by Hitler's determination to restore Germany to the rightful place at the top of the table, and like many other military commanders was taken in by what the more astute cynics called 'the command bug', namely Hitler's ability to inspire confidence in his military commanders. After the initial meeting Dönitz in his cruiser toured the globe to places of interest to the German navy. On arrival back in Germany, Raeder came abroad with the surprise announcement that a new man would take over the *Emden*, because Dönitz was to take command of the new U-boat service. Having served in powerful surface ships with all their grandeur it was not necessarily welcome news for the always aspiring Dönitz, but being Prussian trained he obeyed orders without protest and immersed himself in the new work.

160    Major Blunders of the Second World War

Dönitz ensured his U-boat policy was shared with the navy, stating that unlike the First World War the U-boat war would not be a trade war, but would be an attack on warships and troop transports, indicating he was assuming a war against Britain. He underlined the nature of U-boat war as having an attacking spirit, and not always needing a home port, but a surface support vessel equipped with facilities to support a number of U-boat crews. Raeder and other admirals were pleased with these early plans. Dönitz was soon promoted to the rank of captain as he moved amongst his U-boats, meeting and training the commanders and their crews, and in doing so won their confidence as he tried to wield them into the elite corps he wanted. He also started to plan their tactics, not least acting as a group. It could be seen as the first formulation or embryo of what he would later call his Wolf Packs, though at this stage he was not contemplating a trade war. By 1936 the first Type VII U-boats were ready for service and Dönitz was given the title of *Führer der U-boote* (FdU). He carried out exercises looking at the deployment of the U-boat working alongside the surface fleet, though now there were growing signs that he was beginning to foresee a possibility of a trade war. Based on his First World War experience he also wrote about the dangers of aircraft attack which was prescient given the rapid development of aircraft since 1918. In this post he often took his much-favoured skiing holidays with his family, returning from one as the *Anschluss*, the annexation of Austria occurred.

He started concentrating on the communication systems between U-boats deep in the Atlantic or elsewhere and U-boat headquarters, though some further up the ladder were concerned this could be picked up by an enemy leaving the U-boat vulnerable to attack. Dönitz argued otherwise, pointing out the U-boat was a torpedo weapon, and the days were passing when a U-boat was expected to surface and use guns to attack or sink a ship. Although Dönitz had not at first anticipated a trade war, as the interbellum years unfolded the potential dangers of the British Royal Navy were never far from his thoughts. The Royal Navy's dominance to block and monitor all German ports was a fundamental issue, the British had an extensive coastline and access to the open seas with more ease than the Germans could imagine. None of these worries

U-Boat War, was Dönitz Guilty? 161

were helped by the slow build up not only of capital ships but U-boats, the Army and Luftwaffe were soaking up resources and creating a drain on the economy. The Germans had what they called a Z Plan for a massive naval build-up, but it was all an illusion. Dönitz hoped there would be a rapid increase in U-boat construction because they were cheaper to build. He even wrote a book on the 'U-boat Arm' (*Die U-bootswaffe*) and thereby re-introduced the value of the trade war. His efforts indicated his personal and dedicated belief in the U-boat. By this time, he was 47 years old and already a grandfather, but still with a strong fighting spirit. He started work on a potential Atlantic war, although Hitler had assured Raeder that there would be no war with Britain until 1943 at the earliest. He also proposed large boats giving access beyond the Atlantic. He wrote 'by our geographical position…and inferiority to English sea power the U-boat is the means above all the battle means of our Navy which can be committed to the decisive battle against English sea communications by itself with the greatest security'.[48] An experienced rear admiral queried whether U-boats could succeed against the Royal Navy and whether the prospect of an Asdic immune U-boat appeared very remote. However, Dönitz held firm and pointed out that in a war against Britain, an attack on their sea communications could bring devastation. As such Dönitz proposed the building of U-boat repair ships moored overseas, leaving no doubt that the direction of the interbellum years was indicating a possible war against the Royal Navy.

With Hitler's intentions towards Eastern Europe becoming clearer, and the various treaties between Britain and France with many of these countries, there was for the more politically astute little question about the future. As preparations were made against Poland the U-boats not necessary for the Baltic were disposed in a circle around the British Isles. It is difficult to know for sure Dönitz's views at this stage, there is a sense that he vacillated on whether it meant war with Britain, but he was shocked when it became a reality.

## 162 Major Blunders of the Second World War

### The Second World War

A reminder was sent about what was called the Prize Rules, that a ship should be stopped, and the crew made safe before sinking, which was an almost impossible demand for the security of the U-boat. It has been suggested this demand was made more for the reason of appeasing neutrals, especially the Americans. Dönitz did not make the rules, they came from higher up the ladder of command. However, this did not stop *U-30* under the command of Julius Lemp sinking the liner the *Athenia*. It was a serious blunder as even through the blurred vision of a periscope a liner with lifeboat craft along its length could not look like a warship. As noted above Goebbels used his propaganda machine to shift the blame onto the British, leaving the Americans uncertain for many months. The Kriegsmarine accepted this as either coming under the influence of Nazism or bound by its Prussian sense of obedience to the government or the leader of the country.

The U-boat war started well with the sinking of the aircraft carrier HMS *Courageous* by *U-29*, and many individual merchantmen. The Prize rules were continually under discussion as it was immediately apparent that rapid wireless messages were being sent from the victims, some were becoming armed, and there was always the danger of being rammed. Dönitz knew he had to be tougher in his instructions and was awaiting the time for unrestricted warfare, but he was restrained because of the fear of encouraging America into the conflict. He learned a great deal by his habit of frequently turning up to greet returning U-boats and speaking with their commanders and crew. This not only gave him a good reputation amongst the U-boat crews but fed him the latest information. Dönitz was forever searching for innovations for success, asking for Luftwaffe assistance over Scapa Flow, then planning with Günther Prien for an attack on British warships in that secure mooring. This led to the sinking of the *Royal Oak*, thereby ensuring that Günther Prien, Dönitz, and the U-boats were soon elevated onto the pedestals of heroes and victors. Dönitz continued to press for unrestricted warfare but higher command sensitivities demanded restraint. It was, however, already happening, as

## U-Boat War, was Dönitz Guilty? 163

with Lemp sinking the *Athenia*. The question of unrestrained warfare was and remains a delicate issue, and it will be explored in a later part of this text dealing with Dönitz's trial at Nuremberg.

While Dönitz was becoming concerned about how to deal with the large convoys emerging into the Atlantic War, he was often obliged to move his U-boats around the seas dictated by Hitler in the process of his land wars. The occupation of Norway, provoked by the belief the British had already started to extend their coastline reaches, meant Dönitz had to send U-boats to that area. It was here they discovered the problem of malfunctioning torpedoes, and the Royal Navy appearing to know the areas in which they lurked.

Following the fall of France, Dönitz took the opportunity to increase the chances of victory in the Atlantic by surveying the French ports as U-boat moorings, first choosing Lorient and then others noted above, as this gave him quicker and seemingly safer access to the Atlantic. The first to moor in was Lemp's U-boat, and the number of sinkings rose exponentially and Dönitz was convinced, trying to persuade others of the value of a trade war and the importance of the U-boat service. It was soon agreed that Britain was to be totally blockaded which made official the unrestricted war that had already been in progress for a long time. It was the time for the proposed operation *Sea Lion*, and Dönitz was instructed by Raeder to prepare his U-boats to act as a screen against Royal Navy intruding into the invasion area. As such Dönitz moved his headquarters from Germany to Paris. Dönitz could always be found in his office from the early hours with his staff, checking the whereabouts of every U-boat, and then receiving their news and observations before planning the next move, usually against the convoys. This also included the Italian boats, but they were proving ineffective, with Dönitz and Field Marshal Kesselring putting it down to the non-belligerent Mediterranean temperament of the Italians. Dönitz's constant study enabled him and his men to concentrate the Wolf Packs with growing success. For Dönitz these were his best days and he moved his HQ to just outside Lorient once *Sea Lion* was abandoned, which enabled him to greet most of the returning U-boats

164    Major Blunders of the Second World War

and enhance his popularity and knowledge of his crews. 'The staff of a Luftwaffe general invited to lunch one day were astonished at the free style of the U-boat men with their chief, and the riposte and banter which bounced back and forth across the table'.[49]

However, it was not always success. The British asdic system seemed to be working more effectively, and they had developed a better way of spreading their depth-charges. It was also observed that the convoys were becoming more difficult to find and track, almost as if they knew the whereabouts of the U-boats. This raised the possibility of spies, whether radio messages were being deciphered, but this was believed to be impossible, and it seemed unlikely they could track radio traffic. Unknown to most it was the work of Bletchley untying the configurations of the Enigma code. The naval version had proved difficult until, as mentioned above, *U-110* commanded by Lemp was captured, together with his coding apparatus. The settings were changed once a month, but having triggered the main source of the problem the Bletchley machine did not take long to identify the changes.

When Pearl Harbor occurred on 7 January 1941 the war changed, not least for Dönitz who welcomed the removal of restrictions on attacking American shipping. He used coded messages to U-boats in American waters for some easy pickings. Despite British conferences with the Americans and warning their coast guards, they were slow to react, and it took time for them to come to terms with this style of warfare. By March 1941 the U-boat successes virtually doubled in terms of tonnage sunk. However, Hitler kept demanding U-boats in areas such as Norway, then the Mediterranean and later the Arctic to block convoys to Russia, and Dönitz was aware that the USA under their war construction plan could rebuild the same amount as sunk each year. On the home front Dönitz had been encouraging a Professor Walter with new U-boat innovations, not least one which could travel at 28 knots while submerged, but Hitler's land wars dominated his thinking with tanks and aircraft soaking up the financial resources.

When it came to the U-boat warfare it was reported that Hitler had a conversation with the Japanese Ambassador, and in a nutshell stated that

## U-Boat War, was Dönitz Guilty?    165

the U-boat should not only sink the ship but kill the crew. This would not only make the recrewing of new vessels difficult but argued it would put men off volunteering. Later both Raeder and Dönitz would insist this was Hitler's idea alone. When this was raised at the Nuremberg trial Dönitz simply replied 'No, I received neither a written nor a verbal order. I knew nothing at all about this discussion; I learned about it through the document which I saw here'.[50]

While this policy was raising its head a British commando raid took place at St Nazaire, no U-boats were destroyed, but the possibility of a U-boat command HQ being captured raised concern, and Dönitz's offices were moved back to the relative safety of Paris. Not long afterwards it was reported that a British destroyer had machine gunned survivors from a German minelayer vessel called the *Ulm*, which Raeder promptly investigated. How far this was true is difficult to ascertain, it is believed that many were rescued but others left to die because of the sudden presence of German aircraft. Reports were made on the incident in Britain, but they may well have been incomplete or suffered from the sin of omission.

Aircraft were also appearing in the Bay of Biscay, and the French Admiral Darlan, (an Anglophobe who claimed his grandfather had fought the British as Trafalgar) gave the Germans a device which could detect radar transmissions to warn them of incoming attack planes. Dönitz was desperate to find ways to improve his U-boats with anti-aircraft guns and even hoping for some rockets he knew were being developed at Peenemünde. Then in September Dönitz was called to his HQ because one of his larger U-boats, a Type IX under Hartenstein had sunk a British Troop Carrier called the *Laconia* only to discover it was packed with Italian PoWs and civilians. Dönitz claimed he agreed with Hartenstein for the rescue, and as noted above, ordered the other U-boats in the area to assist. Given the known facts it would appear Dönitz had indeed made those decisions. This was an important incident in understanding the nature of the U-boat war, the human element, and the part played by Dönitz, and as such will be returned to in more detail later in this text.

## 166 Major Blunders of the Second World War

In the meantime, in the upper regions of the Nazi command Raeder was having problems with Hitler who, angry that the surface fleet was not so successful as he wished, instructed that the large battleships should be scrapped, having their guns put ashore for land defence. Raeder was furious and resigned despite Hitler's attempts to appease him. When Hitler asked Raeder who was best to replace him the Admiral offered two names, one of which was Dönitz, which was something of a surprise as the two men had not become close and relationships were often strained, Dönitz having once told Raeder he would not follow one of his given orders. However, Raeder saw in Dönitz a natural and inspiring leader, and so Dönitz became the *Grossadmiral*, the Grand Admiral on 30 January 1943.

Dönitz was now in the upper echelons of the military leadership and met Hitler more often. He had, as noted earlier, been raised in the tradition of Prussian obedience and loyalty to the state, and as far as he was concerned his country was at war, and Hitler was the leader to whom he therefore owed total loyalty. The benefit of hindsight rightly condemns any loyalty to a man as evil as Hitler, but on the human side such condemnation must be monitored alongside the natural human propensity to follow the instincts with which humans are imbued as young people, and reinforced by the belief that one's country is sacred (my country right or wrong) and its enemies unforgiveable. He had always maintained since his youth that a military man belonged to the state, and his honour rested on this belief. For Dönitz no one had a right to a private life, it had to be devoted to the country. In the months to come he lost two sons to the war, and it was noted that each time he showed no emotion. Dönitz was always supported by his wife Ingeborg, who continued to search PoW records in the hope that her first son to be lost in his U-boat had survived, and he was alive as a prisoner. This was not because Dönitz lacked emotion, but for a man of his background duty to the country came first above his own life and those of his family, and he constantly sent messages to his crews that their duties, loyalties and lives belonged to the state. Hitler was aware of these attitudes, always

## U-Boat War, was Dönitz Guilty? 167

wondering about the potential treachery of his generals, but never the navy, and as such valued Dönitz and rarely interfered with naval issues.

As Dönitz reached the top of his navy career the problems were increasing not just at sea, but on nearly all the battle fronts. For Dönitz his driving force was his stubborn belief that the U-boat could still win the war, and he sent instructions of this belief to all his crews. The army during 1943 would be suffering defeats and reverses. Mussolini would be toppled from power and Italy changing sides. The Luftwaffe was not coping with the bombing raids on Germany, and Dönitz arrived at the conclusion that the U-boat service was the only offensive Germany had to rely upon. Amongst the main issues, Germany was faced with limited resources and the major industrial power of America. Unquestionably Hitler was becoming fraught as the war turned against him, but Dönitz was always positive, loyal, and supportive which Hitler needed. He required men who had these leanings and he found this in Dönitz, but in the army there was decreasing support, with the possible exception of Kesselring.

Dönitz moved to Berlin, living in an expensive residence and in an area guarded by the SS. Like others he had received a massive gift from Hitler as he rose to the top rung of the ladder. His task was immense because Germany with its occupied territories had a vastly extended coastline to guard and use, and shipments had to be protected. He was one of the few commanders Hitler appeared to trust enough to agree with his views. Raeder had resigned over the argument of the disposal of capital surface ships, but Dönitz re-opened the debate pointing out that these warships could do much to challenge the convoys to Russia. Hitler was not convinced but agreed that Dönitz could see if this worked, and he gave him half a year to prove which of them was correct. Dönitz was astute in knowing Hitler by mentioning the Russian supply line when raising the issue, but it was apparent that Hitler trusted him. Later the formidable *Tirpitz* was damaged by a clandestine attack and when Dönitz sent the *Scharnhorst* out to tackle a convoy it was pursued and destroyed, with only 36 survivors from a crew of 2,000, proving Hitler had been right about surface ships facing Royal Navy opposition.

168    Major Blunders of the Second World War

In his main theatre of concern, the Atlantic War, and other areas where he could wage his attacks on essential British and Russian imports, life was proving more difficult for the U-boat. One of the concerns was the way the British guided their convoys as if they knew where the Wolf Packs were lurking. There were suspicions of spies and treachery, and he was told by the experts there was no way the British could have broken the Enigma code. He astutely ordered that the naval machine should have an additional rota added, this worked for a time but the experts at Bletchley Park soon understood what had happened. He used the B-Dienst system which had broken the Royal Navy's cypher system in 1941 to try and readdress the balance. This enabled him to have a better insight into the areas in which the convoys would be passing through. This proved successful but alerted the British and Americans that the U-boat was still a serious danger. However, as the U-boats searched the gap in the Atlantic which aircraft could not reach, they soon found the escort vessels had increased in number. In addition to this problem, the Atlantic gap of a no-plane area was diminishing, and some long-range aircraft were appearing which could not be detected by the U-boats' radar system. It was a long impossible haul for Dönitz who managed to convince Hitler for more U-boats, but there was simply not enough steel. The constant air-attacks, especially in the Bay of Biscay, were lowering the morale of the crews. There was also the danger of aircraft carriers providing aerial support where once it was out of the question. Dönitz decided that the larger Type IX were more vulnerable to falling bombs and depth charges, so he ordered them further afield to remoter areas where shipping was still abundant. The danger was that the U-boat known previously for its undetectability was now becoming much more vulnerable, and Dönitz continually hoped that some scientific genius could provide a boat which was immune to Asdic. He sent a message to his crews pointing out that 'at present you alone can take the offensive against the enemy and beat him. The U-boat arm, by continuously sinking ships with war supplies and materials for the island must subdue the enemy by continual bloodletting which must cause even the strongest body to bleed to death'.[51] Despite the growing strength of the Allied counterattacks Dönitz remained determined and certain that his U-boats could eventually win.

He continued every effort to improve his fleet, turning to Professor Walter for larger and larger U-boats, and seeking boats with a higher surface speed. He looked to better anti-aircraft guns and some were fitted with powerful machine guns to their coning towers. The snorkel was researched for improvement and fitted to the latest models. The acoustic torpedo was at first seen as the answer to convoys, but it was not as reliable as hoped, and could often turn back on the U-boat which had fired it in the first place. The Allies also developed a towing device meant to attract such weapons. There were explorations into electric U-boats, and in this frantic search to improve the fleet he had the support of Albert Speer. They also developed a new means of detecting planes; it was called the *Hagenuk*, and it was devised to detect enemy radar beams. However, it was clear that Allied science in this area of research was more advanced than German efforts. One of the main problems was the lack of Luftwaffe support, but Dönitz knew better than to clash with Göring. He managed to convince Hitler of the necessity of the navy having control of its own flying wing, but it was too late and not effective enough given the failing resources of the day.

Following the problems in North Africa, Hitler sent Dönitz to represent his views to Mussolini, which was a sure sign that the dictator was looking towards his Admiral with more than naval eyes, but with political trust. Dönitz realised the Italian navy was less useful than he had anticipated, and they had given up hope of victory in North Africa. He was sent back a second time when Hitler rightly suspected the Italians were losing heart in the war, was concerned for Mussolini, and already wondering whether the Italians would change sides if invaded. While there he met Kesselring who was convinced, unlike most, that Sicily would be the next target for the Allies. Dönitz wondered about involving Spain in the war in order to free Gibraltar from British control. Admiral Canaris, head of the Abwehr was sent to speak to Franco, but Franco remained determined to remain neutral, and it is believed that Canaris who was a part of the German resistance against Hitler, advised him against such a move.

When Sicily was invaded the Italian navy was reluctant to respond and Dönitz suggested the Germans took over the Italian fleet, but Hitler

170    Major Blunders of the Second World War

was unhappy with this idea, always being a supporter of Mussolini who was still in power at that time. During this crisis it was apparent that Dönitz was one of Hitler's advisers. It was equally clear that Dönitz thought highly of the Führer and was impressed by the way Hitler had foreseen the political ramifications in Italy before anyone else. Dönitz continued to visit the U-boat bases to boost the morale of his crews and commanders who were now suffering severe losses.

Curiously a conference was held at Posen where Dönitz gave a speech on his naval matters, but this was followed by Himmler who revealed all about the 'Jewish question'. Turning public on this issue may have been a calculated move by the sinister Himmler to remind others there could be no turning back, and Dönitz's biographer Padfield suggests there is no way that Dönitz could have missed these revelations. His argument is persuasive but there is no concrete evidence one way or the other. This issue of how far Dönitz was aware of Nazi barbarity will be explored later in the text.

Dönitz also attended Hitler at the *Wolfschanze* (the Wolf's Lair) on conferences concerning the course of the war. Here his professional bonding with Speer developed more, and together they managed to persuade Göring to allow Speer's department to look into radar issues. Dönitz continued to gain the trust of Hitler because of his determination to win and his sense of loyalty. When Hitler was too ill to attend the annual Heroes' Memorial Day parade in Berlin, he asked Dönitz to take his place, which may have felt something like a rebuke to men like Göring. Just after this event the news arrived that *U-852* under Eck had machine gunned survivors. This would have been agreeable to Hitler who, as previously noted wanted crews eliminated, but it still sent out shockwaves. This incident brought back memories of the HMHS *Llandovery Castle* Hospital ship with its clearly defined markings, which had been sunk by a German U-boat on 27 June 1918.

As he had once been on holiday and returned to the news of the *Anschluss*, so in June 1944 he was again on holiday when the news of the Normandy invasion arrived. The reality was such that Dönitz could do little when faced with the immense size of the Allied attack, both in their land, air and naval strength, and his meagre forces could offer next to no resistance. The 20 July plot to assassinate Hitler also came as a shock to such a loyal man as Dönitz, and he went straight to the site and joined the extraordinary tea-party Hitler held for Mussolini who had come on a visit. He wrote to his men describing the attempted assassination as 'filling one with holy wrath and bitter revenge', the later element soon finding itself fulfilled by the so-called People's Court. The investigations were brutal and far-reaching, but in the Kriegsmarine only three were pinpointed. For the remaining years it was a matter of turbulence as the Third Reich started to crumble, but Dönitz, unlike many others, never wavered from his hope and belief in Hitler, still hoping that a new U-boat, the XXI and XXIII could help what was a helpless cause. He demanded unquestionable loyalty from all his subordinates, and it was swifty noted by Hitler and Goebbels. Dönitz even offered naval men to the army, and still gave morale boosting speeches to his crews when able. This again reflected his character born in the background of the Prussian belief of the good of the state despite all other circumstances. Even when the Russians were working their way through the streets and avenues of Berlin, he still demanded loyalty and obedience, and it was no surprise that Hitler demanded that all fortress commanders should be naval officers. The rumours of the wonder weapons never materialised, and everyone knew the war was lost. Nevertheless, the Schnell boats and some U-boats still carried out the occasional forays, especially in the Baltic area. The Allied bombers attacked Hamburg and Kiel destroying some 24 U-boats, but Dönitz would not give up. When Rosevelt's death was announced Hitler, Goebbels, and others thought the war would change in Germany's favour, but it was reported that Dönitz did not think it would change the outcome, indicating that despite his loyalty he remained a realist.


### Post-Hitler

Hitler gave Dönitz the responsibility for the defence of north Germany and sent Kesselring to the south for the same reasons. Hitler still trusted

172  Major Blunders of the Second World War

these men, both of whom always defended Hitler's right to rule. Göring was dismissed by Hitler on the dubious grounds of betrayal, and Himmler was seeking a separate peace in the hope he would be treated as the head of state. Dönitz was at least more level-headed and saw no point in trying to negotiate a separate peace with the West. It was not until late April that Dönitz's eternal optimism faded. Dönitz had stationed himself in Plön when he heard that he had been named as Hitler's chosen successor, but at that moment there was no mention of Hitler's suicide; Dönitz was simply stunned. Immediately the question arose as to how Himmler would respond, and guards were placed around Dönitz's headquarters. Himmler arrived, asked to be second to Dönitz who refused the offer and Himmler seemed to accept this message.

Although the death of the Third Reich was clearly apparent, Dönitz's obsessive sense of loyalty and obedience held firm, and although now knowing Hitler had killed himself, he broadcast the message that Hitler had died fighting for the German people. He was equally obsessed with trying to make the West understand the dangers of the communist threat which later became real enough, but in 1945 it was the desperate Nazi effort to portray Nazi Germany holding back the threat of Bolshevist domination on behalf of Europe and the world. As such he tried to use his limited time to save German lives still fighting in the East, and it will never be known how successful this was, as by this stage there was total confusion and much down to the ingenuity of individual soldiers. In his broadcasts he even appealed for God's help, which would have been unheard of in Nazi Germany, where Hitler preferred 'providence'.

The situation was so hopeless there seemed little point in calling for resistance, but he ordered this on the excuse of giving soldiers in the East time, but even his own position was in danger. It was decided to move to the naval cadet school at Flensburg with some fantasy defence line along the Kiel canal. He had the company of Speer who had a keen eye on his future safety, Keitel and Jodl headed towards him as did others. Himmler still persisted around the edges in the anticipation of becoming Dönitz's Chancellor. Dönitz instructed Seyss-Inquart, freshly arrived from the Netherlands, not to carry out a proposal for the destruction

## U-Boat War, was Dönitz Guilty? 173

by flooding in his area of responsibility, indicating he was showing some sense. Common sense ruled, and through Admiral von Friedeberg accepted Montgomery's terms of surrender, and sent other orders not to scuttle ships, and for the U-boat service to surrender. Most did but some scattered to other parts of the world, to Argentina or Japan. There was a general appeal for a humanitarian approach to the Americans and British, but this was ignored, not least on the grounds that news of the barbarity in the concentration camps was spreading like wildfire. This appeal was probably based on hoping for division between the West and the Soviet Union.

For his part Dönitz had no idea what would happen to the Flensberg government he had established. As part of his personal appeal to the West he had dismissed the leading Nazi members, including Göring, Goebbels, and Himmler, the latter proving the most tenacious in his demands for inclusion. Many efforts were made by the Flensberg government to distance itself from the concentration camp horrors, based principally on ignorance, and the belief that the West would need them to counter the Bolshevist threat. Attempts to communicate with Eisenhower met with total silence.

By 22 May it was becoming clear that the Flensberg government was being seen as an Alice in Wonderland side show, and Dönitz, Jodl and Speer were arrested as war criminals. Dönitz had hoped that he would be recognised as the legal leader of Germany, and as such be treated in this way in the anticipated new postwar scenario. The government was dissolved and Dönitz and others were flown to face their trial at Nuremberg, which Dönitz described as 'the continuation of war by other means'.[52] There followed the trial which will be explored in the next section of this account.

### Introduction to Trial

After months of interrogations, interviews with psychologists, and many other formal departments Dönitz was put on trial in May 1946. He always appeared well-dressed and unlike many other defendants managed

174    Major Blunders of the Second World War

to stay dignified throughout the proceedings. They had carried out IQ tests, and Dönitz was found to be the same as Göring with a respectable score of 138. It was interesting to note that when Dönitz met one of the psychiatrists, he proved to speak excellent English, and that he was 'polite, affable in a half-suspicious way...but must be given his own reins or he shuts up with his mouth firmly compressed'.[53]

His appointed defence counsel was Otto Kranzbühler a German Naval lawyer who was also smart and well presented, and who was able to wear his naval uniform as the navy still existed, if only to clear minefields. It was an international trial trying to offer the impression it reflected the collective conscience of mankind. None of the four victors were free of war guilt, not least the Russians who had been Hitler's ally while occupying Poland, and carrying out the Katyń massacres, and both America and Britain had carried out carpet bombing and used two nuclear weapons in Japan. It was, nevertheless, an effort to use the legal system to try and address past wrongs and bring a sense of balance to the postwar years. Kranzbühler knew he was in a better position than other defence counsels because the Kriegsmarine did not have the same reputation as the SS, and Kranzbühler knew the British Admiralty found nothing to condemn, and when compared to the army and Luftwaffe, 'the German navy came much closer to following the rules of chivalry'.[54]

However, on behalf of Dönitz he faced some difficult questions, not least the believed slaughter of U-boat victims, accepting Hitler's Commando Order, and being an accessory to what is now called the Holocaust. Obeying Hitler was not seen as a defence, even in 1921 the German court had ruled that obeying superior orders if criminal would be regarded as illegal. The general feeling was that when German subjects had put their trust in one man, they had to accept both the sweet and the bitter consequences. In reading the trial manuscripts Dönitz was direct and clear in his answers, and indicated he was absolutely certain as to where he stood, showing little regret as he argued that he was a navy man only interested in matters of sea-warfare. There were three major issues which caught the attention of the prosecution, the first was Dönitz's involvement in promoting and preparing for an aggressive war. The second was the military level at which he was accused of war crimes and even crimes against humanity in the conduct of the naval war, based on his direction of the U-boat fleet. He was portrayed as part of the Nazi administration and continuing a hopeless war after succeeding Hitler. It was often a question of whether Dönitz could be believed. There were reams of documents, but the possibility he had been involved in the conspiracy to plan a war held no water, because at the time he was the commander of the light cruiser *Emden* far away in the Indian Ocean. Also, because of his roles, he could not be placed in the category of the secret rearming of German forces contrary to the restrictions of the Versailles Treaty. It was argued that because he was involved in the maritime war against Norway and Denmark, he was a 'planner of war', but this would have indicted every German officer in all their forces. It was pointed out that as the war against Poland started, Dönitz ordered U-boats to encircle Britain, but these were orders directed to him, and Dönitz pointed out they were necessary prophylactic measures. None of the prosecution accusations were strong. Even when tackled about the racist ideology of the Nazis, Dönitz was able, with much loyal support, to claim he was only interested in Naval matters, and in public speaking he supported the Party only for the sake of a sense of national unity, which had become more important as the war turned against them. On the issue of not promptly surrendering in April 1945, he argued that it was a matter of trying to save soldiers and civilians from the communist onslaught, which probably captured a degree of acceptance from the Western Allies, as it was coming to light that the barbarity of the Soviet war had matched that of the Nazis as the Russians sought revenge. It would later be believed, with some substance that the Russian prosecution had anticipated that all the defendants, including Dönitz would be hanged, not least because they had lost so many and suffered the most destruction by the Nazi regime. The French had suffered a humiliating defeat, seen their ports utilised and bombed because of the U-boat threat, and they were equally as angry but not as extreme as the Russians. A favourite theme running through the trial was that the politicians had caused the problems, but now the military sat in the dock because of them. The French constantly challenged this,

# 176 Major Blunders of the Second World War

arguing that a military officer is the representative of the state. The British were recalling the immense losses of their merchant fleets, and although they had armed merchantmen with guns, sometimes with depth charge supplies, ordered wireless signals to be deployed pinpointing the whereabouts of a U-boat and told to fight back, they still tended to see the U-boat activity as murderous and blamed Dönitz.

The British and the American admirals were not so critical as they had deployed similar rules to their submarine fleets and knew that the legal *tu quoque* legal argument, that you did the same thing, could not be utilised, because it had been banned by common consent at the Nuremberg Trial, on the tenuous grounds that because others did the same thing did not make it a justified argument. Kranzbühler cleverly raised the issue not under the argument of *tu quoque* but based on the ambiguities of the London Protocol.

A major boost for Dönitz was when the American Admiral Nimitz explained in a memorandum for the defence counsel that America also had specified war zones, and as a general rule they did not assist survivors, never summoning help from Japanese merchantmen knowing they were also armed. The most difficult part of the accusations levelled at Dönitz was that he had ordered the shooting of survivors, though these orders when read were somewhat confusing. A U-boat captain Moehle had read them as orders to kill, though the evidence was as ambiguous as were the orders, and only Captain Eck stood trial for the one time this happened.

Reading through the trial manuscripts it is immediately clear that Dönitz was well-prepared, and defiant in his belief he had not committed war crimes, knew he would be backed by loyal subordinates, and had been told that some of his enemy's admirals were surprised he was on trial.

## Trial Papers

Kranzbühler raised questions he knew would be asked by the prosecutors and received direct answers. He asked if U-boat commanders voiced objections to his orders, to which Dönitz promptly replied 'No, never'. He was then asked, 'What would you have done with a commander who

## U-Boat War, was Dönitz Guilty?    177

refused to carry out the instructions for U-boat warfare?' Dönitz said he would make sure following an examination he was normal, and if so put him before a court martial. Kranzbühler asked 'You could only have done that with a clear conscience if you yourself assumed full responsibility for the orders which you either issued or which you transmitted?' To which Dönitz replied 'Naturally'.[55] The questions were answered directly with no hesitation, even with questions which later came as a surprise. He was asked if he considered merchantmen crews were civilians or soldiers, and promptly responded 'Germany considered the crews of merchantmen as combatants, because they fought with weapons'.[56]

When questioned about Hitler's views on killing merchantmen crew to stop them being used again or rescuing survivors, Dönitz replied he had already answered this, but added it was a military matter as leaving a U-boat in danger because it was rescuing a merchant crew was his major concern. He added the cutting response that 'the British Navy correctly take up a very clear, unequivocal position in this respect: that rescue is to be denied in such cases; and that is evident also from their actions and commands', later adding 'English U-boats in the Jutland waters, areas which we dominated, showed, as a matter of course and quite correctly, no concern at all for those who were shipwrecked, even though, without a doubt, our defence was only a fraction of the British.'[57] Dönitz had managed to introduce the *tu quoque* answer in answering a question

When Kranzbühler asked about his crews rescuing survivors he answered he was in favour of such brave acts, but he was always concerned for the safety of his men and their boat. This immediately raised the issue of the orders to sink and depart immediately following the *Laconia* Order. He explained that he had backed Hartenstein in his rescue mission until the danger of aerial attacked exposed the dangers. When asked about the case of Eck machine-gunning survivors, he suggested Eck was destroying evidence that a boat had been sunk, and he had no idea that this included survivors. He claimed he had only recently heard of the situation and he did not approve of the actions, and when asked had he heard of similar incidents he replied, 'not a single one'.[58] At his trial Eck had denied that Dönitz had ever given such an order.

178   Major Blunders of the Second World War

On a more delicate issue Dönitz was asked by Kranzbühler that when he accepted the post of commander-in-chief of the Navy, he was associating himself closely with the Nazi Party. Dönitz explained it had 'never entered his head', and like any other soldier it was simply accepting a military command. When further pressed about his relationship with Hitler, Dönitz was evidently prepared for the question, answering it in three parts. He accepted National Socialism for the sake of the honour and dignity of Germany, with its 'subordination of each and every one to the interests of the common weal'... the second point was 'my oath to Adolf Hitler'... 'before I became Commander-in-Chief of the Navy, I believe Hitler had no definite conception of me and my person. He had seen me too few times and always in large circles'.[59] He added later that he attended Hitler's meetings only if he had naval matters to discuss, and 'I never received from the Fuehrer an order which in any way violated the ethics of war. Neither I nor anyone in the Navy – and this is my conviction – knew anything about the mass extermination of people, which I learned about here from the Indictment, or, as far as the concentration camps are concerned, after the capitulation in May 1945'.[60]

Dönitz like the others had seen the films about the concentration camps, and every defendant was trying to distance themselves from the exposure of Nazi brutality. He had bowed his head and tried not to watch the films, asking one of the prison psychiatrists 'how can they accuse me of knowing such things?' When asked about Hitler's Commando Order he admitted he had seen this, and that he had been informed that enemy forces had placed themselves by their actions outside the Geneva Convention, but on further questioning claimed he had nothing to do with the Order or its implementation. When asked about the crew of a motor-torpedo boat taken prisoner in Norway and then shot, Dönitz explained that Nuremberg was the first time he had heard about this, and because they had been wearing civilian clothes they had been taken and shot by the SD, and acknowledged it was wrong, but these victims had never been navy prisoners.

The most difficult moments for Dönitz concerned his knowledge and association with the brutality of the Nazi regime. He was asked why he had given talks to his men which amounted to 'preaching Nationalism'. He argued that it was a matter of morale. 'Therefore in all of my speeches I tried to preserve this unity and the feeling that we were the guarantors of this unity. This was necessary and right, and particularly necessary for me as a leader of troops. I could not preach disunity or dissolution, and it had its effect. Fighting power and discipline in the Navy were of a high standard until the end. And I believe that in every nation such an achievement is considered a proper and good achievement for a leader of troops. These are my reasons for talking the way I did'.[61] When accused of being a fanatical Nazi he argued that until the spring of 1945 he had been a straightforward soldier fulfilling his duties by continuing to fight. He explained the Reich Marshal was Hitler's natural successor but there was a 'regrettable misunderstanding, between Göring and Hitler, and the decision was made about Dönitz while he was not even in Berlin. When questioned on his actions as head of state in continuing the war, he argued that the barbarities in the East were so bad for the women and children it was a soldier's duty to defend. He explained he was aware of the Yalta agreement and did not want his soldiers to fall into the hands of the Soviets.

The British prosecutor Maxwell-Fyfe questioned Dönitz over his relationship with Albert Speer, eventually arriving as to why he was so interested in this man, as Speer knew of the forced labour at the naval dockyards, which included concentration camp victims. Dönitz explained he was only interested in building up his U-boat force and never asked about where the labour came from. He admitted he knew they used foreign workers, but from where they were recruited, he never considered this aspect his business. Maxwell-Fyfe pressed him on conversations he may have had with Gauleiter Sauckel who provided the labour, but Dönitz was able to say he never had a conversation with Sauckel. Dönitz added that 'during my conferences with Hitler and Speer, the system of obtaining these workers was never mentioned at all. The methods did not interest me at all. During these conferences the labour question was not discussed at all. I was interested merely in how many submarines I received, that is, how large my allotment was in terms of ships built'.[62]

180   Major Blunders of the Second World War

Maxwell-Fyfe decided that a point-to-point argument with Dönitz was not worthwhile, but he challenged him about his purported ignorance concerning the forced labour and the treatment of the Jews. Dönitz was equally as sharp in his reply that his lack of knowledge was 'self-evident, since we have heard here how all these things were kept secret; and if one bears in mind the fact that everyone in this war was pursuing his own tasks with the maximum of energy, then it is no wonder at all. To give an example I learned of the conditions in concentration camps only here'.[63] Maxwell-Fyfe pursued the question of the Commando Order but found it was like hitting a brick wall whenever Dönitz responded.

The next day, 14 May 1946, a Colonel Phillimore questioned Admiral Wagner (Chief of the Operational Division) about where he thought Dönitz stood in terms of the charges, to be met by the robust claim that 'I already testified yesterday that the difference is very great. Admiral Doenitz opposed the renunciation of the Geneva Convention and said that even if measures to intimidate deserters or counter measures against bombing attacks on cities were to be taken, the Geneva Convention should not be renounced in any case'.[64]

After a recess Kranzbühler was back on his feet, questioning Admiral Godt, pointing out that he had known Dönitz longer than most and whether Dönitz had much to do with politics. Godt replied 'Nothing at all, to my knowledge, before he was appointed Commander-in-Chief of the Navy. As Commander-in-Chief of the Navy, he made occasional speeches outside the Navy; for instance, he addressed dock workers, made a speech to the Hitler Youth at Stettin, and gave a talk over the air on Heroes' Day on 20 July; I remember no other occasions'.[65] On further questioning Godt insisted whether the speeches were for dock-labourers or Hitler youth they were always orientated around Naval matters. Naturally Kranzbühler questioned those men who he knew would be positive about Dönitz, but it could also be noted that Dönitz's loyalty with his men was paying back benefits to him which he could not have foreseen. He also questioned a U-boat commander Hessler who spoke of times he had helped sunk crews and passengers but when he had tried, he had been attacked by the enemy, thus clearly indicating the dangers of stopping to assist survivors.

On reading the trial notes it was clear that Dönitz was supported by his men, colleagues, and his naval opponents in America and Britain. There is also the distinct impression from the written record that Dönitz's instant and knowledgeable replies indicated he was aware of the facts as he saw them, or he had brilliantly prepared himself for all questions. This latter possibility, for many seemed unlikely, as the prosecution was sharp enough in other defendant cases to unpick lies or challenge them with evidence indicating they were not telling the truth. This was not a feature of Dönitz's trial.

## Final Judgement

It was concluded that from 1943 Hitler had always consulted Dönitz, and evidence indicated he was active in waging aggressive war. In terms of unrestricted warfare, he was found not guilty. There was a lack of certainty in the provided evidence of Dönitz giving orders for killing survivors, as they were ambiguous. It was accepted that although he allowed the Commando Order to stay in place, he claimed he knew nothing of the MTB crew handed over to the SD, and seemed to have no knowledge of shipyard labour, or how they were procured. Basically, the two indictments of which he was found guilty were crimes against peace and war crimes, he was found innocent of the indictment of conspiring for war and innocent of crimes against humanity. Dönitz and many others were surprised that he was found guilty at all and felt it was an injustice. Dönitz was equally annoyed at hearing how little Raeder regarded him, having referred to him during the trial 'as Hitler's boy'. Dönitz was a man who felt important, tended even in prison to see himself as the leader of Germany, and felt he was no more guilty of war crimes and crimes against peace than his enemies. The debate vacillates to this day, some thinking with the benefit of hindsight and new evidence he was guilty, and a ten-year sentence was light, others that he was just a good naval officer doing his job and therefore was not guilty.

## 182  Major Blunders of the Second World War

### Observations on the Trial

Running through the trial of Dönitz were several dangerous issues for him. The first was the U-boat campaign, but Admiral Nimitz had used the *tu quoque* argument, stating the Allies had the same policies, and it was known that the British Admiralty felt the same way. The most difficult task Dönitz faced was over the killing of survivors. The evidence on this issue was always weak. A Lieutenant Peter Heisig who had heard Dönitz lecture as a young man may well have misunderstood what Dönitz was saying about this issue. The second was Captain Karl Moehle who was equally weak as a witness, because he had been captured and accused of issuing the *Laconia* Order; he was regarded as 'saving his own neck' and not reliable. Dönitz said in court that he 'regretted that Moehle did not find occasion to clarify these doubts immediately'.* Since there was only one known incident of shooting survivors the prosecution lacked sufficient evidence. The question of sinking without warning was always difficult. The witnesses Admirals Gerhardt Wagner and Eberhard Godt gave support, and Dönitz's son-in-law, Captain Günter Hessler, explained in the training naval officers received they had all the terms of measuring whether a ship should be attacked explained. It was Hessler who had pointed out that a sinking ship often fired on a U-boat as it was coming to help, and everyone knew that the British Admiralty was unhappy about the case against Dönitz. The prosecution summation addressed Dönitz as the 'legatee of defeat' allowing his U-boat commanders the freedom to act as if they were in the jungle, but Nimitz's support was well-used by his defence counsel.[66] In his final words to the court, Dönitz not only denied any criminality or that he had made any mistakes, but also stated that he would 'have done the same all over again'. He repeated his main themes that the German U-boat warfare had been honourable, that the conspiracy charge was mere political dogma, and as the last technical head of state, he took full responsibility.

The second issue was his association with the Nazi leadership and how far he supported not just their war policies, but their racial discrimination

---

\* Moehle was sentenced to five years for passing on the *Laconia* Order; he died in 1996.

and barbaric treatment of people born Jewish. He had argued that he had supported Nazism in his occasional speeches to act as a source of morale boosting. There was the distinct possibility that he had the usual (sadly) social attitude of not liking Jews, but how far or how deep this ran is impossible to clarify. When he saw the filmed horrors and heard the witnesses from the concentration camps, he was clearly distressed, asking how people could think he would be involved in such behaviour. When he was pushed about possible anti-Semitic attitudes, he pointed out that one of his vice-admirals, Bernhard Rogge, was Jewish, along with many others. Rogge had written an affidavit on his behalf, and he claimed he had resisted calls from Hitler about having Jews in the navy. Rogge's father was a Lutheran Minister but with a Jewish grandparent which for the fanatical Nazi was sufficient for condemnation. Dönitz's claim that he knew nothing about slave-labour in the dockyards all simply rested on whether he was to be believed or not. In his favour was the general impression that he was totally obsessive about his professional naval life and trying to win the war at sea, and such was his passion he was in the Indian Ocean during the time the Nazi leaders were planning war.

The third question was his leadership of the so-called Flensburg government where the American prosecutor Jackson accused him of taking over Hitler's role. In taped conversations between senior German officers, this tended to be the main point of criticism against Dönitz, not his naval conduct.[67] One accusation levelled against Dönitz was when Hitler had designated him as head of state, the war continued. Following a discussion with Jodl, he explained why it was necessary to delay surrender, stating that had they capitulated too early, two million soldiers in the East would have fallen into Russian hands. Given the developing friction with Stalin's regime, this must have rung bells that some two million men would have been at the mercy of the Russians; 'having saved life on this scale it made Dunkirk look a very minor achievement'.[68] As a general impression, most of the prosecution charges in naval matters were well defended, as was Dönitz's continuation of the war for the safety of German troops. He could not understand why he had been indicted, a typical 'why me' question asked by many who believe they are genuinely

## 184   Major Blunders of the Second World War

innocent. He was a man used to being in command and confused as to why he was indicted. He questioned why the trial was prosecuting all organisations, which, he argued, involved a major proportion of the population, who would be criminalised. It was explained to him that the prosecutors were only after the leaders, but Dönitz had a valid point. During the Frick trial, when Gisevius had given witness about Göring's involvement in all the dirty dealings (especially Generals Blomberg and Fritsch), Dönitz told his medical visitor Gilbert that the witness should keep talking because it 'showed how the politicians got themselves in a hole and then expected the generals to pull them out'.[69] It was becoming a major battle between the military and political defendants, which the French prosecution tried to expose as non-sensical because they were all dedicated Nazis. Whether he was non-political or not could be regarded as an ongoing debate, with some claiming he was disingenuous, others he was politically naïve, and some accepting his claim.

Opinions were sharply divided both at the trial and long afterwards. The prosecutor Shawcross was especially vitriolic, referring to the sinking of the *Laconia* as brutal, even though the attacking U-boat had spent two days rescuing survivors and had been attacked during these efforts. Many have often queried as to whether the charge on count two was right in the first place. Telford Taylor and many others at the time and since have wondered whether he should have been acquitted.[70] Even in 1946 it was regarded by many as a matter of naval honour, and after the trial Dönitz and Raeder had a hundred or more British and American naval officers who deplored the Dönitz verdict.[71]

### Spandau then Freedom

When the trial finished seven prisoners remained in prison and were banned from speaking to one another, but they were soon allowed to chat casually a few months later while in the exercise yard. On 18 July they were moved to Spandau, a prison built in 1876 which immediately prior to the Second World War had housed those who dared to oppose Nazism. They were only known as numbers, Dönitz was known as number two, Raeder was number four, and they were given clothes once worn by concentration camp victims. Dönitz managed to draw closer to Speer as the trial had separated them, he was seen talking to Raeder, but it was known that they remained somewhat hostile. They were eventually allowed to look after their patches of garden where Dönitz specialised and became an expert in tomatoes. The U-boat association paid for his wife Ingeborg to visit him, but he heard she was suffering from a poor pension because he had owed his rank to Hitler, and that his house had been looted of his naval treasure by a British Colonel. Ingeborg worked as a nursing sister in Hamburg Hospital to help pay her way.

Apart from this they were cut off from the outside world and not allowed any news, though they were aware of the emerging Cold War and the Berlin airlift. In his considerable time for reflection, he still believed the war could have been won had he had enough U-boats, and a leaked British report supported his view.[72] He miscalculated his time for release because the prisoners had all believed the time spent in custody for the trial would be considered. Curiously his son-in-law told him that in a recent survey some 46 per cent of the public had a good view of him, and Dönitz wondered if Germans still saw him as their leader.

After his release he and his wife lived in an apartment, no longer a grand house, but it was convenient for U-boat reunions, and walks in the country. He also managed to have his pension raised to that of an admiral, making them more comfortable but not well off. He used his freedom to write an account of his life but, as with many others, it was full of self-justification, acknowledging he would have joined the resistance against the Nazis had he known then what he learnt later about the demonic policies, and distanced himself from the despised Himmler. This did not stop him criticising the Allies for demanding total surrender, and if they had not intended to partition Germany the war may well have stopped sooner. In May 1962, Ingeborg died, but Dönitz still enjoyed life with his family, and was a regular congregational member at his local church. In 1968 he wrote another volume called *My Changeful Life*, in which he turned his attack on the Nuremberg Trials. He died on 24 December 1980, aged 89. The Bonn Government refused a state funeral and there were to be no uniforms.

## 186  Major Blunders of the Second World War

### Dönitz, A Misjudgement or Not

To this day it is difficult to find on what grounds the guilty verdicts were based, not least because waging an aggressive war could hardly be considered a crime given the nature of human history, and Dönitz's role was at sea where behaviour had not been as outrageous as elsewhere. There were no clear indications for war crimes and insufficient evidence to say he ordered the shooting of survivors, and it was decided he had not been responsible for shooting the MTB crew.

Even Padfield, whose biography of Dönitz was far from being a hagiography, wrote that 'the judgement and sentence do not fit; they read like the result of an inept committee compromise'.[73] The Russians wanted him dead, the British, apart from the admiralty were probably happy with this, less can be speculated about American and French feelings, but it raises the possibility the verdict was possibly a compromise. The American Judge Biddle thought he should be acquitted, whereas his biographer Padfield, wrote that by today's evidence he would have been hanged. Dönitz would have been pleased when the historian J.F.C. Fuller said of the judgement that it was 'a flagrant travesty of justice resulting from hypocrisy'.[74] Then the British Sea Lord Admiral Lord Cunningham wrote in the *Sunday Times* that 'Karl Dönitz was probably the most dangerous enemy Britain had to face since de Ruyter [seventeenth century Dutch Admiral]…it was extremely fortunate for us his advice was so little heeded by his political leaders'.[75] Stephen Roskill in his official history wrote 'the small total number [of U-boats] available early in the year [1942], combined with diversions to unprofitable purposes, now seems to have been a decisive factor in the Atlantic battle'.[76] More recent German historians have been less kind to Dönitz, and Michael Salewski 'exposed Dönitz's total identification with the Nazi State'.[77]

Many feel the judgement more reflected Dönitz's apparent willingness to take over following Hitlers' death, but when asked by what he considered the legitimate head of state, and as a man accustomed to obedience, he could hardly have regarded this as a criminal order. He had told a medical psychologist that he was chosen because others were either dead or in disgrace. He may have felt important being given this charge, but that is common with many politicians and cannot be deemed as criminal. The charge that he should have surrendered promptly was countered by his wish and that of Jodl to save Germans from the Soviet onslaught, which may not have pleased the Russian judges, but would have rung the necessary bells with the Americans, French, and British. His association with the Nazis, he claimed, was purely naval, and he used their so-called ideals simply to booster public and military morale on the few public occasions he gave speeches. It may well have been that he was closer to the Party ethos than he claimed, but this accusation could be aimed not only at other military leaders not sent for trial, but much of the population. The Nazis had promised to restore Germany's rightful place amongst nations following the Versailles Treaty, at first accomplished without bloodshed, then successful wars all of which encouraged many ordinary Germans in their support of the Nazi regime. As the tide turned against them it became a matter of what must have felt like justifiable defence. Most people must have known about the concentration camps established as soon as Hitler took power, and the unforgivable persecution of Jews. Dönitz had a Jewish Vice-Admiral Rogge, but he probably had the unfortunate traditional anti-Jewish views. The knowledge of the bestial behaviour in concentration camps came to Dönitz, as to many others, as a horrific eye-opener. For many, including Dönitz it changed their views. It took these trials and the later Eichmann trial in the early 1960s to bring these horrors out into the open, yet anti-Semitism still exists. Overall, it appears that Dönitz may have suffered the usual prejudice, but he was not involved in the Holocaust, except by supporting the Nazi regime which millions of others did to their later regret.

However, he was found guilty of charges of waging aggressive war and war crimes. This casts serious doubt on the court's judgement. This charge implied than any senior officer who obeyed his government's instructions could be tried for this crime, amounting to thousands. More to the point the four prosecuting countries, Russia, Britain, France, and America all had a history of aggressive war and have had such wars since 1946.

# 188   Major Blunders of the Second World War

The *tu quoque* argument had been banned, as mentioned, not least because of the embarrassing bombing of civilians done by both sides, but much greater by the Western Allies even when it was no longer necessary. The Soviets had also carried out major massacres in Katyń following the Polish invasion. *Tu quoque* was banned on the grounds that because another did the same action does not justify the fact. The *tu quoque* issue is often seen as an *ad hominem* device such as 'I did this because you did the same thing', often interpreted as two wrongs do not make a right. It does not hold the same logic when in war both sides fought the same way, which could in theory make both sides guilty. Nevertheless, not using the *tu quoque* argument was a relief to the prosecution.

It is now widely accepted there was only one incident of a U-boat shooting survivors out of thousands of sinkings and doing so on Eck's own initiative or misunderstanding. It was also accepted that many U-boats rescued or helped survivors, they were doing this in the *Laconia* incident, which Dönitz supported until the U-boat was attacked by American bombers. Other U-boats suffered the same experience of being attacked one way or another while rescuing men in the water. The American Admiral Nimitz had made this crystal clear with his unquestionable support of Dönitz. It was also widely known that the British did not rescue when their submarines were operating, and they had armed some merchantmen not only with guns but depth charges making rescue out of the question; that is the nature of war. In terms of war crimes, the conduct of German U-boat commanders was the same as that of their enemies, but there were more recognised German attempts at rescuing survivors by U-boat commanders than their enemy. The whole concept of sinking merchantmen vessels is for most repugnant, but no more so than carpet bombing civilian cities to break the morale of the targeted population, in which any effort of saving survivors is impossible.

Sending Dönitz to prison for 10 years was the lightest sentence given to those found guilty of any of the indictments. For many it was a misjudgement given the facts raised during the trial. It tended to reflect a general distaste of a man who had been a danger to the enemies, which had been his job, that he was sympathetic to the Nazi causes for war, and he had taken over from Hitler. Given the circumstances of Nazi behaviour, the distaste for Nazi commanders in 1946 was perhaps understandable, but had Dönitz been judged by his naval enemies, he would have been released without charge. The Nuremberg Trial was unquestionably necessary but based on the banned *tu quoque* clause and the behaviour of many U-boat commanders it did not make sense, especially in the light of the *Laconia* incident. Passing judgement of guilty on Dönitz and his conduct of sea warfare was not just a misjudgement but reflected the primal desire for revenge.

# Final Observations on Case Studies

In the first chapter there were moments of sheer incompetence such as an American destroyer releasing an armed torpedo towards Roosevelt's battleship, and the time when a German pilot flew beyond German frontiers carrying top-secret documents. Such blunders occur in every sphere of human life, but this raises the question of incompetence in the training of personnel which is a misjudgement at the highest levels of command. It could be argued that in the emergency of war insufficient time could be giving for training men, but despite the current urgent needs for qualified doctors it would be morally wrong to ask a surgeon to perform a life and death operation until he or she had been fully tested and proved capable. It would be the same with a busy nurse asking the floor cleaner to take blood samples because the nurse was busy. To allow an untested surgeon to operate raises the question of misjudgement at a higher level, and for the nurse to ask a cleaning lady to carry out medical procedures is a misjudgement at the junior but professional level. Blunders are not always the result of incompetence; a chess player may give a critical piece away because he or she was over-tired or distracted by noise. A pilot may bomb the wrong area being distracted by bad weather, flak, and attacks by fighter pilots. Nevertheless, more often than not incompetence tends to show a degree of misjudgement at one level or another.

More often than not it can be difficult to pinpoint '*whatever happened and why*'. In the case of Rommel who seemed to know the British plans in detail, it was simply because the German and Italian Intelligence had broken the code, but the blame was not put on Colonel Fellers who was acting under command orders. However, it raised other questions at a higher level. First, when it was known that Rommel appeared to know his enemy's plans it must have raised some questions as to his possible source.

Sometimes rarely used languages were used in radio communications such as Welsh speakers. This did not work, and it needed deeper digging. First, whether it was necessary for such detailed information to be sent to George Marshal, and secondly, the assumption that the enemy could not break a code raises the issue of misjudgement, especially as it cost so many lives.

The attack on Bari resulting in the Allied gas stocks killing their own people was a series of misjudgements. Primarily it was poor administration of leaving such dangerous weapons open to attack and uncertain as to their whereabouts. This was more than a mistake or blunder, but an act of incompetence based on a misjudgement as to their potential extremely dangerous exposure. It was a politically and military dangerous area where not only was top secrecy required but constant vigilance was essential, and this was lacking. There were other spheres of incompetence in this episode, the assumption that the Luftwaffe was finished simply because they had lesser number of aircraft then the Allies, which amounted to a serious misjudgement in underestimating the enemy. This led to the assumption that it could not happen, and Bari port was lit up at night like a funfair.

There are occasions when a misjudgement is more than apparent. General Patton expending the lives of his own men to save a son-in-law was one of his more serious mistakes, and quite how he would have escaped serious censure without Eisenhower's support is questionable. The bombing of Monte Cassino caused more damage to the Allies and civilians than to the enemy, and this bombing raid assisted the Germans in prolonging their defence. It is difficult to ascertain how many in the top command agreed to this bombing attack, as many after the war tried to distance themselves from this life wasting misjudgement.

In exploring misjudgements, apart from acknowledging that such incidents are shared by most human beings, especially in times of crisis, there are some which remain contentious to this day. An early example in the first chapter was the occasion when the British Royal Navy was ordered to attack the French fleet at Mers-el-Kébir killing over a thousand French sailors. There are those who argue that it was brutal but

## 192  Major Blunders of the Second World War

necessary under the circumstances of the day. Others that it was a serious misjudgement killing Allied sailors, that it led to a breakdown between France and Britain, which has not been forgotten to this day, and when the French scuttled their ships in Toulon before German forces arrived, proved for some, but not all, that France was honourable. The debate of whether it was a misjudgement or not is unlikely to be resolved, and this writer tends to vacillate on this event.

The second chapter concerned the disaster of the raid on Dieppe, which was unquestionably a major misjudgement, costing many lives, and causing both military and political embarrassment. When the original Operation *Rutter* had been abandoned, it was undoubtedly the correct decision from the military perspective, and although it was conceived because of political demands, it was undeniably immoral to sacrifice men just to impress British allies. It appears that the main thrust of resurrecting the abandoned project falls to the misjudgement of Mountbatten, a man who once said, 'it is a curious thing, but a fact, that I have been right in everything I have done and said in my life'.[1] Even the highly respected historian Andrew Roberts described Mountbatten as a 'mendacious, intellectually limited hustler, whose negligence and incompetence resulted in many unnecessary deaths', and this view was reinforced by Mountbatten's official biographer, who wrote that Mountbatten's 'vanity, though child-like, was monstrous, his ambition unbridled. The truth in his hands was swiftly converted from what it was to what it should have been'.[2] The leading British military authorities of the day had no trust in Mountbatten's judgements, but his royal connections gave him full support from Churchill and the Americans. Mountbatten was undeniably central to the disaster, but the misjudgement elements had wider circumferences. The fact that he was supported because of his royal connections, this gave him too much leeway to 'do his own thing'. Even after the disaster, when the event had clearly indicated it was a major misjudgement, he was able to avoid blame. There were unbelievable misjudgements at planning level which Mountbatten tried to sweep under the carpet as a learning exercise for D-Day Normandy, which was too incredulous to be regarded as a rational explanation. This episode reflected the misjudgement of a man who did

# Final Observations on Case Studies 193

not have the military expertise and experience, and who should have been used in a diplomatic office in America, instead of being supported at the highest level in military operations beyond his ability, making the misjudgement widespread at the highest level.

The third chapter was not a life and death situation but created major problems for Britain just at the time when Nazi Germany was ringing alarm bells, and further mayhem during the war years. This involved a misjudgement at the highest levels of the country, the royal household, and the government. This was the critique of King Edward VIII who abdicated the throne, dividing the country and unsettling Britain with divided opinions. Although Britain was governed by elected politicians the assumed head of state is the constitutional monarchy, and their influence has always been deemed important albeit diminishing as time passes. Edward VIII, and as an ex-king, has been viewed by many as a traitor, and for many it was a relief that his brother George VI came to the throne.

This chapter queried the long-held belief that the ex-king was a traitor, concluding it would not have led to a legal court judgement against him, but his serious misjudgements created major problems and many unwanted issues. His personal behaviour with married women, his racist (including anti-Semitism) views, his attitudes towards other nationalities, his personal greed for money and status made him unfit for kingship.

As an ex-king because of his royal status these issues continued. His almost paranoid and continuous requests that his wife should be addressed as HRH, his demands for money, status and recognition pestered the government at a time when their attention was demanded elsewhere on the highly critical international stage. The royal family had a well-known Germanic background leading to a hurried change of names during the First World War, but with his ceaseless ill-considered social chatter, he made it clear he had some form of sympathy for Nazi Germany. Questions arose during the phoney war that he might have passed on secrets about the French defence; although probably not deliberate with his constant social chatting and somewhat dubious friends it may well have happened. The Nazi leadership appreciated his attitudes, and they may have seen

194    Major Blunders of the Second World War

him as a means of driving a wedge between Churchill and the public. His conduct in fleeing his military post would have meant a court martial for anyone else, and his meanderings in Spain and Portugal left question-marks over his sense of loyalty. Even in the relative obscurity of the Bahamas he was of some concern, not least with his demands for peace, with the British government concerned that his views might be possibly reverberating in America during their period of isolationism. His sense of defeatism was well-known, which Churchill had to warn him against, and the claim that bombing Britain would bring instant peace, sounded disloyal to his country suffering war while he lived the life of a playboy.

He may not have been defined as a traitor by the British legal system, but his behaviour throughout his life indicated he was in a continuous state of misjudgement. He had become a major embarrassment to his country, and because he was an ex-king it was a highly delicate situation for Churchill and the government of the day, which took up too much of their time during the crisis of war. The question was what to do with a royal loose cannon. His father George V and his private secretary Lascelles thought he was unfit for the crown, socially his wife Wallis Simpson was blamed, but such was the British unwritten constitution, the eldest son automatically became the next monarch.

Although Edward VIII and as an ex-king was a major misjudgement in himself, the next problem was how to deal with this issue. Misjudging a misjudgement is not unusual, but given the facts of the situation, although a hopeless conundrum, something firm had to be done.

Having him in Europe before and during the start of the Second World War was a mistake, putting him in the relative safety of the Bahamas was too close to America. The best place was at home in Britain where he may have witnessed the onslaught of the war first hand, which may have made him think twice, and where he could be closely monitored if not regulated. His brother King George VI feared his brother's popularity and would not agree, perhaps a misjudgement in itself. As noted in this chapter, perhaps Churchill was too kind in first supporting Edward during the abdication, and then treating him with kid gloves for the sake of protecting the royal family. A firmer hand was needed, perhaps placing him in a safe commonwealth country away from the European and American spheres of activity, such as a remote spot in New Zealand where he could be watched and regulated, while being given some minor post.

The final chapter explored the nature of the submarine (U-boat) warfare and the German Admiral Dönitz who was responsible for its operations and conduct. At the well-known Nuremberg Trial, of those found guilty he was given ten years in prison, the shortest period for those imprisoned, but finding him guilty has remained a contentious point at the time and ever since. It gave strength to the often-heard criticism that the trial was victors' judgement and underlined the hypocrisy of the victors. The question must be asked whether this was a serious misjudgement, both in terms of condemning a German admiral who was supported by his naval opposites in the enemy camp, and, in doing so, increased the slurs often cast upon the Nuremberg Trial. The question is whether Dönitz was condemned founded on wartime bigotry and a sense of revenge. It was found impossible to condemn him for being part of the Nazi conspiracy plan as he was commanding a light cruiser in faraway waters when these embryo plans were hatched. There was no evidence that he was associated with crimes against humanity, which left him answering his role for waging an aggressive war and war crimes. On waging an aggressive war this indictment could have included all senior officers who had been released from prison camps in their droves.

The hub for the prosecution boiled down to the conduct of the U-boat war, but also his association with the Nazi regime, and being selected by Hitler to replace him following his suicide. When Lemp sank the *Athenia* it was a commander's misjudgement not an order from Dönitz, and when Eck the U-boat commander machine-gunned survivors he admitted it was not under Dönitz's orders, and it was the only known incident of this type. The history of the U-boat is inundated with known examples of U-boats rescuing victims, in the *Laconia* incident it was done with Dönitz's full support, until an Allied bomber attacked the rescuing U-boat and survivors. One U-boat commander was invited to Britain in the postwar years in gratitude for his help. It took the American Admiral Nimitz to support Dönitz in arguing that the Allies had the same policy

## 196 Major Blunders of the Second World War

of not helping survivors in order to keep their submarines safe. It should also be noted there were more examples of U-boats helping survivors than in the British and American submarine forces. Given the known facts portrayed in this chapter, it appears that the German U-boat commanders were more chivalrous than their opponents, and accusing Dönitz of perpetrating war crimes made little sense. The main problem for Dönitz was his U-boat success, noted at the time by Churchill, and later naval historians recognised that had Dönitz had the number of U-boats he asked for, then the problems for the British Isles would have become dangerously serious. Carpet bombing was indiscriminate with no chance of helping survivors, whereas U-boat warfare could select targets and often came to the rescue. The wartime propaganda could be persuasive and lasted deep into the postwar years. It portrayed U-boats as villains and Allied bombers crews over enemy cities as striking back and doing their duty, and the efforts in U-boat commanders rescuing survivors was only known by those who lived to tell the tale, and not publicly broadcast, as U-boat commanders could not be seen as men of compassion. The hatred against the U-boat was well-known, and it is quite possible there was a sense of revenge at the trial, but notably not by Dönitz's naval opponents.

The *tu quoque* argument as noted in the relevant chapter was used by Nimitz, but the nature of war raised the question as to whether it was justified in an international court of war. If in a boxing match the two fighters administer illegal blows then both should be judged. While true that two wrongs do not make a right, those involved in the fight should not be passing judgement as both were potentially guilty. The normal criminal and even civil courts are right to be sceptical about *tu quoque*, but a war sometimes changes the logic of the traditional arguments, and this was underlined in the case of Dönitz and the U-boat war, raising the issue of hypocrisy.

A point of rancour was that Dönitz had taken over from Hitler, but again he had not tried to do this as with Himmler and Göring, and his and Jodl's idea of fighting on was not based on a ridiculous notion of an eventual victory, but to save lives of those facing Soviet fury. His association

Final Observations on Case Studies 197

with the Nazi regime, his knowledge of the sources of dockyard labour, his relationship with Speer, his knowledge of the horrors of the concentration camps were all raised. He was like too many in Europe probably leaning towards anti-Semitism, but a vice-admiral with a Jewish background witnessed that he had received Dönitz's protection. It was clear that as a person of the monarchical Wilhelmine era, brought up in the Prussian tradition of obedience and service to his country, he was not appreciated in accepting the Nazi regime. However, it had to be understood that he was single-minded and obsessed with playing his military role as a naval man, and he was personally and totally committed to having oversight of the U-boat war, little else caught his attention. At the time and since, many have thought that finding him guilty was a misjudgement, which indicated elements of victor's justice and revenge, which cast a shadow over an international trial which simply had to take place.

The unhappy nature of human misjudgement comes to light all too vividly and significantly in war, at the individual, national, and international level as can be seen in these selected case studies. The tragedy is that as humans we fail to recall the lessons of history.

# Notes

**Chapter 1**

1. Axelrod, A., *Patton* (London: Palgrave, 2006), p.1.
2. Axelrod, A., *Patton*, p.141.
3. Roberts, Andrew, *The Storm of War* (London: Allen Lane, 2009), p.305.
4. Roberts, Andrew, *The Storm of War*, p.514.
5. Axelrod, A., *Patton*, p.2.
6. Alanbrooke, Field Marshal Lord, *War Diaries 1939–45* (London: Weidenfeld & Nicolson, 2001), pp.360–1.
7. Hastings, Max, *All Hell Let Loose* (London: Harper, 2011), p.445.
8. Blumenson, M., *The Patton Papers* (New York: De Capro Press, 1998), p.663.
9. Blumenson, M., *The Patton Papers*, p.667.
10. Kershaw, A., *The Liberator* (London: Hutchinson, 2012), p.236.
11. Bradley, Omar, *A General's Life* (London: Sidgwick & Jackson, 1983), p.415.
12. Kershaw, A., *The Liberator*, p.234.
13. Kershaw, A., *The Liberator*, p.243.
14. Harper, G. & Tonkin-Covell, J., *The Battles of Monte Cassino* (Auckland: Allen & Unwin, 2013), p.7.
15. Detweiler, Burdick, Rohwer (eds), *German Military Studies WWII, Kesselring's remarks on Med Campaign 4 July 1948* Vol 14 (London: Garland, 1979), pp.3–4.
16. Harper, G. & Tonkin-Covell, J., *The Battles of Monte Cassino*, p.196.
17. Atkinson, R., *The Day of the Battle, The War in Sicily and Italy 1943–44* (London: Abacus, 2013), p.432.
18. Hodges, Richard, *History Today*, 'Tempting providence: The Bombing of Monte Cassino' (Volume 44, Issue 2, 1994).
19. Carver, Tom, *Where the Hell Have You Been?* (London: Short Books, 2009), p.144.
20. Alexander of Tunis, *The Alexander Memoirs, 1940–1945* (Barnsley, Frontline Books, 2010), pp.119–20.
21. Porch, Douglas, Hitler's Mediterranean Gamble: The North African and the Mediterranean Campaigns in World War II (London: Weidenfeld & Nicolson, 2004), p.522.
22. Westphal, Siegfried, *The German Army in the West* (London: Cassell, 1951), p.155.
23. Hodges, *History Today*, 'Tempting', p.246.
24. Senger und Etterlin, Frido von, *Neither Fear Nor Hope* (London: Macdonald, 1963), p.187.
25. Harper, G. & Tonkin-Covell, J., *The Battles of Monte Cassino*, p.35.
26. Ibid., p.36.
27. Hodges, *History Today*, 'Tempting', pp.246, ff.
28. Vassiltchikov, Maries, *The Berlin Diaries 1939–45* (London: Pimlico, 1999), p.151.

## Notes    199

29. *The Times*, 20 April 1944, p.3.
30. Kesselring, Albert, *The Memoirs of Field-Marshal Kesselring* (London: William Kimber, 1953), p.195.
31. Senger und Etterlin, Frido von, *Neither Fear Nor Hope*, p.202.
32. Harper, G. & Tonkin-Covell, J., *The Battles of Monte Cassino*, p.54.
33. Atkinson, R., *The Day of the Battle, The War in Sicily and Italy 1943–44*, p.439.
34. Harper, G. & Tonkin-Covell, J., *The Battles of Monte Cassino*, p.64.
35. Ellis, John, *Cassino: The Hollow Victory* (London: Sphere Books, 1985), p.406.
36. Hodges, *History Today*, 'Tempting'.
37. Harper, G. & Tonkin-Covell, J., *The Battles of Monte Cassino*, pp.52–3.
38. Salmaggi, C. & Pallavisini, A., *2194 Days of War – Chronology* (Milan: Galley Press, 1977), p.498.
39. Harper, G. & Tonkin-Covell, J., *The Battles of Monte Cassino*, p.149.
40. Ibid., p.78.
41. Ellis, John, *Cassino: The Hollow Victory*, p.20.
42. Harper, G. & Tonkin-Covell, J., *The Battles of Monte Cassino*, p.144.
43. Keegan, J., *The Second World War* (London: Arrow Books, 1990), p.359. Stated by Montgomery and quoted in Harper, G. & Tonkin-Covell, J., *The Battles of Monte Cassino*, p.105. Alexander and Wilson did not get on, Harper, G. & Tonkin-Covell, J., *The Battles of Monte Cassino*, p.110.
44. Ellis, John, *Cassino: The Hollow Victory*, p.475.
45. Weinberg, Gerhard, *A World at Arms* (Cambridge: CUP, 1994), p.145.
46. Beevor, Antony, *The Second World War* (London: Weidenfeld & Nicolson, 2012), p.124.
47. Arthur, Max, *Lost Voices of the Royal Navy* (London: Hodder, 2005), p.256.
48. Weinberg, Gerhard, *A World at Arms*, p.145.
49. Ibid., p.146.
50. Burleigh, Michael, *Moral Combat* (London: Harper Press, 2010), p.171.
51. Beevor, Antony, *The Second World War*, p.125.
52. Hastings, Max, *All Hell Let Loose*, p.187.
53. Forczyk, Robert, *We March Against England: Operation Sea Lion, 1940–41* (Oxford: Osprey Publishing, 2016), p.36.
54. Muggeridge, Malcolm (ed.), *Ciano's Diary* (London: Heinemann, 1947), p.274.
55. See Forczyk, Robert, *We March Against England*, pp.35–6.
56. Forczyk, Robert, *We March Against England*, p.36
57. Mallet, Alfred, *Pierre Laval* (Paris, 1954), p.217 note.
58. See Michel, Henri (translated by D. Parmée) *The Second World War* (London: Andre Deutsch, 1975), p.150.
59. Thomas, R.T., *Britain and Vichy: The Dilemma of Anglo-French Relations 1940–1942* (London: Macmillan, 1979), p.171.
60. *Psychological Medicine*. 38(10): 1419–1426, October 2008.
61. *Alan Brooke's Diary*, p.251.
62. Sangster, Andrew, *Alan Brooke: Churchill's Right-Hand Critic* (Oxford: Casemate, 2020), pp.76–7.
63. Overy, Richard, *The Bombing War: Europe 1939–1945* (London: Allen Lane, 2013), p.33.
64. Infield, Glen, *Disaster at Bari* (New York: Bantam, 1988), pp.29–30.
65. Atkinson, R., *The Day of the Battle: The War in Sicily and Italy 1943–44*, p.34
66. Ibid., p.340.

## 200 Major Blunders of the Second World War

67. Infield, Glen, *Disaster at Bari*, p.14.
68. Ibid., p.14.
69. Ibid., p.135.
70. KNA-HW/1/3715-p.3.
71. KNA-18/4/1945-HW/1/3715-pp.1–2.
72. Beevor, Antony, *The Second World War*, p.534
73. Infield, Glen, *Disaster at Bari*, p.194.
74. Ibid., p.207.
75. Ibid., p.205.
76. Ibid., p.237.
77. Glen Infield.

**Chapter 2**
1. Atkin, Ronald, *Dieppe 1942: The Jubilee Disaster* (London: Book Club Associates, 1980) and Bishop, Patrick, *Operation Jubilee, Dieppe 1942: The Folly and the Sacrifice* (London: Penguin Books, 2022).
2. Bradley, Omar, *A General's Life*, p.159.
3. Aspinall-Oglander, Cecil, *Roger Keyes* (London: Hogarth, 1951), p.383.
4. Beevor, Antony, *The Second World War*, p.339.
5. Aspinall-Oglander, Cecil, *Roger Keyes*, p.406
6. Ziegler, Philip, *Mountbatten: The Official Biography* (London: Collins, 1985), p.168.
7. Alanbrooke, Lord, *War Diaries 1939–45*, p.236.
8. Alanbrooke, Lord, *War Diaries 1939–45*, p.357.
9. Aspinall-Oglander, Cecil, *Roger Keyes*, p.408.
10. Alanbrooke, Lord, *War Diaries 1939–45*, p.536.
11. Lownie, Andrew, *The Mountbattens: Their Lives and Loves* (London: Blink Publishing, 2020) p.139.
12. Davies, Norman, *No Simple Victory* (London: Viking, 2006), p.102.
13. Hastings, Max, *Catastrophe* (London: William Collins, 2013), p.326.
14. Gilbert, Martin, *Second World War* (London: Weidenfeld & Nicolson, 1989), p.354.
15. Quoted in Lownie, Andrew, *The Mountbattens*, p.143.
16. Villa, Brian Loring, *Unauthorized Action* (Oxford: OUP, 1989), p.4.
17. Bradley, Omar, *A General's Life*, p.230
18. Ibid., p.230.
19. Ibid., p.159.
20. Villa, B.L., *Unauthorized Action*, p.94.
21. Ziegler, Philip, *Mountbatten*, p.195.
22. Alanbrooke, Lord, *War Diaries 1939–45*, p.357.
23. Aspinall-Oglander, Cecil, *Roger Keyes*, p.383.
24. Alanbrooke, Lord, *War Diaries 1939–45*, p.275.
25. Ibid., p.309 and p.317.
26. Ibid., p.322.
27. Villa, B.L., *Unauthorized Action*, p.20.
28. Knight, Nigel, *Churchill: The Greatest Briton Unmasked* (Cincinnati; D & C, 2009), p.217.
29. See Ziegler, Philip, *Mountbatten*, p.195.
30. Liddell Hart Centre, King's College London, Ismay Papers. Ismay: 2/3/254a.
31. Alanbrooke, Lord, *War Diaries 1939–45*: 2/3/256 and 2/3/260.

## Notes   201

32. Villa, B.L., *Unauthorized Action*, p.28.
33. Ibid., p.206.
34. Ibid., p.229.
35. Ziegler, Philip, *Mountbatten*, p.162
36. Ibid., p.165.
37. Villa, B.L., *Unauthorized Action*, p.187.
38. Ibid., p.200.
39. Picknett, Prince, Prior, Brydon, *War of the Windsors* (London: Mainstream, 2002), p.182.
40. Villa, B.L., *Unauthorized Action*, p.210.
41. Ibid., p.240.
42. Hough, Richard, *Mountbatten: Hero of Our Time* (London: Weidenfeld & Nicolson, 1980), p.157.
43. Roberts, Andrew, *The Storm of War*, p.319.
44. Roberts, Andrew, *Eminent Churchillians* (London: Weidenfeld & Nicolson, 1994), p.133.
45. Picknett et al., *War of the Windsors*, p.43.
46. Roberts, Andrew, *Eminent Churchillians*, p.55.
47. Ziegler, *Mountbatten*, p.701.
48. Ibid., p.215.
49. Quoted Hastings, Max, *All Hell Let Loose*, p.656.
50. Davies, Norman, *No Simple Victory*, p.102.

### Chapter 3

1. See Ziegler, Philip, *King Edward VIII* (London: Harper Press, 2012), p.31.
2. Ibid., p.199.
3. See Pasternak, Anna, *The American Duchess: The Real Wallis Simpson* (London: William Collins, 2020), p.15.
4. Godfrey, Rupert (ed.), *Letters from a Prince: Edward to Mrs Freda Dudley War* (London: Little Brown & Co, 1998).
5. Ziegler, Philip, *King Edward VIII*, p.139.
6. Picknett et al., *War of the Windsors*, p.63.
7. Lascelles, Sir Alan (ed. Duff Hart-Davis) *King's Counsellor* (London: Weidenfeld & Nicolson, 2006), p.104.
8. Ibid., p.105.
9. Ibid., p.109.
10. Ibid., p.110.
11. Shawcross, William, *Queen Elizabeth The Queen Mother: The Official Biography* (London: Macmillan, 2009), p.358.
12. See Pasternak, Anna, *The American Duchess*.
13. See Pasternak, Anna, *The American Duchess*, p.xvii.
14. Bouverie, Tim, *Appeasing Hitler* (London: The Bodley Press, 2019) pp.108–9.
15. Shawcross, William, *Queen Elizabeth*, p.385.
16. See Picknett et al., *War of the Windsors*, pp.57–8.
17. Ziegler, Philip, *King Edward VIII*, p.338.
18. See Pasternak, Anna, *The American Duchess*.
19. See Bouverie, Tim, *Appeasing Hitler*, p.118.
20. Shawcross, William, *Queen Elizabeth*, p.423.
21. See Ziegler, Philip, *King Edward VIII*, p.382.

## 202 Major Blunders of the Second World War

22. Shawcross, William, *Queen Elizabeth*, pp.358–9.
23. See Lownie, Andrew, *Traitor King* (London: Blink Publishing, 2021), p.15.
24. Shawcross, William, *Queen Elizabeth*, p.366.
25. Ziegler, Philip, *King Edward VIII*, p.392.
26. Lownie, Andrew, *Traitor King*, p.63.
27. Ibid., p.76.
28. Shawcross, William, *Queen Elizabeth*, p.494.
29. Pasternak, Anna, *The American Duchess*, p.211.
30. Weinberg, Gerhard, *A World at Arms*, pp.143–4.
31. Ibid., p.144.
32. Picknett et al, *War of the Windsors*, p.154.
33. See Costello, John, *Mask of Treachery* (New York: William Morrow & Co, 1988), p.452.
34. See Allen, Martin, *Hidden Agenda: How the Duke of Windsor Betrayed the Allies* (London: Macmillan, 2000).
35. Lownie, Andrew, *Traitor King*, p.96.
36. See Ibid., p.112.
37. Ibid., p.121.
38. Michel, Henri, *The Second World War*, pp.147–8.
39. Ziegler, Philip, *King Edward VIII*, p.425.
40. Ibid., p.426.
41. Ibid., p.431.
42. Ibid., p.456.
43. Taylor, Fred (ed.), *The Goebbels Diaries, 1939–41* (London: Hamish Hamilton, 1982), p.34.
44. Ibid., p.345.
45. Pasternak, Anna, *The American Duchess*, p.232.
46. Ziegler, Philip, *King Edward VIII*, p.469.
47. *New York Times*, 16 April 1951, and also quoted in Lownie, Andrew, *Traitor King*, p.295.
48. Pasternak, Anna, *The American Duchess*, p.255.
49. Lownie, Andrew, *Traitor King*, p.372.

### Chapter 4

1. Padfield, Peter, *Dönitz: The Last Führer* (London: Harper & Row, 1984).
2. Werner, Herbert A., *Iron Coffins: A U-Boat Commander's War 1939–1945* (London: Cassell Military Paperbacks, 1999).
3. Ibid., p.42.
4. Ibid., p.43.
5. Ibid., p.280.
6. Ibid., p.66.
7. Ibid., p.167.
8. Ibid., p.158.
9. Ibid., p.149.
10. Ibid., p.309.
11. Ibid., p.309.
12. See Edwards, Bernard, *Dönitz and the Wolf Packs* (Barnsley: Pen & Sword, 2014), p.10.
13. Ibid., p.16.
14. Hoyt, Edwin P., *U-boats: A Pictorial History* (London: Stanley Paul and Co. Ltd, 1987), p.2.
15. Ibid., p.6.

# Notes 203

16. See Ibid., p.21.
17. Hoyt, Edwin P., *U-boats*, p.24.
18. Quoted in Edwards, Bernard, *Dönitz and the Wolf Packs*, pp.19–20.
19. Hoyt, Edwin P., *U-boats*, p.96.
20. Ibid., pp.191–2.
21. See Ibid., p.200.
22. See Ibid., p.75.
23. Kaplan, P., Currie, J., *Wolfpack U-boats at War 1939–1945* (London: Aurum Press, 1999), p.7.
24. Ibid., p.219.
25. See Ibid., p.219.
26. See Showell Mallman, Jak (Foreword writer), *Führer Conferences on Naval Affairs 1939–1945* (London: Chatham Publishing, 1990), p.57.
27. Grossmith, Frederick, *The Sinking of the Laconia* (Stamford: Paul Watkins, 1994), p.16.
28. Duffy, James, *The Sinking of the Laconia and the U-boat War* (London: Nebraska Press, 2013), p.5.
29. Showell Mallman, Jak, *Führer Conferences on Naval Affairs*, p.39.
30. Taylor, Fred (ed.), *The Goebbels Diaries, 1939–41*, p.25.
31. McLoughin & Gibb, *One Common Enemy* (London: National Maritime Museum, 2006), p.77.
32. Quoted in Duffy, James, *The Sinking of the Laconia and the U-boat War*, p.5.
33. Mentioned in Steinhilper, Ulrich, *Spitfire on my Tail* (Bromley: Independent Books, 1989).
34. Quoted in Duffy, James, *The Sinking of the Laconia and the U-boat War*, p.11.
35. Showell Mallman, Jak, *Führer Conferences on Naval Affairs*, p.39.
36. Showell Mallman Jak, *Führer Conferences on Naval Affairs*, pp.51–2.
37. *Life Magazine*, 16 October 1939.
38. Grossmith, Fred, *The Sinking of the Laconia*.
39. McLoughin & Gibb, *One Common Enemy*, p.77.
40. Duffy, James, *The Sinking of the Laconia and the U-boat War*, p.85.
41. Grossmith, Fred, *The Sinking of the Laconia*, p.107.
42. Quoted in Duffy, James, *The Sinking of the Laconia and the U-boat War*, p.81.
43. McLoughin & Gibb, *One Common Enemy*, p.197.
44. Edwards, Bernard, *Dönitz and the Wolf Packs*, p.20.
45. Padfield, *Dönitz: The Last Führer*, p.7.
46. Ibid., p.92.
47. Quoted in Ibid., p.125.
48. Quoted in Ibid., p.176.
49. Ibid., p.227.
50. Nuremberg Trial Manuscript, 9 May 1946.
51. See Padfield, *Dönitz: The Last Führer*, p.301.
52. Quoted in Padfield, *Dönitz: The Last Führer*, p.435.
53. Goldensohn, Leon, edited by Robert Gellately, *The Nuremberg Interviews* (London: Pimlico, 2007), p.3.
54. Taylor, Telford, *The Anatomy of the Nuremberg Trials: A Personal Memoir* (New York: Alfred Knopf, 1992), p.86.
55. Nuremberg Trial Manuscript, 9 May 1946.
56. Ibid.

# 204 Major Blunders of the Second World War

57. Ibid.
58. Ibid.
59. Ibid.
60. Ibid.
61. Ibid.
62. Ibid.
63. Ibid.
64. Nuremberg Trial Manuscript, 14 May 1946.
65. Ibid.
66. Nuremberg Trial Manuscript, 9 May 1946.
67. Neitzel, Sönke (ed.), *Tapping Hitler's Generals: Transcripts of Secret Conversations 1942–45* (Barnsley, Frontline Books, 2007), pp.153–8.
68. Tusa, Ann and Tusa, John, *The Nuremberg Trial* (London: BBC Books, 1995), p.353.
69. Gilbert, G.M., *Nuremberg Diary* (New York: Da Capo Press, 1995), p.296.
70. Taylor, Telford, *The Anatomy of the Nuremberg Trials*, p.631.
71. Neave, Airey, *Nuremberg* (London: Biteback Publishing, 2021) p.221.
72. See Padfield, *Dönitz: The Last Führer*, pp.473–4.
73. Ibid., p.445.
74. Ibid., p.484.
75. *Sunday Times*, 25 January 1959.
76. Padfield, *Dönitz: The Last Führer*, p.484.
77. Ibid., p.486.

### Final Observations on Case Studies
1. Hough, Richard, *Mountbatten*, p.157.
2. Ziegler, Philip, *Mountbatten*, p.701.

# Bibliography

**Diaries, Memoirs**

Alanbrooke Field Marshal Lord, *War Diaries 1939–45* (London: Weidenfeld & Nicolson, 2001)

Alexander Earl of Tunis, *The Alexander Memoirs 1940–1945* (London: Frontline Books, 2010)

Arthur Max, *Lost Voices of the Royal Navy* (London: Hodder, 2005)

Blumenson M *The Patton Papers* (New York: De Capro Press, 1998)

Bradley Omar, *A General's Life* (London: Sidgwick & Jackson, 1983)

Gilbert, G. M. *Nuremberg Diary* (New York: Da Capo Press, 1995)

Godfrey, Rupert (Ed), *Letters from a Prince: Edward to Mrs Freda Dudley War* (London: Little Brown & Co, 1998)

Goldensohn, Leon, edited by Robert Gellately. *The Nuremberg Interviews* (London: Pimlico, 2007)

Kesselring Albert, *The Memoirs of Field-Marshal Kesselring* (London: William Kimber, 1953)

Lascelles Sir Alan (Ed. Duff Hart-Davis) *King's Counsellor* (London: Weidenfeld & Nicolson, 2006)

Muggeridge Malcolm (Ed), *Ciano's Diary* (London: Heinemann, 1947)

Senger von und Etterlin, *Neither Fear nor Hope* (London: Macdonald, 1963)

Showell Mallman Jak, (Forward writer) *Führer Conferences on Naval Affairs 1939–1945* (London: Chatham Publishing, 1990)

Steinhilper, *Ulrich, Spitfire on my Tail* (Bromley: Independent Books, 1989)

Taylor Fred Ed., *The Goebbels Diaries,1939–41* (London: Hamish Hamilton, 1982)

Taylor, Telford. *The Anatomy of the Nuremberg Trials: A Personal Memoir* (New York: Alfred Knopf, 1992) p.86.

Vassiltchikov Maries, *The Berlin Diaries 1939–45* (London: Pimlico, 1999)

Werner, Herbert A, *Iron Coffins, A U-Boat Commander's War 1939–1945* (London: Cassell Military Paperbacks, 1999)

Westphal Siegfried, *The German Army in the West* (London: Cassell, 1951)

**Cited Publications**

Allen Martin, *Hidden Agenda: How the Duke of Windsor Betrayed the Allies* (London: Macmillan, 2000)

Atkin, Ronald, *Dieppe 1942, The Jubilee Disaster* (London: Book Club Associates, 1980

Atkinson R, *The Day of the Battle, The War in Sicily and Italy 1943–44* (London: Abacus, 2013)

Aspinall-Oglander Cecil, *Roger Keyes* (London: Hogarth,1951)

Axelrod A, *Patton* (London: Palgrave, 2006)

Beevor Anthony, *The Second World War* (London: Weidenfeld & Nicolson, 2012)

Bishop, Patrick, *Operation Jubilee, Dieppe 1942: The Folly and the Sacrifice* (London: Penguin Books, 2022)

## 206  Major Blunders of the Second World War

Bouverie Tim, *Appeasing Hitler* (London: The Bodley Press, 2019)

Burleigh, Michael, *Moral Combat* (London: Harper Press, 2010)

Carver Tom, *Where the Hell have you Been?* (London: Short books, 2009)

Costello, John, *Mask of Treachery* (New York: William Morrow & Co, 1988)

Davies Norman, *No Simple Victory* (London: Viking, 2006)

Duffy James, *The Sinking of the Laconia and the U-boat War* (London: Nebraska Press, 2013)

Edwards, Bernard, *Dönitz and the Wolf Packs* (Barnsley: Pen & Sword, 2014)

Ellis John, *Cassino: The Hollow Victory* (London: Sphere Books, 1985)

Forczyk Robert, *We March Against England, Operation Sea Lion, 1940–41* (Oxford: Osprey Publishing, 2016)

Gilbert Martin, *Second World War* (London: Weidenfeld & Nicolson, 1989)

Grossmith Frederick, *The Sinking of the Laconia* (Stamford: Paul Watkins, 1994)

Harper G &Tonkin-Covell J, *The Battles of Monte Cassino* (Auckland: Allen & Unwin, 2013)

Hastings Max, *All Hell Let Loose* (London: Harper, 2011)

Hastings Max, *Catastrophe* (London: William Collins, 2013)

Hough A Richard, *Mountbatten: Hero of our Time* (London: Weidenfeld & Nicolson, 1980)

Hoyt, Edwin P., *U-boats, A Pictorial History* (London: Stanley Paul and Co. Ltd, 1987)

Infield, Glen, *Disaster at Bari* (New York: Bantam, 1988

Kaplan P, Currie J, *Wolfpack U-boats at War 1939–1945* (London: Aurum Press, 1999)

Keegan J, *The Second World War* (London: Arrow Books, 1990)

Kershaw A, *The Liberator* (London: Hutchinson, 2012)

Knight, Nigel, *Churchill, The Greatest Briton Unmasked* (Cincinnati; D & C, 2009)

Lownie, Andrew, *The Mountbattens, Their Lives and Loves* (London: Blink Publishing, 2020)

Lownie Andrew, *Traitor King* (London: Blink Publishing, 2021)

Mallet Alfred, *Pierre Laval* (Paris, 1954)

McLoughin and Gibb, *One Common Enemy* (London: National Maritime Museum, 2006)

Michel Henri (translated by D Parmée) *The Second World War* (London: Andre Deutsch, 1975)

Neave, Airey. *Nuremberg.* (London: Biteback Publishing, 2021)

Neitzel, Sönke (ed.). *Tapping Hitler's Generals: Transcripts of Secret Conversations 1942–45.* (Barnsley, Frontline Books, 2007)

Overy, Richard, *The Bombing War, Europe 1939–1945* (London: Allen Lane, 2013)

Padfield, Peter, *Dönitz, The Last Führer* (London: Harper & Row, 1984)

Pasternak Anna, *The American Duchess, The Real Wallis Simpson* (London: William Collins, 2020)

Picknett, Prince, Prior, Brydon, *War of the Windsors* (London: Mainstream, 2002)

Porch Douglas, *Hitler's Mediterranean Gamble* (London: Weidenfeld & Nicolson, 2004)

Roberts Andrew, *Eminent Churchillians* (London: Weidenfeld & Nicolson, 1994)

Roberts Andrew, *The Storm of War* (London: Allen Lane, 2009)

Salmaggi C & Paallavisini A, *2194 Days of War – Chronology* (Milan: Galley Press, 1977)

Sangster, Andrew, *Alan Brooke: Churchill's Right-Hand Critic* (Oxford: Casemate, 2020)

Shawcross William, *Queen Elizabeth, The Queen Mother, The Official Biography* (London: Macmillan, 2009)

Thomas *RT, Britain and Vichy, The Dilemma of Anglo-French Relations 1940–1942* (London: Macmillan, 1979)

Tusa, Ann and John Tusa. *The Nuremberg Trial* (London: BBC Books, 1995)

Villa L Brian, *Unauthorised Action* (Oxford: OUP, 1989)

Weinberg, Gerhard, A World at Arms (Cambridge: CUP, 1994)

Bibliography 207

Ziegler, Philip, *Mountbatten, The Official Biography* (London: Collins, 1985)
Ziegler Philip, *King Edward VIII* (London: Harper Press, 2012)

**Newspapers**
*The Times*, 20 April 20, 1944.
*New York Times*, 16 April 1951.
*Sunday Times*, 25 January 1959.
*Life Magazine*, 16 October 1939.

**Articles**
*Psychological Medicine.* 38(10): 1419–1426, October 2008
Hodges Richard, *History Today*, 'Tempting providence: The Bombing of Monte Cassino' (Volume 44, Issue 2, 1994.

**Primary Sources**
Kew National Archives: KNA-HW/1/3715-p.3
KNA-18/4/1945-HW/1/3715-pp.1-2
Liddell Hart Centre, King's College London, Ismay Papers. Ismay: 2/3/254a
Nuremberg Trial Manuscripts, 9 May 1946. 14 May 1946

# Index

Albert, Prince 82
Alexander, Field Marshal Lord 13, 14, 17, 18, 198, 199
Alexander, Lieutenant Colonel Stewart 35
*Athenia* 137, 145, 148, 162, 163, 195

Baldwin, Prime Minister 93, 94, 96, 100, 101, 102, 103, 109
Baum, Captain Abraham 10, 11
Beaton, Cecil 100
Beaverbrook, Lord 49, 60, 61, 100, 104
Bedaux, Charles 103, 107, 108, 111, 112
Bohmler, Major Rudolf 16
Bradley, General Omar 9, 11, 39, 63, 198, 200
Brooke, General Alan 6, 9, 30, 39, 41, 42, 49, 50, 51, 53, 55, 63, 64, 65, 66, 67, 68, 70, 73, 74, 75, 76, 199

Canaris, Admiral Wilhelm 158, 169
Channon, Chips 100, 106
Churchill
  and Dieppe Raid 38, 39, 53, 55, 62, 66, 67, 73, 74, 77
  and Edward VIII 100, 102, 114, 116, 117, 120, 122
  and Monte Cassino 14, 17
  and sinking French Fleet 22, 23
  on U-boat warfare 136, 137, 141, 147
  silence on gas incident 37
Ciano, Italian Foreign Minister 5, 23, 199
Clark, General Mark 7, 8, 13, 16, 17
Coningham, Sir Arthur 32
*Courageous*, HMS 162
Crerar, General Harry 50, 51, 69
Cunningham, Admiral 25, 186

Darlan, Admiral 21, 22, 23, 165
de Gaulle, Charles 23, 24, 25, 26, 124
Dieppe Battle 57
Donahue, Jimmy 124
Dönitz, Admiral Karl 132, 136, 137, 138, 139, 140, 141, 152, 153
  and the Nazis 170, 171, 172, 175, 178, 180, 182
  as British PoW, WWI 157
  character 161, 162, 163, 165, 171, 174
  early life 155, 156, 157
  head of government 172, 173
  his attitudes 162, 166, 167, 168, 169, 171, 174, 177
  his work 160, 163, 165, 168, 169
  interbellum years 158, 159
  meets Mussolini 169
  on trial 173, 174, 175, 176, 177, 178, 179, 180, 181, 182, 184
  postwar 185
Dönitz, Ingeborg 156, 166, 185
Dresky, Hans-Wilhelm von 138, 150
Duke, *see* Edward VIII

Eck, Heinz Wilhelm 145, 148, 149, 170, 176, 177, 188, 195
Eden, Anthony 72, 114, 125, 127
Edward VII 83, 84, 102
Edward VIII
  and his Royal Family 92
  character 89, 92, 93, 104, 105, 118, 119, 121, 122
  company he kept 103, 104, 112, 118
  early life 88
  his views 91, 98, 105
  indiscretions 99, 101, 103, 104, 105, 106, 107, 109, 111, 112, 115, 116, 120, 123, 124, 125

## Index 209

misbehaviour 89, 90, 92, 94, 96, 102
political blunders 107, 108, 114, 119, 120
racialism 91, 118, 127
royal background 81, 82, 83, 84, 85, 86, 87
views on 94, 100, 101, 103
Eisenhower, General Dwight 11, 12, 34, 48, 173, 191
Elizabeth, wife of George VI 96, 99, 110, 122
*Emden* 159, 175
Enigma machine 57, 139, 143, 164, 168
Ex-king, *see* Edward VIII

Fellers, Colonel Bonner Frank 3, 4, 190
Freyberg, General 13, 14, 17
Friedeberg, Admiral von 173
Furness, Thelma 96

Gamelin, French Commander 6, 7
Geneva protocol, on gas 29
Gensoul, Admiral 20, 21
George, Duke of Kent 93, 98, 100, 114, 120
George V 84, 85, 86, 87, 88, 94, 96, 98, 99
George VI 49, 54, 70, 87, 92, 96, 99, 100, 101, 102, 105, 109, 110, 112, 118, 121, 125, 193, 194
Godt, Admiral 180, 182
Goebbels, Joseph 119, 137, 138, 146, 162, 171, 173, 202
Göring, Hermann 5, 107, 118, 169, 170, 172, 173, 174, 179, 184, 196
Gort, Lord 6, 112
*Greer*, USS 147

Hague Declaration, on gas 29
Harris, Bomber 43, 58
Hartenstein, Werner 151, 152, 153, 165, 177
Henry, Duke of Gloucester 98, 100
Hessler, Captain Günter 180, 182
Himmler, Heinrich 2, 28, 170, 172, 173, 185, 196
Hitler
and U-boats 141, 163, 164

and use of gas 34, 35
meets the Windsors 107
Hoare, Samuel 24, 111
Hoenmanns, Major Erich 4
Holland, Captain Cedric 20, 21
Hughes-Hallett, Captain John 44, 69, 71
Huntziger, General 24

Ismay, General 54, 66, 67, 68, 73, 77, 200

Jardine, Reverend Anderson 104
Jodl, General 5, 172, 173, 183, 187, 196
*John Harvey*, SS 33, 35
Juin, General 13, 17

Kesselring, Field Marshal 5, 13, 14, 15, 16, 17, 18, 31, 32, 37, 48, 52, 163, 167, 169, 171, 198
Keyes, Sir Roger 6, 41, 49, 70, 200
King, Admiral 3, 74
Knowles, Captain Elwin 33
Kranzbühler, Otto 174, 176, 177, 178, 180

*Laconia*, RMS 145, 146, 151, 153, 154, 165, 177, 182, 184, 188, 189, 195, 203
Lang, Archbishop Cosmo 100
Lascelles, Tommy 93, 94, 122, 194, 201
Laval, Pierre 22, 24, 25, 199
Leigh-Mallory, RAF Air Vice-Marshal 52, 54, 56, 69
Lemp, Fritz-Julius 137, 145, 162, 163, 164, 195
Leopold III, King of Belgium 5, 6
Ley, Robert 107
*Llandovery Castle*, HMHS 149, 170
Lloyd George 86
London Protocol 135, 176
*Lusitania*, RMS 134, 146, 156

Mackenzie King, Canadian PM 50, 69
Maisky, Ivan, Russian Ambassador in London 44
Marshall, George 3, 11, 40
Maxwell-Fyfe, British Prosecutor 179, 180
McNaughton, General Andrew 50, 67, 69
Mechelen incident 4
Mers-el-Kébir, sinking the French fleet 19

## 210  Major Blunders of the Second World War

Metcalfe, Major Edward Dudley 104,
110, 113
Mitford, Diana 99
Moehle, Captain Karl 176, 182
Molotov, Soviet Foreign Minister 42
Monckton, Walter 110, 112, 117
Monte Cassino battle 12
Montgomery, Field Marshal 7, 8, 9, 48,
51, 52, 53, 54, 56, 61, 63, 67, 69, 70, 72,
173, 199
Mosley, Sir Oswald 99, 104, 106
Mountbatten, Louis
character 53, 59, 61, 64, 67, 69, 70, 71
his royal reputation 48, 49, 52, 70,
72, 75
views on 41, 49, 65, 71, 72
Mussolini, Benito 5, 28, 31, 39, 48, 101,
106, 125, 133, 158, 167, 169, 170, 171

Nicholas II, Tsar 84, 86
Nimitz, Admiral 176, 182, 188, 195, 196
Nye, General Archibald 68, 76

Oakes, Sir Harry 118, 120
Operation Barbarossa 137
Operation Catapult 20, 22, 23, 25, 26
Operation Husky 33
Operation Jubilee 55, 56, 64, 65, 67
Operation Rutter 46, 47, 48, 49, 53, 54
Operation Sledgehammer 40, 41, 42, 48
Operation Torch 55, 75
Oster, Colonel Hans 6

Paget, General 69
Patton, General George 8, 9, 10, 11, 12,
48, 149, 191, 198
Pearl Harbor 164
Pétain, Marshal 22, 23, 24, 25
Portal, Air Marshal 58, 65
Porton Down 30, 35
Pound, Admiral Dudley 41, 65
Prien, Günther 138, 150, 162
Pug, *see* Ismay, General

Queen Elizabeth II 125

Raeder, Admiral 50, 141, 142, 159, 160,
161, 163, 165, 166, 167, 181, 184, 185

Ramsay, Admiral 45, 55, 69
Reinberger, Major Helmuth 5
Ribbentrop, German Ambassador 23, 95,
97, 103, 106, 113, 119
Richthofen, Manfred von 32, 33
Rogge, Vice-Admiral Bernhard 183, 187
Rommel, Field Marshal 1, 3, 4, 8, 73, 190
Roosevelt, President xiii, 1, 2, 3, 15, 22,
34, 39, 40, 49, 70, 74, 75, 78, 119, 147,
148, 190
*Royal Oak*, HMS 138, 150, 162
Rundstedt, Field Marshal von 8, 46

Saint-Nazaire, attack on docks 41
Schellenberg, Walter 117
Schulz, Kapitänleutnant Georg-Wilhelm
150, 151
Senger und Etterlin, General von 14, 15,
16, 198, 199
Seyss-Inquart, Arthur 172
Simmerforce 51
Simpson, Ernest 96, 103
Simpson, Wallis 80, 89, 90, 94, 95, 96, 97,
98, 100, 101, 110, 194, 201
Somerville, Admiral 20, 23
Sparks, Colonel Felix 12
Speer, Albert 169, 170, 172, 173, 179,
185, 197
Spencer, Earl Winfield 95
Stalin, Joseph xii, 8, 38, 39, 40, 41, 44, 49,
51, 55, 57, 62, 63, 73, 74, 78, 183

Tuker, Major-General 13
*tu quoque* 176, 177, 182, 188, 189, 196

U-boat warfare
attitudes 131, 133
nature of this war 132, 133, 143,
144, 145
objectives 134, 135, 140
propaganda 138, 145, 146, 147, 154
rescuing survivors 135, 138, 147, 149,
150, 151, 152, 154

Victoria, Queen 80, 81, 82, 83, 85, 122

Wagner, Admiral 180, 182
Walter, Professor 164, 169

## Index    211

Ward, Mrs Freda Dudley  89, 95, 96
Waters, Colonel John  10, 12
Weizsäcker, Ernst von  121
Wenner-Gren, Axel  118
Werner, Herbert A.  132, 133, 134, 138, 151, 202

Westphal, General  14, 198
Wilhelm II  83, 84
*William D Porter*, USS  2, 3
Windsor, *see* Edward VIII

Dear Reader,

We hope you have enjoyed this book, but why not share your views on social media? You can also follow our pages to see more about our other products: facebook.com/penandswordbooks or follow us on X @penswordbooks

You can also view our products at www.pen-and-sword.co.uk (UK and ROW) or www.penandswordbooks.com (North America).

To keep up to date with our latest releases and online catalogues, please sign up to our newsletter at: www.pen-and-sword.co.uk/newsletter

If you would like a printed catalogue with our latest books, then please email: enquiries@pen-and-sword.co.uk or telephone: 01226 734555 (UK and ROW) or email: uspen-and-sword@casematepublishers.com or telephone: (610) 853-9131 (North America).

We respect your privacy and we will only use personal information to send you information about our products.

Thank you!